Web Programming for Business

Web Programming for Business: PHP Object-Oriented Programming with Oracle focuses on fundamental PHP coding, giving students practical, enduring skills to solve data and technical problems in business.

Using Oracle as the back-end database, the book is version-neutral, teaching students code that will still work even with changes to PHP and Oracle. The code is clean, clearly explained, and solutions-oriented, allowing students to understand how technologies such as XML, RSS, and AJAX can be leveraged in business applications. The book is fully illustrated with examples, and includes chapters on:

*   database functionality;
*   security programming;
*   transformation programming to move data.

PowerPoint slides, applied exam questions, and the raw code for all examples are available on a companion website. This book offers an innovative approach that allows anyone with basic SQL and HTML skills to learn PHP object-oriented programming.

David Paper is a professor of management information systems at Jon M. Huntsman School of Business, Utah State University, USA. With experience at major companies including Texas Instruments and IBM, David teaches both undergraduate and graduate students of computer science and business.

A range of further resources for this book are available on the Companion Website at www.routledge.com/cw/paper

Web Programming for Business
PHP Object-Oriented Programming with Oracle

David Paper

 Routledge
Taylor & Francis Group

NEW YORK AND LONDON

First published 2015
by Routledge
711 Third Avenue, New York, NY 10017

and by Routledge
2 Park Square, Milton Park, Abingdon, Oxon OX14 4RN

Routledge is an imprint of the Taylor & Francis Group, an informa business

© 2015 Taylor & Francis

Library of Congress Cataloging in Publication Data
Paper, David.
Web programming for business : PHP object-oriented programming with
Oracle / David Paper.
pages cm
Includes bibliographical references and index.
ISBN 978-0-415-81804-9 (hardback : alk. paper) – ISBN 978-0-415-81805-6
(pbk. : alk. paper) – ISBN 978-0-203-58208-4 (ebook : alk. paper) 1. PHP
(Computer program language) 2. Oracle (Computer file) 3. Web sites–
Design. I. Title.
QA76.73.P224P37 2014
006.7'6–dc23
2014002227

ISBN: 978-0-415-81804-9 (hbk)
ISBN: 978-0-415-81805-6 (pbk)
ISBN: 978-0-203-58208-4 (ebk)

Typeset in Times New Roman
by Cenveo Publisher Services

Printed and bound in Great Britain by CPI Group (UK) Ltd, Croydon, CR0 4YY

This book is dedicated to my mother Radine and great friend Malik. My mother was always there when I needed a shoulder to cry on during the writing process. She never ceased to amaze me with her unwavering support even when I would babble on about technology outside of her realm of experience. Malik is always encouraging me by telling me that I can doing anything I set my mind to accomplishing. I am lucky to have such wonderful people in my life!

Contents

Illustrations

Figures

Tables

Preface

Audience

I wrote this book for people who want to be web programmers. Web programming is not trivial, but it is definitely not astrophysics or neuroscience. In over two decades of teaching technologies of various sorts and 18 years of teaching PHP (with Oracle), I believe that almost anyone can learn how to do it.

I teach between 10 and 20 students in my PHP class. My students tend to be graduate management information systems (MIS) majors, but I always let a few undergraduate students attend. Some semesters, I even have a few computer science students in my class. My students tend to have some programming experience, but some have little to none. Nevertheless, students who work hard tend to come out of my class with marketable PHP programming skills.

Admittedly, students with at least one or two programming classes under their belt (preferably of the object-oriented variety) tend to learn faster. But, I know of many students with no programming experience who have thrived in my class. The profile of *successful* students is that they possess a great attitude for learning. They want to be in the class and they want to gain a skill that will help them succeed.

Coverage

Topics for the book were chosen based on many years teaching web programming, consultation with industry experts in the field, reading numerous white papers and programming books, and talking to students about course content. Some of my former students have working experience, which adds even more credence to their suggestions. I invite alumni, programmers, consultants, and managers to speak in my class whenever possible. My experience, student comments, and industry comments help ensure the timeliness, relevance, and quality of course content.

Teachers' Guide

The book is intended as a source of simple to advanced tested and working code pieces to help students learn PHP web programming in a modular and systematic fashion with Oracle 12c as the back-end database. The emphasis is on precision using practice-feedback loops to enrich knowledge and understanding. With practice-feedback loops, an example is presented, students load the code in a browser, the expected result is shown, and then feedback and explanation of what the code accomplished is provided.

The companion website provides all code from the book, accompanying assignments for each chapter, and PowerPoint slides for each chapter. The PowerPoint slides are what I use to teach the MIS 6650 Advanced Web Development (graduate) class, which is in its 18th year of being offered. Students have commented to me every semester that the slides are an excellent supplement that helps them complete the assignments, fare well in exams, and get them ready for the job market. The book offers much deeper explanations (than the slides) of what the code accomplishes (feedback) as well as definitions of terms and symbols.

Although I recommend that students have attended at least one course related to object-oriented programming, I have taught students with little to no programming background. I believe that students with a 'positive' attitude toward learning can gain the programming skills I teach in the book. Acquiring programming skills is not magic. It requires a lot of hours sitting in front of a computer beyond taking a class or reading a book. I don't think that there is any other way to learn programming skills!

The book expresses the knowledge I have acquired in over 20 years of working with Oracle, PHP, PL/SQL, AJAX, and SQL. I purposely include as many code modules as possible because this is how I teach students PHP (with Oracle) and many of my students have gone on to have successful careers. I emphasize practice, practice, and more practice because this is how I learned and how my students have learned. Over the years, I have received many positive endorsements from students who took this course. They inform me that my instruction on PHP web development was instrumental in their careers; from getting their first job to advancing their MIS careers.

I reserve the first week of class for creating and testing Linux and Oracle student accounts. I have each student login to their Linux and Oracle accounts, and run simple PHP scripts. I have an information technology (IT) expert who installs and maintains a Linux server instance and an Oracle 12c instance. My IT expert also creates all student accounts and maintains the software. Prior to class, I tell students to read the chapter we will cover, attempt to run the code, and – when and where problems occur – to prepare questions to bring to class. I recommend teaching the chapters sequentially from beginning to end.

Students' Guide

The course is intended for students with some working knowledge of relational databases and programming. Once students have working Linux and Oracle accounts, they are ready to begin coding. Each chapter in the book provides 'tested' PHP modules that students can load into a web browser (via its URL) to see results. All code is available on the companion website so the code need not be retyped. However, I suggest that, once the code is working, students should make some changes to better understand how the language works.

The best way to transfer PHP code to a Linux account is to use 'WinSCP', which is free file transfer software. I discuss how to install this software in Chapter 1. 'WinSCP' transfers files should be used exactly as typed. If students try to do this by copying and pasting, they may encounter serious spacing problems.

The companion website includes PowerPoint slides, assignments, and PHP code for each chapter. When I teach, I assume that my students have read all chapters prior to lectures and attempted to get all code examples to work. When problems are encountered, I encourage students to bring questions to the next lecture.

The first week of class is reserved for creating and testing Linux and Oracle student accounts. As I said previously, students should login into their Linux and Oracle accounts, and test simple PHP scripts to ensure that all is well. Once Linux and Oracle accounts are working properly, students are set up to run any code provided in the book.

In my classes, I have a dedicated IT expert who installs and maintains a Linux server instance and an Oracle 12c instance. The IT expert also creates all student accounts and maintains the software. If technical problems arise, I try to solve them. If I cannot, I have students contact the IT expert.

I recommend that students follow the chapters sequentially from beginning to end. I also recommend that students spend a substantial amount of time getting familiar with the code. From my more than 20 years' experience of teaching programming classes, I can emphasize that programming skill is only obtained through rigorous practice (which takes many hours of hard work and many times is not really a lot of fun). As one of my colleagues always says, "You have to spend a lot of time in front of a computer screen to learn how to program."

If students embrace hard work, practice, and dedication to the craft of programming, they will very likely be a successful programmer. I know I sound a bit preachy, but this is how I became a proficient programmer. I just don't know of any other way to achieve excellence.

Companion Website

The book has a companion website that includes assignments, code, and PowerPoint slides for each chapter. The assignments include definition questions and coding questions. The code is included so that students don't have to retype each code snippet to test. The PowerPoint slides provide bulleted information and code illustrations, but do not delve deeply into explanation. The book provides explanation and feedback.

Pedagogy

I tell students on the first day of class to carefully read and digest every word, paragraph, and page of the book. My next advice is to tell them to work through each code example. That is, load the URL that points to the code in a web browser, look at the results, and go back to the code to make sure that each line makes sense. Finally, I tell them to make some changes to the code and see if they can get it to work with their own customizations.

The best advice I can give a student is to practice, practice, and practice some more. The only way, in my opinion, that a student can become a good programmer is to sit in front of a computer screen and spend hours coding.

To enrich learning, I use *practice-feedback loops*. **Practice-feedback loops** follow a three-step process. First, a concept is introduced. Second, an example is provided. Third, feedback is given. I use this pedagogy because this is how I have learned many languages and technologies, and this is how many of my students have learned how to program and secure excellent jobs.

Information Technology

Going on my 21st year of teaching various technologies and programming languages, I have always had an IT expert install and maintain software as well as create student accounts. The platform I currently use includes Oracle 12*c* database, Linux (Fedora) server, and PHP 5.3.14. This platform allows students to login to a central server to complete their work.

I keep in touch with several former students and friends, who inform my platform decisions. These people currently work in the technology industry. They tell me that the platform I use for my class gives students a somewhat realistic environment to work with PHP. They use the word 'somewhat' because so many configurations are used in industry that it makes it difficult to set up a single representative IT configuration. However, my industry contacts agree that using a centralized Linux server with Oracle and PHP (the one I use for my classes) is a minimum for preparing students for interviews and the job market.

Prerequisites

Students should possess basic programming knowledge. Some object-oriented programming knowledge or experience is even better. Basic knowledge of HTML and SQL is also recommended. However, the book covers all that a student needs to know. From my experience of teaching web programming, I notice that people with basic programming skills tend to learn faster and be more comfortable with learning technical content. However, I have had numerous students in my class with no programming experience who have done extremely well!

Acknowledgments

Although I have been teaching PHP with Oracle for many years, a few years ago I found a book by David Powers entitled *PHP Object-Oriented Solutions*. This book was an inspiration because it helped me become inculcated into the world of object-oriented programming. Before acquiring this book and poring over it for many months, I had no background in object-oriented programming. Of course, I consulted the Internet for a lot of help, but this book helped me adhere to a structure for converting my class from procedural to object-oriented programming and acted as a guide to build real-world Oracle examples related to the ones Powers built with MySQL.

1 Linux, HTML, PHP, and JavaScript Basics

Overview

The 2014 Fall semester marks my 18th year teaching PHP web scripting (programming) with Oracle as the back-end database. Over the years, many of my students have commented on programming skills developed, ability to secure a good job and discipline to help advance careers acquired by successfully completing the course. This book is based on what I have learned, how I have learned, continuous interactions with industry experts (web developers, database engineers, and application programmers), my experiences as a programmer, consultant, and analyst, and clear and concise programming fundamentals. Although technology changes rapidly, programming fundamentals remain relatively constant. The code included in these chapters has changed little over the years and still works even with new distributions of Linux, PHP, JavaScript, and Oracle. Of course, I tweak and add new code as I learn more.

In my technology teaching experiences, I have learned that clean, clear, concise, and systematic code examples with explanations go a long way in helping students learn, digest, and apply technologies, such as various types of programming and database activities. Also, teaching fundamentals has proven to be key in establishing a strong technological base in my students. Feedback from numerous industry employers who hire our students have indicated that my classes offer excellent and enduring technology fundamentals (which is one of the most important reasons why they hire our students).

So, this book strives to offer programming fundamentals presented in a clear, concise, and practical manner. In later chapters, I include applications using the fundamentals included in these chapters.

Web programming is only possible with an appropriate information technology (IT) platform. An IT platform can take many forms, but must include an operating system (OS), programming (or scripting) language, web browser, web server, and database management system (DBMS). The platform I use includes Linux as the OS, PHP as the scripting language, a web browser (Google Chrome is my preference), and Oracle as the DBMS.

I have an IT expert install and maintain Oracle, Linux, and PHP on a computer server. Our industry advisory board endorses the IT platform I have just described. My current platform includes Oracle 12c, Linux (Redhat Fedora), and PHP 5.3.14. My IT expert creates Linux and Oracle accounts on a server for each student. Students create and save PHP scripts on their Linux accounts using PuTTY (or MobaXterm), and use Oracle SQL Developer to interact with Oracle. When students need to securely transfer files, they use WinSCP.

Chapter 1 covers Linux, HTML, JavaScript, and PHP basics. Although basics are covered, I recommend visiting w3schools' or other websites for tutorials to deepen knowledge of Linux, HTML, PHP, and JavaScript. The w3schools' URL is www.w3schools.com/.

Learning Objectives

After completing this chapter, you will gain a fundamental understanding of Linux, HTML, PHP, and JavaScript through explanation and code examples. The following objectives summarize the skills the chapter will help you develop:

1   Learn how to install and use 'PuTTY'.
2   Learn how to install and use 'WinSCP'.

3   Learn how to install and use 'Oracle SQL Developer'.
4   Learn the basics of Linux (as an end user).
5   Learn the basics of HTML.
6   Learn the basics of PHP.
7   Learn the basics of JavaScript.

Install and Use PuTTY

'PuTTY' is a free and open-source terminal emulator application that can act as a client program for SSH, Telnet, and Rlogin network protocols. 'PuTTY' is used to connect to a user account on Linux. 'PuTTY' opens a window where anything typed is sent straight to the Linux machine and the response from Linux is sent back to the open window. So, you can work on the Linux machine as if you were sitting at its console, while actually sitting in a remote location. To download 'PuTTY', Google the keywords 'putty download' and choose the hyperlink 'PuTTY Download Page' (Figure 1.1). The version may change over time. Feel free to use another site if you wish. The site is only recommended because it is the one that I use.

Figure 1.1 PuTTY Download Page

On the 'PuTTY Download Page' (Figure 1.2), choose the 'putty.exe' link. This is the first link under 'For Windows on Intel x86'. Click the down arrow (to the right of the downloaded file 'putty.exe') and choose 'Show in folder'. Your computer automatically opens the 'Downloads' directory. Find the 'putty' icon in this directory and open it. Click 'Run' to open 'PuTTY'.

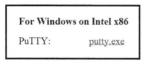

Figure 1.2 Hyperlink to PuTTY Download Page (http://www.chiark.greenend.org.uk/~sgtatham/putty/download.html)

The 'PuTTY Configuration' window opens automatically. Type the name of the server for 'Host Name' and the 'Port' for the port where Linux is listening for requests. Your IT expert should provide this information. In my case, I use 'SSH' to enhance security, which is recommended. So, after you type in the host and port information be sure to click the 'SSH' button (if you use SSH). Click 'Open' to begin your session. Now, you should see the console. To access Linux account information, enter your 'username'. When Linux prompts you for your password, enter it. Your IT expert will provide this information (Figure 1.3). If username and password are accepted, you are logged into Linux (Figure 1.4). Type 'exit' to close the session.

```
login as: paper
paper@mis6330.go.usu.edu's password:
```

Figure 1.3 Username and Password to SSH into Linux Server

```
login as: paper
paper@mis6330.go.usu.edu's password:
Last login: Thu Mar 12 11:58:16 2015 from 129.123.44.162
[paper@server1 ~]$
```

Figure 1.4 Command Prompt with Successful Login

Install and Use WinSCP

'WinSCP' is a free and open-source SFTP, SCP, and FTP client for Microsoft Windows. Its main function is secure file transfer between a local and a remote computer. To download 'WinSCP' onto your computer, Google the keywords 'winscp download' and choose the hyperlink 'WinSCP Download' (Figure 1.5). The version may change over time. Feel free to use another site if you wish. The site is only a recommendation because it is the one that I use.

WinSCP :: Download
winscp.net/eng/**download**.php ▾
Open source freeware SFTP, SCP and FTP client for Windows.

Figure 1.5 Hyperlink to WinSCP Download Page (http://winscp.net/eng/download.php)

On the 'WinSCP Download' page, choose 'Installation package' (Figure 1.6). This hyperlink is on the left of the page under 'WinSCP 5.1.7'. This is the version as of writing this chapter; it may change over time.

Downloading WinSCP

WinSCP 5.1.7

Installation package (4.8 MiB; 183,764 downloads to date)

Figure 1.6 WinSCP Installation Package

Click the down arrow (to the right of the downloaded file 'winscp517setup.exe') and choose 'Show in folder'. Your computer automatically opens the 'Downloads' directory. Find the 'winscp517setup' icon in this directory and open it. Click 'Run' to open the program. Click 'Yes' to allow the program to make changes to your computer. Click 'OK' to select 'English'. Click 'Next' to begin 'WinSCP Setup Wizard'. Accept the agreement and click 'Next' (accept what is 'recommended'). Click 'Install' and then click 'Finish'. Keep in mind that minor changes may occur during the installation process with future versions of the software.

To launch 'WinSCP', choose 'File protocol' using the down arrow (I use 'SCP'). Type in your Linux 'Host name', 'port number', 'User name', and 'Password', and click the 'Login' button (this information should be the same that was provided by your IT expert for using 'PuTTY'). You have established a new session. The right panel contains your account information on the remote Linux server. The left panel contains your local computer information. The 'WinSCP' software works like 'FTP', but it is much more secure. Using the software is also easy because it works like a 'Windows' directory. Close the session by clicking on the 'X' on the top right of the window.

Install and Use Oracle SQL Developer

Oracle SQL Developer is a free integrated development environment that simplifies the development and management of the Oracle database. To download 'Oracle SQL Developer' onto your computer, Google the keywords 'Oracle SQL Developer' and choose hyperlink 'Oracle SQL Developer Downloads' (Figure 1.7). The version may change over time. Click the 'Downloads' tab to the right of the 'Overview' tab. Click the 'Accept License Agreement' button (Figure 1.8).

Oracle SQL Developer Downloads
www.**oracle**.com/technetwork/**developer**-tools/**sql-developer**/downloads/ ▾
Nov 1, 2012 - Platform. Windows 32-bit - zip file includes the JDK1.6.0_35, Download 209 M. Windows 32-bit - Installation Notes, Download 174 M. Windows ...
Oracle SQL Developer - Installation Notes - Documentation - Here

Figure 1.7 Hyperlink to Download Oracle SQL Developer

Figure 1.8 Oracle SQL Developer License Agreement Page (http://www.oracle.com/technetwork/developer-tools/sql-developer/downloads/index.html)

Scroll down the page and choose the appropriate platform for your computer (Figure 1.9). The only version that I have experience with is the 'Windows 32-bit' version, which includes the 'JDK' (Java development kit).

Platform	
Windows 32-bit - zip file *includes* the JDK1.6.0_35	⬇ Download 209 M
Windows 32-bit - Installation Notes	⬇ Download 174 M
Windows 64-bit - Installation Notes	⬇ Download 174 M
Mac OS X - Installation Notes	⬇ Download 173 M
Linux RPM - Installation Notes	⬇ Download 173 M
Other Platforms - Installation Notes	⬇ Download 174 M

Figure 1.9 Oracle SQL Developer Download Options

Oracle will ask you for a username and password. So, click the 'Sign Up' hyperlink to create a new account (unless you already have one). Fill out the online form completely and click the 'Create Account' button on the bottom of the form. On the 'Account Verification' page, click the 'Continue' button. Now, sign in with your new username and password. Wait for the download to complete, which may take some time (so be patient). Click the down arrow (to the right of the downloaded file) and choose 'Show in folder'. Your computer automatically opens the 'Downloads' directory.

Find the 'sqldeveloper' icon in this directory and open it. Open the 'sqldeveloper' folder. Click on the 'sqldeveloper' icon. Click the 'Extract all' button. Click 'Extract' button to place software in the 'Downloads' directory. Be patient while the software is being downloaded because the process will take several minutes. Double click on the 'sqldeveloper' folder. Open the software with the 'sqldeveloper' icon. When prompted, click 'Run'. Choose the first option 'SQL Source (.sql)' and click 'OK'. Click the green '+' button and enter the 'Connection Name', 'Username', 'Password', 'Hostname', 'Port', and 'SID' information. Ask your IT expert for this information.

Keep in mind that the 'Username' and 'Password' is for access to the Oracle database, not the Linux OS. To keep it simple for my students (and me), their Linux and Oracle accounts have identical usernames and passwords. Click 'Test' to see if you have a successful connection. If successful, click the 'Connect' button to establish a connection to the database. Close the connection by either closing the pop-up window or using 'File' and then 'Exit' on the menu. Once a connection has been established, the next time you open the software just click on the '+' symbol to the left of the connection to open a session.

Linux Basics

This section explains and illustrates with examples how an end user works with Linux to display content on the Internet. To log into your Linux user account, open a 'PuTTY' session as demonstrated earlier in the 'PuTTY' section (Figures 1.3 and 1.4). Figure 1.10 illustrates a successful 'SSH' login with the cursor on the command line. The ***command line*** is where you tell Linux what is needed by typing commands at the cursor position.

```
login as: paper
paper@mis6330.go.usu.edu's password:
Last login: Thu Mar 12 11:58:16 2015 from 129.123.44.162
[paper@server1 ~]$
```

Figure 1.10 Command Prompt with Successful Login

Let's begin by creating a directory to display content. This directory is where all files that you wish to be displayed on the Internet ***must*** reside. Type the following on the command line and press 'Enter':

mkdir public_html

Command 'mkdir' tells Linux to create a new directory. In this case, the new directory is called 'public_html'. Typically, 'public_html' is where Linux looks for information to display on the Internet. Now, set permissions for the directory (type the following on the command line and press 'Enter'):

```
chmod 705 public_html
```

Command 'chmod' tells Linux to change permissions to '705' for the directory listed. I will explain what '705' means in a moment. To see what happened, type the following command:

```
ls-la
```

Command 'ls' lists the contents of a directory. In this case, you are at the highest level of your directory structure. With 'ls', two options are included – 'l' and 'a'. Options are preceded by a hyphen '-'. Option 'l' tells the list command to use a long list format. Option 'a' tells it to not hide anything. Look to the left of directory 'public_html' to see its permissions.

```
drwx---r-x
```

Letter 'd' tells you that 'public_html' is a directory. The next three letters 'rwx' are permissions for the owner (you) of the directory. The following three '---' are permissions for the group. Don't worry about group permissions in this book, because we won't discuss them. The final three 'r-x' are permissions for the world (Internet). Before explaining permissions more deeply, let's look inside the 'public_html' directory. To do this, enter the following on the command line:

```
cd public_html
```

Command 'cd' changes directories to your choice. In this case, you are changing to 'public_html'. Now, list contents with no options:

```
ls
```

You see nothing because you have yet to create content in 'public_html'. Command 'cd' followed by a directory moves you down your directory tree. To move up your directory tree, type the following on the command line:

```
cd ..
```

You should now be back at the top of your directory tree. Type the following:

```
ls
```

You should see only the 'public_html' directory that you created. Earlier in this section, you typed 'ls-la' to see permissions of 'public_html'. Permissions for your display directory are 'drwx---r-x'. The first bit 'd' means directory. The next three bits 'rwx' mean that the owner (you) has read, write, and execute privileges. So, you can read from this directory, write to this directory, and execute from this directory. The next three bits '---' are for group privileges. The hyphen '-' means that no permissions are provided. The group therefore has no privileges on this directory. The final three bits 'r-x' mean that anyone on the Internet can read from the directory and execute from it, but cannot write to it. If you wish to secure a directory or file from the world, *never* provide 'write' privileges, otherwise *anyone* with access to the Internet can potentially write to your file or directory!

Table 1.1 Octal to Binary Conversion

Octal	Binary
0	000
1	001
2	010
3	011
4	100
5	101
6	110
7	111

Octal (Base Eight) Permissions

Linux permissions are based on octal numbering (or base eight). When you changed permissions to '705', each number was in base eight. The reason Linux uses base eight is because it translates easily into binary, but represents more bits in less space than binary. Base eight number '7' translates into binary '111'. A binary '1' means on. A binary '0' means off. Since all three binary numbers are '1', read, write, and execute are on. The leftmost bit '1' corresponds to 'r', the next bit '1' corresponds to 'w', and the rightmost bit '1' corresponds to 'x'. Base eight number '0' translates into binary '000', which means that all permissions are off. Finally, base eight number '5' translates into binary '101'. Since the leftmost bit represents 'read' and is on, the Internet can read. The rightmost bit represents 'execute' and is on, which means the Internet can execute. The middle bit represents 'write' and is off, which means the Internet cannot write. Notice that 'r', 'w', and 'x' are positional, which makes Linux permissions relatively easy to understand. Table 1.1 is provided to facilitate easy conversion from base eight to binary (and vice versa). Conversion is necessary because command 'chmod' accepts base eight numbers only, while Linux permissions are represented by binary numbers.

Two caveats are in order. First, be sure that all content (files and directories) that you wish to be displayed in a browser are located within the 'public_html' directory. Second, do not allow the Internet 'write' permissions. In most cases, you do not want the world to be able to 'write' to your directory or file. To close a remote connection to Linux, enter the 'exit' command (type 'exit' on the command line and press 'Enter').

Display Content

With a bit of Linux knowledge, you can create a PHP script that can display content on the Internet. Open a web browser of your choice. I use 'Google Chrome', so the examples will be from this browser. Use 'PuTTY' to open an SSH Linux session and change to the 'public_html' directory. Next, use command 'vi' to open a new file. Be sure to enter each command on a separate command line.

```
cd public_html
vi test.php
```

To enter command mode, press the escape key 'Esc'. To enter commands, press the colon ':' key. You should see a colon ':' bottom left of the screen. **Command mode** is the command environment for Linux files. Turn on line numbering with the following command:

```
:set nu
```

Figure 1.11 shows that line numbering is turned on. If you wish, you can turn off line numbering with the following command:

:set nonu

Figure 1.11 Editing a New File with 'vi' Command and Turning Line Numbering On

To edit a file, press 'Esc' and change to input mode by typing the letter 'i'. ***Input mode*** is the editing environment for Linux files. Enter the text shown in Figure 1.12 line by line (press 'Enter' after each line).

Figure 1.12 Input Mode with 'vi' Command

Be sure to start typing on the first line leftmost column to eliminate spurious errors. Begin every PHP script with beginning tag '<?php' and end with ending tag '?>'. Remove any additional blank lines after ending tag '?>'. To exit insert mode, press the 'Esc' key. To save the file, enter colon ':', 'w', and press 'Enter'. To return to the directory structure, press 'Esc', enter ':q', and press 'Enter'. Enter 'ls' to see the file in 'public_html'. To verify that the contents of 'test.php' are what you expect, enter 'vi test.php'. To display 'test.php' on the Internet, enter the correct path:

servername/~username/test.php

The 'servername' is the name of the host computer where the PHP engine resides. Your IT expert can help you with this. The tilde '~' must precede your Linux user account name. Do not include 'public_html' in the path because the PHP engine already knows that the file is within this directory. Figure 1.13 shows what should be displayed.

My first PHP display

Figure 1.13 Displaying PHP Content on a Web Browser

Again, since Linux knows that 'public_html' is the display directory, do not include it in the path. To create a new file, use 'vi filename'. The basic file commands are entered by preceding them with the colon ':' key. However, edit commands are not preceded by the colon ':' key. Edit commands are available when you first edit a file, but if the colon key has been pressed or you are in insert mode, press the 'Esc' key. Now, you can use edit commands such as copy, cut, and paste. To copy code, enter 'vi test.php', a colon ':', command 'set nu', and move cursor to line 2 (if necessary). Moving to a line is easy in Linux because you can use the up, down, left, and right arrows on your keyboard. Type letters 'yy' (consecutively) and letter 'p'. Letters 'yy' mean copy and letter 'p' means paste. Figure 1.14 shows that the line was copied.

```
1  <?php
2    echo "My first PHP display";
3    echo "My first PHP display";
4  ?>
```

Figure 1.14 Copying Lines in a File

To copy multiple lines of code, move the cursor to line '2' and type '2yy'. Move the cursor to line '3' and enter 'p' to copy two lines (Figure 1.15). Typing a number followed by 'yy' enables copying of any number of lines.

```
1  <?php
2    echo "My first PHP display";
3    echo "My first PHP display";
4    echo "My first PHP display";
5    echo "My first PHP display";
6  ?>
```

Figure 1.15 Copying Multiple Lines in a File

To cut (delete) a line of code, move the cursor to the line and enter 'dd'. To delete multiple lines, type a number followed by 'dd'. Let's delete lines 3, 4, and 5. Move cursor to line '3', and enter '3' followed by 'dd' (Figure 1.16).

```
1 <?php
2  echo "My first PHP display";
3 ?>
```

Figure 1.16 Deleting Lines from a File

Now, let's copy, rename, and remove files. First, get out of 'vi' by pressing the 'Esc' key followed by the colon ':' key and type 'wq' to save and then quit the file. Next, enter the following:

cp test.php new_test.php

The 'cp' command copies the first file to the name of the second file. Type 'ls' to see that the file was copied correctly. To view contents of the new file without editing, type the following:

cat new_test.php

To clean clutter from the screen, type the following:

clear

To rename a file, type the following:

mv new_test.php second_test.php

To verify, use the 'ls' command. To remove a file, type the following:

rm-rf second_test.php

Be careful when removing files because they cannot be recovered once the command is entered. Table 1.2 summarizes the basic Linux commands and Table 1.3 summarizes the basic 'vi' commands.

Table 1.2 Basic Linux Commands

mkdir	create new directory
chmod	change permissions
ls	list (files and directories)
ls-la	list with hidden content
cd	change directory
cd ..	move up tree structure
vi (vim)	create or edit new file
cp	copy file
mv	rename file
rm	remove file
clear	clear screen clutter

Table 1.3 Basic 'vi' Commands

:	change to file mode
:set nu	turn on line numbering
:set nonu	turn off line numbering
i	insert mode
esc	end insert mode
yy	copy (yank) line
#yy	copy (yank) # lines
p	paste yanked line(s)
dd	cut (delete) line
#dd	cut (delete) # lines
:w	write file
:wq	write file and quit
:q	quit (no changes)
:q!	forced quit

Linux is *case sensitive*. As such, 'W' and 'Q' do not work. To write (save) a file, use lowercase 'w'. To quit, use lowercase 'q'. I can't tell you how many times I've typed 'W' only to have Linux not respond as I expect!

In the Linux sections, Linux basics to enable an end user to create, modify, and display PHP script content on the Internet were introduced. Linux permissions and how to modify them were also introduced. Finally, Linux and 'vi' basic commands were presented. The next section introduces HTML basics.

HTML Basics

This section introduces the HyperText Markup Language (HTML) used in this book. A more comprehensive introduction can be found at www.w3schools.com, which also includes tutorials for CSS, SQL, XML and other languages that might prove useful for students with little or no experience of web programming. Since this book teaches programming, not design, HTML5 and CSS3 are not covered. To *program* with PHP at a very high level, only basic HTML and CSS are required. HTML5 and CSS3 are essential for those with interest in web design.

Markup

Markup is additional text inserted into an HTML document. Inserted text has three characteristics. First, it is not usually visible to the reader. Second, it is not part of the document's content. Third, it enhances the document in some manner.

An HTML document is a text file containing small markup tags. The file extension for an HTML document must be 'htm' or 'html', unless the markup is contained within a scripting language such as PHP. Markup text inserted into an HTML document has meaning to the HTML interpreter.

HTML Tags

HTML tags mark up the structure of a document and embed basic information that tells the web browser how to display content. HTML tags are always enclosed in angle brackets and are *not* case sensitive. (Linux commands are case sensitive.) HTML tags divide a web page into its basic sections, such as header and body. HTML tags generally have a beginning and matching ending tag. This matching tag strategy contains all document content between a set of tag pairs. As such, content within a container follows the rules of that container. The advantage is that containerization forces tags to be balanced and clearly delineates the rules applied to any given content within the HTML document.

Nesting tags is legal, but containers should always be nested within each other appropriately. White space in the document does not matter to the HTML interpreter. I do, however, recommend that you use whitespace to make the document look as clean as possible to the naked eye. Not every tag in HTML is paired (containerized). Some tags don't require a closing tag. The break tag '<br />' is one such example.

Markup Types

HTML uses two types of markup – tags and character entities. A ***character entity*** is a reference to a particular kind of character that has been predefined or explicitly declared in a document type definition. A ***document type definition*** (DTD) is a set of markup declarations that define a document type for HTML. The purpose of a character entity is to provide a way to refer to a universal character in a limited character encoding (e.g., ASCII). Character entities include international characters as well as characters usually included in tags as markup. A character entity begins with an ampersand, followed by the entity name, and ends with a semicolon. The character entity for an ampersand follows:

```
&amp;
```

A useful character entity is the one for a nonbreaking space.

```
 
```

Three character entity references that deserve special attention are '<' (less than), '>' (greater than), and '"' (double quote). To apply, replace '<' with '<', '>' with '>', and '"' with '"' when necessary. The availability of these three references is important because HTML uses '<' and '>' to enclose HTML tags, and '"' to enclose strings. PHP also uses '"' to enclose strings. You can therefore use a character entity reference instead of the actual character to mitigate confusion and errors. The character entity references are as follows:

```
&lt;
&gt;
&quot;
```

HTML tags have four components – attributes, values assigned to attributes, contents, and end tags. Tags don't necessarily have to have all four components because some tags lack content, attributes or even end tags. ***Attributes*** provide additional information about HTML elements. An ***HTML element*** is an individual component of an HTML document. An HTML matched pair tag acts as a container for an HTML element. An example should help you understand. The 'input' tag is used for data input as follows:

```
<input type="text" name="username" />
```

The HTML element is 'input'. The attributes are 'type' and 'name' with values of 'text' and 'username' respectively. The 'input' tag does not contain any content and does not require an end tag.

Document-Wide Tags

Document-wide tags are those that apply to the whole HTML document. Let's discuss three of them now. All tags are elements of the '<html>' tag. The first and last tags in a document should ***always*** be the HTML tags. The '<head>' tag conveys header information for a document. The '<body>' tag contains document text to be displayed in a browser.

A web page should include '<html>', '<head>', and '<body>' tags as a minimum. The '<div>' tag defines a division or section within an HTML document. Its purpose is to group HTML elements together. One use of '<div>' is to format a block of HTML elements. Another use is to lay out a web page together with CSS. **CSS** is used to control the style and layout of multiple web pages all at once. The **comment tag** is used to insert comments into the source code. Comments are not displayed in the browser.

Load File in a Web Browser

To display content on the Internet, web browsers need to access the file by its URL. The appropriate URL consists of the name of the server (host server), followed by your Linux user name preceded by the '~' (tilde) symbol, and ending with the path to the file preceded by the '/' (forward slash) symbol. The path is pretty simple. It is the path to the file inside the 'public_html' directory. Do *not* include 'public_html' in the path.

```
servername/~username/test.php
```

As a *hypothetical* path, the following URL displays 'one.htm' located in 'book' directory (inside 'public_html' directory) within user 'paper' on server 'http://dnet.brigham.usu.edu'.

```
<URL>
http://dnet.brigham.usu.edu/~paper/book/one.htm
```

The following HTML document includes document-wide tags, the '<div>' tag, and a comment tag. Save the contents in a file and load the URL in a web browser.

```
1  <html>
2  <head><title>Minimal</title></head>
3  <body>
4  <div style="text-align:center;">
5  <!-- The remaining part is the body. -->
6  Nothing!
7  </div>
8  </body>
9  </html>
```

Nothing!

Figure 1.17 Displaying Different PHP Content on a Web Browser

Since the 'attribute' for the '<div>' tag is 'align:center' (line 4), the word 'Nothing!' (line 6) is centered and displayed (Figure 1.17). Notice that the comment (line 5) was not displayed.

Various HTML Tags

The next HTML example illustrates '<body>', '<h2>', and '<p>' tags. Tag '<h2>' is for a second level heading and '<p>' is the paragraph tag. Notice the use of the 'style' attribute (lines 3–6) for setting various background colors (Figure 1.18).

```
1  <html>
2  <head><title>Body Style Example 1</title></head>
3  <body style="background-color:yellow;">
4  <div style="text-align:center;">
5  <h2 style="background-color:red;">This is a heading</h2>
6  <p style="background-color:green;">This is a paragraph.</p>
7  </body>
8  </html>
```

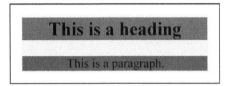

Figure 1.18 HTML Display from a PHP File

Let's look at one more example using various tags.

```
1   <html>
2   <head><title>Body Style Example 2</title></head>
3   <body style="background-color:burlywood;">
4   <div style="text-align:center;">
5   <h2 style="background-color:indigo; font-family:arial;color:white;
6   font-size:20px;"> If you click on the link, you see an alien</h2>
7   <p style="background-color:coral;">
8   <a href="alien.gif">Link</a>
9   </p>
10  </div>
11  </body>
12  </html>
```

The anchor tag '<a href="alien.gif">' in line 8 allows insertion of an image (in this case a gif image). 'WinSCP' can be used to move a downloaded image into the 'public_html' directory. Figure 1.19 shows the page. Assuming the image is located in 'public_html', clicking on the link displays it. Notice how the '<h2>' tag is split on two separate lines (lines 5 and 6). This is perfectly fine because whitespace doesn't matter.

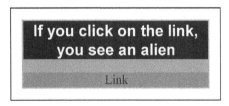

Figure 1.19 HTML Display with a Hyperlink

Heading tags emphasize text in the body of an HTML document. The second level heading '<h2>' was introduced earlier. Heading tags have nothing to do with the '<head>' tag structure. HTML supports six levels of headings. This code example demonstrates all six heading levels (Figure 1.20).

```
1  <html>
2  <head><title>Heading Levels</title></head>
3  <body style="background-color:burlywood;">
4  <div style="text-align:center;">
5  <h1>Heading 1</h1>
6  <h2>Heading 2</h2>
7  <h3>Heading 3</h3>
8  <h4>Heading 4</h4>
9  <h5>Heading 5</h5>
10 <h6>Heading 6</h6>
11 </div>
12 </body>
13 </html>
```

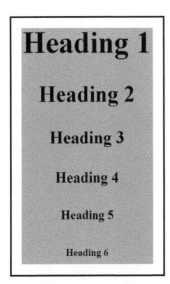

Figure 1.20 HTML Display of Headers

Paragraph tags separate blocks of text in a meaningful manner. Notice that the '<div>' tag contains the style for centering text (lines 4 and 15). As a result, all HTML between the '<div>' tags centers text when displayed in a web browser. This code example illustrates usage of the '<p>' tag (Figure 1.21).

```
1  <html>
2  <head><title>Paragraphs</title></head>
3  <body style="background-color:burlywood;">
4  <div style="text-align:center;">
5  <p>
```

```
 6 Paragraphs can be any length.<br />
 7 They contain blocks of text.<br />
 8 </p>
 9 <p>
10 This is the second paragraph.
11 </p>
12 <p>
13 This is the third paragraph.
14 </p>
15 </div>
16 </body>
17 </html>
```

Paragraphs can be any length.
They contain blocks of text.

This is the second paragraph.

This is the third paragraph.

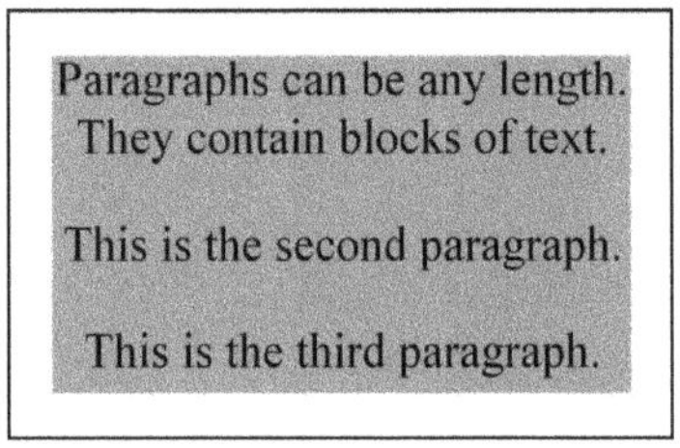

Figure 1.21 HTML Display of Paragraphs

The next example again uses the 'style' attribute within a '<div>' tag (line 4) to center content (Figure 1.22).

```
 1 <html>
 2 <head><title>Center Content</title></head>
 3 <body style="background-color:burlywood;">
 4 <div style="text-align:center;">
 5 <p>
 6 Center within 'div' tags
 7 </p>
 8 </div>
 9 </body>
10 </html>
```

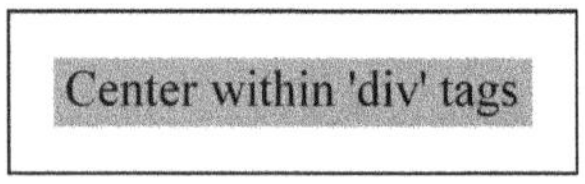

Center within 'div' tags

Figure 1.22 HTML Display of Centered Text

Line break tags '<br />' force a line break in the browser (lines 5–7). The code example uses this tag (Figure 1.23).

```
 1  <html>
 2  <head><title>Line Break Example</title></head>
 3  <body style="background-color:burlywood;">
 4  <div style="text-align:center;">
 5  Here is one line of text.<br />
 6  Here is another line of text.<br />
 7  Here is yet another line of text.<br />
 8  </div>
 9  </body>
10  </html>
```

```
Here is one line of text.
Here is another line of text.
Here is yet another line of text.
```

Figure 1.23 HTML Display of Multi-Line Centered Text

In the next example (Figure 1.24), the **preformatted tag** '<pre>' (lines 5 and 10) generates text in a fixed-width font. This tag displays text information as typed in the document. Notice how its style attribute overrides the centering style defined by the '<div>' tag.

```
 1  <html>
 2  <head><title>Preformatted Tag</title></head>
 3  <body style="background-color:burlywood;">
 4  <div style="text-align:center;">
 5  <pre style="text-align:left;">
 6  some commands
 7  some more commands
 8  even a few more commands
 9  fin
10  </pre>
11  </div>
12  </body>
13  </html>
```

```
some commands
some more commands
even a few more commands
fin
```

Figure 1.24 HTML Display Using '<pre>' Tag

Logical style tags define the relative appearance of text. They allow the browser to define how to display information. All browsers are able to interpret logical style tags correctly because the associated logical function provides meaning for the tag. The next code example demonstrates emphasis '<em>', strong '<strong>', and cite '<cite>' (lines 5 and 8) logical style tags (Figure 1.25).

```
 1  <html>
 2  <head><title>Logical Style Tags</title></head>
 3  <body style="background-color:burlywood;">
 4  <div style="text-align:center;">
 5  This <em>silly</em> sentence <strong>shows</strong><br />
 6  how logical style tags operate.<br />
 7  <p>
 8  <cite>Paper, D. (2003) How to Fly. Journal, 1, 1, 20-30.</cite>
 9  </div>
10  </body>
11  </html>
```

This *silly* sentence **shows** how logical style tags operate.

Paper, D. (2003) How to Fly. Journal, 1, 1, 20-30.

Figure 1.25 HTML Display of Logical Style Tags

Physical style tags define the precise appearance of text. They do *not* allow the browser to define how to display information because no logical functions are associated with them. Browsers may interpret differently, so use logical style tags whenever possible. The code example illustrates use of italics '<i>', bold '<b>', and citation '<tt>' (lines 5 and 8) physical style tags (Figure 1.26).

```
 1  <html>
 2  <head><title>Physical Style Tags</title></head>
 3  <body style="background-color:burlywood;">
 4  <div style="text-align:center;">
 5  This <i>silly</i> sentence <b>shows</b><br />
 6  how physical style tags operate.<br />
 7  <p>
 8  <tt>Paper, D. (2003) How to Fly. Journal, 1, 1, 20-30.</tt>
 9  </div>
10  </body>
11  </html>
```

This *silly* sentence **shows**
how physical style tags operate.

Paper, D. (2003) How to Fly.
   Journal, 1, 1, 20-30.

Figure 1.26 HTML Display of Physical Style Tags

Although italics and bold worked as expected, the citation did not. Images can be clip art, icons, animated art or pictures in one of the following formats – jpeg, xbm, gif, and png. The image '<img>' tag (line 5) is used to display images. In the code example, a gif is displayed as an image rather than as part of an anchor tag. (Note: I used 'WinSCP' to copy 'alien.gif' to my Linux account.)

```
1  <html>
2  <head><title>Image Example</title></head>
3  <body style="background-color:burlywood;">
4  <div style="text-align:center;">
5  <img src="alien.gif" title="Gnome" />
6  </div>
7  </body>
8  </html>
```

HTML tables are defined with the '<table>' tag. A table is divided into rows (with the '<tr>' tag), and each row is divided into data cells (with the '<td>' tag). The letters 'td' stand for table data and the <td> tag holds the content of a data cell. A '<td>' tag can contain text, links, images, lists, forms, and other tables. The following example creates a simple table. The '<style>' tag contained in the '<head>' tag includes CSS (lines 4–7) to center the table and create good margins. The 'class' attribute in the '<table>' tag (line 12) makes use of the CSS style (Figure 1.27).

```
1  <html>
2  <head>
3  <style type="text/css">
4  table.center {
5  margin-left:auto;
6  margin-right:auto;
7  }
8  </style>
9  </head>
10 <body style="background-color:burlywood;">
11 <div>
12 <table class="center" border="2">
13 <caption>Simple Table</caption>
14 <tr><th>Heading 1</th><th>Heading 2</th><th>
15 Heading 3</th></tr>
16 <tr><td>100</td><td>200</td><td>300</td></tr>
```

```
17  <tr><td>150</td><td>250</td><td>100</td></tr>
18  </table>
19  </div>
20  </body>
21  </html>
```

	Simple Table	
Heading 1	Heading 2	Heading 3
100	200	300
150	250	100

Figure 1.27 HTML Display of Simple Table

HTML Forms

HTML forms are used to select different kinds of user input. A form requests input from a user. It contains normal content and controls. Controls allow users to interact with forms. The input tag '<input>' specifies simple input inside a form. The '<form>' tag specifies a fill-out form. You can use attributes of both tags ('<form>' and '<input>') to customize the displayed form.

Multiple forms can exist within a single document, but cannot be nested. Forms use two attributes – 'action' and 'method'. 'Action' specifies the URL to which the form's contents will be submitted. If this attribute is absent, the web browser will use the current URL. 'Method' is the means by which form data are sent between web pages.

Two types of methods can be used – 'get' and 'post' – to pass data between web pages. Both methods are discussed next.

Get and Post

The default is 'get'. The 'get' method causes the fill-out form contents to be appended to the URL as if they were a normal query. This makes the 'get' less secure because users can see the data appended to the URL. The 'post' method causes the fill-out form contents to be sent to the server in a data body rather than as part of the URL, which makes it more secure than 'get'.

Input Tag

The '<input>' tag is standalone, which means that no closing tag is needed. The more useful attributes of this tag include 'type', 'name', 'value', 'checked', 'size', and 'maxlength'.

The 'type' attribute is the type of input and can be 'text', 'password', 'checkbox', 'radio', 'submit' or 'reset'. The 'name' attribute is the symbolic name of the input field. The 'value' attribute is the value based on the type of input from the 'type' attribute. The 'checked' attribute is for a 'checkbox' or 'radio' type of input. The 'size' attribute indicates the size of the input field in characters. The 'maxlength' attribute indicates the maximum number of characters that are acceptable. The code example illustrates how to implement a checkbox (lines 12 and 15). Output is shown in Figure 1.28.

```
 1  <html><head>
 2  <style type="text/css">
 3  table.center {
 4  margin-left:auto;
 5  margin-right:auto;
 6  }
 7  </style></head>
 8  <body style="background-color:burlywood;">
 9  <div style="text-align:center;">
10  <form>Please make your choice:<br/>
11  <table class="center"><tr>
12  <td><input type="checkbox" name="apples" /></td>
13  <td>I like fruit!</td>
14  </tr><tr>
15  <td><input type="checkbox" name="carrot" /></td>
16  <td>I like veggies!</td>
17  </tr></table>
18  </form>
19  </div></body></html>
```

Figure 1.28 HTML Display of Checkbox

The following code illustrates how to implement a drop-down menu (lines 12–16). Output is shown in Figure 1.29.

```
 1  <html><head>
 2  <style type="text/css">
 3  table.center {
 4  margin-left:auto;
 5  margin-right:auto;
 6  }
 7  </style></head>
 8  <body style="background-color:burlywood;">
 9  <div style="text-align:center;">
10  <form method="post" action="next_page.html">
11  <table class="center"><tr>
12  <td><select name="menu1">
13  <option selected>Choice one</option>
14  <option>Choice two</option>
15  <option>Choice three</option>
```

```
16  </td></select></tr>
17  </table>
18  <table class="center"><tr>
19  <td><input style="text-align:center;" type="submit"
20  value="Submit" /></td>
21  <td><input style="text-align:center;" type="reset"
22  value="Reset" /></td>
23  </tr></table></form>
24  </div></body></html>
```

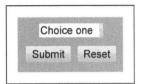

Figure 1.29 HTML Display of Drop-Down List

Drop-down menus are very useful when working with data from a database. The following code illustrates how to implement a radio button (lines 12–17). Output is displayed in Figure 1.30.

```
1   <html><head>
2   <style type="text/css">
3   table.center {
4   margin-left:auto;
5   margin-right:auto;
6   }
7   </style></head>
8   <body style="background-color:burlywood;">
9   <div style="text-align:center;">
10  <form method="post" action="handle_card.php">
11  <table class="center"><tr>
12  <td>Visa:</td><td><input type="radio" checked name="card"
13  size=4 /></td></tr><tr>
14  <td>Mastercard:</td><td><input type="radio" name="card"
15  size=20 /></td></tr><tr>
16  <td>Discover:</td><td><input type="radio" name="card"
17  size=20 /></td></tr>
18  </table>
19  <table class="center"><tr>
20  <td><input align="text-align:center;" type="submit" name="submit"
21  value="Submit" /></td>
22  <td><input align="text-align:center;" type="reset" name="reset"
23  value="Reset" /></td></tr>
24  </table></form>
25  </div></body></html>
```

Figure 1.30 HTML Display of Radio Button

In this section, HTML was introduced with examples to help you understand how it works. Website www. w3schools.com offers a more comprehensive introduction to HTML as well as other technologies like PHP, JavaScript, CSS, SQL, and XML. The next section introduces the basics of PHP. With PHP, you will learn how to make use of HTML forms and the data that are passed to them.

PHP Basics

PHP is a server-side scripting language, which means that PHP scripts are run on the server. The file extension for a PHP script *must* be 'php'. In my experience of teaching PHP, students who have a basic understanding of HTML and JavaScript fare much better. However, knowledge of HTML is more critical.

PHP works very well with Oracle. Oracle has committed significant resources in developing, testing, optimizing, and supporting open-source technologies such as PHP. Actually, PHP is Oracle's web scripting language of choice.

PHP files can contain text, HTML tags, and scripts. PHP can run on different platforms, but I only have experience working with the language on Linux. So, the book assumes you are running PHP on Linux. However, all PHP scripts provided in this book should run on any platform.

Syntax

A PHP file must begin with '<?php' and end with '?>'. To reduce spurious errors, be sure to place the beginning '<?php' tag on the first line, first (leftmost) column of the file. Also, be sure to leave no blanks or lines after the ending '?>' tag.

A PHP file typically contains HTML tags and PHP scripting code. In later chapters, I add SQL and JavaScript to PHP files. Each code line in PHP must end with a semicolon ';'. To display text on a web browser, two statements can be used – 'echo' and 'print'. I prefer using 'echo' because it is a bit shorter in length. PHP comments include '//' for a single-line comment and a matching pair of '/*' and '*/' to enclose a comment block. PHP file 'first.php' includes comments and displays some text (Figure 1.31). The file contains no HTML.

```
1  <?php
2  // File first.php
3  /* This file uses an 'echo' statement to display
4  simple output to the browser
5  */
6  echo "Hello World";
7  ?>
```

```
Hello World
```

Figure 1.31 PHP Display of Simple Text

I like to begin each PHP file with a single-line comment that contains the name of the file (line 2). In this case, the file is named 'first.php'. Although not required, I explicitly name each PHP file with a single-line comment to avoid confusion as I build multiple PHP files throughout the course of this book. I used blocked commenting to add multi-line comments (lines 3–5). Finally, I used 'echo' to display some simple text (line 6).

Variables

Variables are containers for storing information. PHP variables start with a '$' sign followed by the name of the variable. A variable must begin with a letter or the underscore character and can only contain alphanumeric characters and underscores. A variable name cannot contain spaces. Finally, variable names in PHP are case sensitive. A PHP variable is created the moment you first assign it a value. PHP file 'variable.php' shows how variables work.

```
1  <?php
2  // File variable.php
3  $username = 'dave';
4  $password = 'paper';
5  echo "The username is: $username<br />";
6  echo "The password is: $password";
7  ?>
```

```
The username is: dave
The password is: paper
```

Figure 1.32 PHP Display Variables Interpreted

The variable '$username' and '$password' are assigned 'dave' and 'paper', respectively (lines 3 and 4). The strings are displayed with two 'echo' statements (lines 5 and 6). Figure 1.32 shows what is displayed by loading the URL for the PHP code in a browser.

Be careful with quotation marks because single and double quotes are interpreted differently in 'echo' statements. In the next example, single quotes are used instead of double quotes.

```
1  <?php
2  // File variable.php
3  $username = 'dave';
4  $password = 'paper';
5  echo 'The username is: $username<br />';
6  echo 'The password is: $password';
7  ?>
```

```
The username is: $username
The password is: $password
```

Figure 1.33 PHP Display with Variables Not Interpreted

Figure 1.33 shows that variables are not interpreted by the PHP engine when single quotes are used (lines 5 and 6). So, use double quotes if you want the PHP engine to interpret variable values. However, you can use either single or double quotes when assigning a string to a variable.

Concatenation

The concatenation operator '.' is used to put two string values together. PHP file 'concatenate.php' uses concatenation to join strings 'dave' and 'paper' (line 5). Notice that in line 5, I place a space between first and last names to improve what is displayed (Figure 1.34).

```php
1  <?php
2  // File concatenate.php
3  $fname = 'dave';
4  $lname = 'paper';
5  echo "The name is: " . $fname . " " . $lname;
6  ?>
```

```
The name is: dave paper
```

Figure 1.34 PHP Display with Concatenated Variable

Functions

PHP supports two types of function – built-in and custom. **Built-in functions** provide a simple way to use functionality without having to build your own code. PHP file 'function.php' introduces three useful functions – 'strlen()', 'strpos()', and 'substr()'.

The 'strlen()' function returns the length of a string and accepts one parameter (the string). The 'strpos()' function searches for a character or text within a string and accepts two parameters (the string and a string to search for within it). The 'substr()' function returns part of a string and accepts either two or three parameters (the string, starting position (within the string), and length (characters beginning from the starting position). If the length parameter is omitted, the substring starting from the starting position until the end of the string is returned. A **parameter** is used in a function to refer to one of the pieces of data provided as input to the function. Parameters can also be referred to as *arguments*.

```php
1  <?php
2  // File function.php
3  $db = "Oracle 12c";
4  $search1 = "Oracle";
```

```
 5  $search2 = "12c";
 6  echo strlen($db) . '<br />';
 7  echo strpos($db,$search1) . '<br />';
 8  echo substr($db,0) . '<br />';
 9  echo substr($db,1) . '<br />';
10  echo substr($db,7,3) . '<br />';
11  echo substr($db,0,3) . '<br />';
12  echo substr($db,0,-4) . '<br />';
13  ?>
```

```
10
0
Oracle 12c
racle 12c
12c
Ora
Oracle
```

Figure 1.35 PHP Display with String Functions

As shown in Figure 1.35, 'Oracle 12c' has a length of '10' (line 6) and position of 'Oracle' in 'Oracle 12c' begins at '0' (line 7). In PHP, strings begin at index '0' rather than index '1'. The substring of 'Oracle 12c' starting at position '0' (line 8) is 'Oracle 12c'. The substring of 'Oracle 12c' starting a position '1' is 'racle 12c' (line 9). The substring of 'Oracle 12c' starting at position '7' and going forward three characters is '12c' (line 10). The substring of 'Oracle 12' starting at position '0' and going forward three characters is 'Ora' (line 11). Finally, the substring of 'Oracle 12c' starting at position '0' while removing the last four characters is 'Oracle' (line 12). Using a negative number as the third parameter in a 'substr()' function indicates the number of characters to omit from the end of the string.

A ***custom function*** is one that is built by the programmer to automate a set of tasks. A custom function can also be referred to as a *user-defined function*. The following example creates a custom function that returns the average of the elements in an array. An ***array*** is a variable that holds multiple values of the same type. I put 'custom.php' in one file and 'invoke_custom.php' in another file to enhance modularity. To display results, load 'invoke_custom.php' (URL pointing to the file) in a web browser (Figure 1.36).

```
1  <?php
2  // File custom.php
3  function calc_avg_array($arr)
4  {
5  $avg = array_sum($arr)/count($arr);
6  return $avg;
7  }
8  ?>
```

```
1  <?php
2  // File invoke_custom.php
3  require_once('custom.php');
4  $array = array(10,20,30,40,50);
```

```
5 $result = calc_avg_array($array);
6 echo "Average is: " . $result;
7 ?>
```

```
Average is: 30
```

Figure 1.36 PHP Display with Calculated Average

PHP file 'custom.php' includes function 'calc_avg_array' (lines 3–7), which accepts a parameter assumed to be an array (line 3), calculates the average of the array elements (line 5) and returns the result to the calling environment (line 6). Built-in function 'array_sum()' (line 5) returns the sum of array elements and built-in function 'count()' (line 5) returns the number of array elements. Using these two built-in functions, it is easy to calculate the average.

PHP file 'invoke_custom.php' includes the contents of 'custom.php' with the 'require_once()' function (line 3) so that the custom function is within scope of the invoking program. That is, to use code from another file you must include the contents of the other file in the calling program. Variable '$array' holds the array contents (line 4). Variable '$result' invokes function 'calc_avg_array()' with the array '$array' as parameter (line 5). The 'echo' displays results (line 6).

Arrays

A PHP array is actually an ordered map that associates values to keys. A *key* points to an array element (value). Keys can be named or numbered. Numbered keys are the default and begin with index '0', so you need not define numbered keys explicitly. PHP file 'simple_array.php' illustrates how array keys map to array elements (values). Figure 1.37 displays the results.

```
 1  <?php
 2  // File simple_array.php
 3  $arr1 = array
 4  (
 5  "dog" => "dalmation",
 6  "cat" => "persian",
 7  "bird" => "cockatoo"
 8  );
 9  $arr2 = array
10  (
11  "dalmation",
12  "persian",
13  "cockatoo"
14  );
15  echo "<strong>named key</strong><br />";
16  echo "My new cat is a: " . $arr1["cat"] . '<br />';
17  echo "<strong>number key</strong><br />";
18  echo "My new cat is a: " . $arr2[1];
19  ?>
```

```
named key
My new cat is a: persian
number key
My new cat is a: persian
```

Figure 1.37 PHP Display with Arrays

The first array '$arr1' (lines 3–8) uses 'named' keys, while the second array '$arr2' (lines 9–14) uses 'numbered' keys. You don't need to provide keys explicitly when using the 'numbered' (default) option. Keep in mind that numbered keys start with index '0', so the key to access the 'cat' element (line 18) is index '1'(second position in the array). The key to access 'cat' element using a named key is "cat" (line 16).

Conditional Statements

Conditional statements are used to perform different actions based on different conditions. PHP uses 'if', 'else', and 'elseif' statements to perform conditional branches. PHP file 'if_else.php' illustrates how to use conditional branching (Figure 1.38).

```php
1  <?php
2  // File if_else.php
3  $val = 10;
4  if($val < 10)
5  {
6  echo "Value less than 10";
7  }
8  elseif($val > 10)
9  {
10  echo "Value greater than 10";
11  }
12  elseif($val == 10)
13  {
14  echo "Value equal to 10";
15  }
16  else
17  {}
18  ?>
```

```
Value equal to 10
```

Figure 1.38 PHP Display with Conditional Statements

The first condition (lines 4–7) tests whether '$val' is less than '10'. Since it is not, PHP moves to the second condition (lines 8–11), which tests whether '$val' is greater than '10'. Since it is not, PHP moves to the third condition (lines 12–15), which tests whether '$val' is equal to '10'. Notice in line 12 that two consecutive equal symbols '==' are required to test for equivalency. Since '$val' is equal to '10', the condition is true and the echo is executed.

Be *very careful* with equivalency because two consecutive equal symbols '==' are required. Using only one equal sign actually assigns the value to the variable, which means that the condition will always be true! Notice that the last condition 'else' (lines 16 and 17) includes empty curly brackets '{}', which means that no action is taken if this condition is true.

PHP Iteration

PHP supports three types of iteration (looping) – 'while', 'for', and 'foreach'. *Loops* execute a block of code a specified number of times, or while a specified condition is true.

A 'while' loop iterates through a block of code while a specified condition is true. A 'for' loop iterates through a block of code a specified number of times. A 'foreach' loop iterates through a block of code for each element in an array or object. PHP file 'loop.php' illustrates each type of loop.

```php
1  <?php
2  // File loop.php
3  $i = 1;
4  echo "<strong>while loop</strong><br />";
5  while($i <= 2)
6  { echo "The number is " . $i . '<br />';
7  $i++; }
8  echo "<strong>for loop</strong><br />";
9  for($i=1; $i<=2; $i++)
10 { echo "The number is " . $i . '<br />'; }
11 $array = array
12 ( "ford" => "mustang",
13 "chevrolet" => "camaro",
14 "mazda" => "miata" );
15 echo "<strong>foreach loop</strong><br />";
16 foreach($array as $key=>$value)
17 { echo $key . ' => ' . "$value<br />"; }
18 ?>
```

```
while loop
The number is 1
The number is 2
for loop
The number is 1
The number is 2
foreach loop
ford => mustang
chevrolet => camaro
mazda => miata
```

Figure 1.39 PHP Display with Loops

The 'while' and 'for' loop are very similar, except 'while' continues as long as the value meets the condition, but 'for' knows in advance how many times the script should run. The 'while' loop continues as long as variable '$i' is less than or equal to 2 (line 5). Variable '$i' is incremented by one with '$i++' (line 7). The 'for' loop begins with value of '1', continues until it is less than or equal to '2', and is incremented by one (line 9). The 'foreach' loop is designed to work with arrays and objects. The 'foreach' loop (line 16) displays the 'key' and 'value' pairs (line 17). Run the code to see what is displayed (Figure 1.39).

PHP '$_GET' Variable

The predefined '$_GET' variable is used to collect values in a form where information sent is displayed in the address bar of the browser. There is a limit on the amount of information that can be sent.

   The following example illustrates how this variable is used. There are two files. The first file contains the HTML form, but is named 'get.php' to adhere to the naming convention I use in this book. A comment to name the file is the only logic contained between the PHP tags (lines 1–3). The form's 'method' and 'action' are defined in line 13. So, the form uses 'get' to send data to the file 'handle_get.php' (identified with the 'action' attribute) upon submission. User inputs are defined in lines 15 through 18 with 'input' tags. The 'input' tags define data to be passed with 'type' as text and 'name' as "username" and "password", respectively. Form submission is defined in lines 21 and 22 with an 'input' tag.

```
1  <?php
2  // File get.php
3  ?>
4  <html><head>
5  <style type="text/css">
6  table.center {
7  margin-left:auto;
8  margin-right:auto;
9  }
10 </style></head>
11 <body style="background-color:burlywood;">
12 <div style="text-align:center;">
13 <form method="get" action="handle_get.php">
14 <table class="center"><tr>
15 <td>User:</td><td><input type="text"
16 name="username" /></td></tr><tr>
17 <td>Password:</td><td><input type="text"
18 name="password" /></td></tr><tr>
19 </table>
20 <table class="center"><tr>
21 <td><input align="text-align:center;" type="submit"
22 name="submit" value="Submit" /></td>
23 <td><input align="text-align:center;" type="reset"
24 name="reset" value="Reset" /></td></tr>
25 </table></form>
26 </div></body></html>
```

The second file contains logic to handle the information sent with the form and is named 'handle_get.php'. Lines 3 and 4 set 'get' input from the form to variables with '$_GET', which holds key–value pairs (where keys are the names of the form controls and values are the input data from the user).

```
1  <?php
2  // File handle_get.php
3  $username = $_GET["username"];
4  $password = $_GET["password"];
5  echo "The username is: " . $username;
6  echo "<br />The password is: " . $password;
7  ?>
```

Load 'get.php' in a browser, enter a 'username' and 'password', and click the 'submit' button. Figure 1.40 shows the form with data entered just prior to submission. Figure 1.41 shows the data passed by the form. Notice that the values of 'username' and 'password' are visible within the URL in the browser bar.

Figure 1.40 PHP Display with 'GET' Form

Figure 1.41 PHP Display with 'GET' Form Result

PHP '$_POST' Variable

The predefined '$_POST' variable is used to collect values in a form where information sent is invisible to others. There are no limits on the amount of data that can be sent.

The following example illustrates how this variable is used. There are two files. The first file contains the HTML form and is named 'post.php'. A comment to name the file is the only logic contained between the PHP tags (lines 1–3). The form's 'method' and 'action' are defined in line 13. So, the form uses 'post' to post data to 'handle_post.php' (identified with the 'action' attribute) when the form is submitted. User inputs are defined in lines 15 through 18 with 'input' tags. The 'input' tags define data to be passed with 'type' as text and 'name' as "username" and "password", respectively. Form submission is defined in lines 21 and 22 with an 'input' tag.

```
1  <?php
2  // File post.php
3  ?>
4  <html><head>
5  <style type="text/css">
6  table.center {
```

```
 7  margin-left:auto;
 8  margin-right:auto;
 9  }
10  </style></head>
11  <body style="background-color:burlywood;">
12  <div style="text-align:center;">
13  <form method="post" action="handle_post.php">
14  <table class="center"><tr>
15  <td>User:</td><td><input type="text"
16  name="username" /></td></tr><tr>
17  <td>Password:</td><td><input type="text"
18  name="password" /></td></tr><tr>
19  </table>
20  <table class="center"><tr>
21  <td><input align="text-align:center;" type="submit"
22  name="submit" value="Submit" /></td>
23  <td><input align="text-align:center;" type="reset"
24  name="reset" value="Reset" /></td></tr>
25  </table></form>
26  </div></body></html>
```

The second file contains logic to handle the information sent with the form and is named 'handle_post.php'. Lines 3 and 4 set 'post' input from the form to variables with '$_POST', which holds key–value pairs (where keys are the names of the form controls and values are the input data from the user).

```
1  <?php
2  // File handle_post.php
3  $username = $_POST["username"];
4  $password = $_POST["password"];
5  echo "The username is: " . $username;
6  echo "<br />The password is: " . $password;
7  ?>
```

Load 'post.php' in a browser, enter a 'username' and 'password', and click the 'submit' button. Figure 1.42 shows the form with data entered just prior to submission. Figure 1.43 shows the data passed by the form. Notice that values of "username" and "password" are not visible within the URL in the browser bar.

Figure 1.42 PHP Display with 'POST' Form

The username is: david
The password is: paper

Figure 1.43 PHP Display with 'POST' Form Result

JavaScript Basics

JavaScript is the most popular object-oriented programming language in the world. It allows developers to control the behavior of web pages. In this section, I will cover JavaScript basics. A more comprehensive coverage can be found at www.w3schools.com/js/default.asp.

HTML Document Object Model (DOM)

The *HTML DOM* is the W3C standard for accessing HTML elements. JavaScript can change HTML content by manipulating the DOM. The first example demonstrates how JavaScript can change the value of the source attribute (src) of an HTML 'image' element.

The first file is 'light.js'. It contains a function defining an 'image' variable that points to a location within an HTML document, uses two 'gif' files (one image is an 'on' light, the other is an 'off' light), and runs an 'if-else' branch to control processing. Line 1 uses a comment to identify the file name as 'light.js'. Line 2 uses the 'function' keyword to define the function name 'light'. The variable 'image' (line 4) points to 'myImage' inside an HTML document. The 'if' condition 'image.src.match("bulbon")' (line 5) uses method 'match' on the 'src' attribute (within the 'image' tag of the HTML document) to check if the bulb is on or off. If true, the 'off' light image is displayed (line 6). The 'else' condition (line 7) runs if the bulb is 'off' and displays the 'on' light (line 8).

```
1  // File light.js
2  function light()
3  {
4  var image = document.getElementById('myImage');
5  if(image.src.match("bulbon"))
6  { image.src = "pic_bulboff.gif"; }
7  else
8  { image.src = "pic_bulbon.gif"; }
9  }
```

The second file 'on_off.php' uses the 'script' tag to identify the external file 'light.js' (line 7). The image tag (line 8) use attribute 'id' to define the image, the 'onclick()' event handler (line 8) to identify the function to be run when the image is clicked, and the source file of the 'off' image (line 9).

```
1  <?php
2  // File on_off.php
3  ?>
4  <html>
5  <body>
6  <div style="text-align:center">
7  <script src="light.js"></script>
8  <img id="myImage" onclick="light()"
```

```
 9  src="pic_bulboff.gif" width="50" height="50">
10  <p>Click to turn on/off</p>
11  </div>
12  </body>
13  </html>
```

The 'gif' images are included on the companion website (Chapter 1 folder). Both 'gif' images must be copied to your Linux account for the scripts to work. Be careful to use the '.js' file extension for external JavaScript files.

Load the 'on_off.php' URL in a web browser. Figure 1.44 shows the light bulb in the 'off' state. Click the image. Figure 1.45 shows the bulb in the 'on' state.

Figure 1.44 Light Bulb 'Off' Using JavaScript

Figure 1.45 Light Bulb 'On' Using JavaScript

Validate Data

JavaScript can validate input data. To demonstrate, two files are used for this example – 'validate.php' and 'validate.js'.

The 'validate.js' file checks whether a number is between 1 and 10 or whether it is an illegal number with function 'isNaN()'. Specifically, line 4 defines variables 'x' and 'text'. Line 5 assigns the value of the input field with id="number" in the HTML document to 'x'. The 'if' condition (lines 6 and 7) checks whether the number is less than 1 or greater than 10 (that is, whether it is an illegal number). If true, "Input not valid" is assigned to 'text'. Otherwise (lines 8 and 9), "Input OK" is assigned to 'text'. Finally, the 'text' value is placed in the HTML document where id="doit", which is the second paragraph tag (<p>).

```
1  // File validate.js
2  function validate()
3  {
4  var x, text;
5  x = document.getElementById("number").value;
```

```
 6  if(isNaN(x) || x < 1 || x > 10)
 7  { text = "Input not valid"; }
 8  else
 9  { text = "Input OK"; }
10  document.getElementById("doit").innerHTML = text;
11  }
```

The 'validate.php' file includes 'validate.js' (line 7) and a button tag with the 'onclick()' event handler (line 10). The 'input' tag (line 9) enables user input and the paragraph with id="doit" (line 12) is where output is directed from the JavaScript function 'validate()'.

```
 1  <?php
 2  // File validate.php
 3  ?>
 4  <html>
 5  <body>
 6  <div style="text-align:center">
 7  <script src="validate.js"></script>
 8  <p>Input a number between 1 and 10:</p>
 9  <input id="number" type="text">
10  <button type="button" onclick="validate()">
11  Submit</button>
12  <p id="doit"></p>
13  </div>
14  </body>
15  </html>
```

Load the 'validate.php' URL in a web browser. Figure 1.46 shows the initial state. Figure 1.47 shows what happens when a valid number is entered.

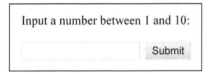

Figure 1.46 Initial State Using JavaScript

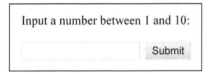

Figure 1.47 After Valid Number Entered Using JavaScript

JavaScript is case sensitive, so 'x' and 'X' are two different variables. The same is true with function names. Functions 'light()' and 'Light()' are two different functions.

JavaScript Statements

In HTML, JavaScript statements are 'commands' to the web browser. That is, they tell the browser what to do. The following example takes a number as user input and returns the number squared to the browser. It also includes a means to clear the returned number from the browser.

The 'square.js' file contains two functions. The 'square()' function assigns the value of the input field with id="in" in the HTML document to 'x' (line 5). It then squares the value of 'x' (line 6) and places the result in the HTML document paragraph tag (<p>) with id="out" (line 7). The 'clr()' function places an empty string in the HTML document where id="out" (the paragraph tag), which clears the result from the browser (lines 11 and 12).

```
1  // square.js
2  function square()
3  {
4  var x;
5  x = document.getElementById("in").value;
6  x = x * x;
7  document.getElementById("out").innerHTML = x;
8  }
9  function clr()
10 {
11 var p = document.getElementById("out");
12 p.innerHTML= "";
13 }
```

The 'square.php' file includes 'square.js' (line 7), a button tag for handling the 'square()' function (lines 9 and 10), and a button tag for handling the 'clr()' function (lines 11 and 12). User input is handled by the 'input' tag (line 8) with id="in". The result is handled by the 'paragraph' tag (line 13) with id="out".

```
1  <?php
2  // File square.php
3  ?>
4  <html>
5  <body>
6  <div id="all" style="text-align:center">
7  <script src="square.js"></script>
8  <input id="in" type="text">
9  <button type="button" onclick="square()">
10 Submit</button>
11 <button type="button" onclick="clr()">
12 Clear</button>
13 <p id="out"></p>
14 </div>
15 </body>
16 </html>
```

Load the 'square.php' URL in a web browser. Figure 1.48 shows the initial state. Enter '7' and click on 'Submit'. Figure 1.49 shows what happens when a number is entered. Click on 'Clear' to remove what is displayed (Figure 1.50).

Figure 1.48 Initial State Using JavaScript

Figure 1.49 After Number Entered Using JavaScript

Figure 1.50 Clear Screen Using JavaScript

Summary

The goal of this chapter was to facilitate a fundamental understanding of Linux, HTML, PHP, and JavaScript. I defined concepts as they were discussed in the chapter. Code examples with explanations were used throughout to reinforce learning.

2 Object-Oriented Concepts and Fundamentals

Overview

Object-oriented programming (OOP) is a design philosophy that uses objects and methods rather than linear concepts of procedures and tasks (procedural programming) to accomplish programmatic goals. An *object* is a self-sustainable construct that enables reusability of code. A *method* specifies one operation without providing any details to describe how the operation should be carried out. This chapter covers OOP fundamentals, including classes, properties, methods, and objects. In addition, encapsulation, polymorphism, inheritance, abstract classes, interfaces, aggregation, and supplemental OOP concepts are covered.

Learning Objectives

After you complete this chapter, you will gain a fundamental understanding of OOP concepts through explanation and code examples. The following objectives summarize the skills the chapter will help you develop:

1 Learn the main advantages of OOP.
2 Learn the building blocks of OOP.
3 Learn how to create and instantiate a class.
4 Learn OOP fundamentals.
5 Learn about getters and setters.
6 Learn about the constructor, destructor, and 'toString' methods.
7 Learn about constants and static methods and properties.
8 Learn about type hinting.
9 Learn about exception handling.
10 Learn about debugging.

Advantages of OOP

Object-oriented programming (OOP) has four main advantages over procedural programming – modularity, code reusability, information-hiding, and debugging ease.

Modularity is when a piece of code is independent of other pieces of code. *Reusability* is when code can be used, without modification, to perform a specific service regardless of what application uses the code. OOP facilitates code reusability by making it easy to break down complex tasks into generic modules (classes) and separate files that contain classes from the main PHP script. *Information-hiding* is when the details of the internal implementation of a module (class) remain hidden from the outside world. *Debugging ease* means that when a problem occurs, it is much easier to fix because the module (class) is independent from other pieces of code. Independent modules (classes) facilitate easier maintenance because the code is modular by nature. So, modifying one piece of code doesn't impact other pieces of code in the application. Reliability is also enhanced because the natural modularity of OOP helps ensure consistency of the code. Once a module (class) has been tested, it can be thought of as a 'black box' and relied upon to produce consistent results. Such consistency means that you only have to fix a coding problem in one place.

Class

The fundamental building block of OOP is a class. A *class* is a collection of related properties and methods wrapped in a pair of curly braces and labeled with its name. A *property* is what we normally think of in procedural programming as a variable. A *method* is what we normally think of as a function in procedural programming. Properties and methods, however, are much more flexible than their procedural programming counterparts.

Object

An *object* is a data structure consisting of data fields and methods together with their interactions. To use the properties and methods of a class, an object (an instance of a class) must be created. Creation of an object from a class is generally referred to as instantiation (or creating an instance) of a class.

Encapsulation

Encapsulation is an OOP fundamental that ensures that each part (class) of an application is self-contained and doesn't interfere with any others, except in a clearly defined manner. This means that encapsulation prevents the values of important properties from being changed except by following the rules laid out by the class.

Encapsulation allows you to prevent unauthorized access to a class by hiding its properties and methods. To implement encapsulation, a property or method can be defined as public, private, or protected.

Public allows access from both inside and outside the class. *Protected* can only be accessed from within an object's method. *Private* is even more restrictive because, like protected, it can only be accessed from within the object's method, but it is inaccessible from a derived object's method. That is, private properties or methods cannot be used with inheritance. We will talk about inheritance shortly, so don't worry about this distinction because it will be explained with examples later in the chapter.

Inheritance

Inheritance is a way to reuse the code of existing objects. That is, an object is able to inherit characteristics from another object. So, once a class has been developed, you don't have to reinvent the wheel. You can create a new (child) class that inherits either some or all of the characteristics of the parent class without having to rewrite the code already tested in the parent. Inheritance is therefore most useful when the parent's properties and methods can be reused in different contexts.

Polymorphism

Polymorphism is the ability to create a property or method of an object that has more than one form. While inheritance allows you to pass the characteristics of a parent class to a child class, polymorphism allows you to override existing properties and methods. That is, you can use the same property or method names, but modify them to suit your needs.

OOP vs. Procedural Programming

When properly applied, polymorphism, encapsulation, and inheritance combine to produce a programming environment that supports the development of far more robust and scalable programs than does procedural programming. I have already mentioned that OOP better facilitates modularity, code reusability, information-hiding, and debugging ease. Before we can start OOP, you need to understand the 'new' keyword and 'this' identifier.

New

The *new* keyword creates an instance of a class. When an instance (object) is created (instantiated), the new object must be assigned to a variable. The new object is allocated its own copies of the properties and methods defined in the class, and then the constructor of the object is called if one was defined. I will talk about constructors later in the chapter.

This

The *this* pseudo-variable is built into all objects and points to the current object. It allows access to properties and methods within the object instance. PHP automatically sets '*this*' to point to the object you are currently working on. Let's look at an example to help you understand how '*this*' works.

PHP file 'use_this.php' contains class 'use_this' (lines 3–15) that encapsulates private property '$_array' (line 5), public method 'sum()' (lines 6–10), and public method 'avg()' (lines 11–14). The purpose of '$_array' is to hold the array passed into the class. It is convention (and recommended) to use '_' before the variable name when using 'protected' or 'private' properties. The purpose of method 'sum()' is to return the sum of array elements (passed to the class). The purpose of method 'avg()' is to return the average of array elements.

```php
1  <?php
2  // File use_this.php
3  class use_this
4  {
5  private $_array;
6  public function sum($array)
7  {
8  $this->_array = $array;
9  return array_sum($array);
10 }
11 public function avg()
12 {
13 return $this->sum($this->_array)/count($this->_array);
14 }
15 }
16 ?>
```

From top to bottom, method 'sum()' assigns the array passed into the class to the '$this->_array' property (line 8) and returns the sum of array elements. Once assigned, '$this->_array' can be used anywhere in the class. Built-in PHP function 'array_sum()' (line 9) automatically sums array element values. Method 'avg()' returns the average of array elements (line 13) and is calculated by dividing the sum of array elements by the number of array elements. Summing array elements is done by invoking method 'sum()' with '$this->sum' and using the array as parameter with '$this->_array'. Using 'this' with method 'sum()' allows you to invoke the method anywhere within the class. Counting array elements is done by using the built-in PHP function 'count()' with the array as parameter. The array is referred to with '$this->_array'.

Notice that PHP uses the keyword 'function' to refer to OOP methods. Also notice how 'this' is used to make properties available inside the class and invoke methods inside the class.

Now, I use a script to instantiate the class and display results. I always place a class in its own PHP file to enhance modularity. This way, other applications and classes can use the class. I also recommend naming a class and PHP file similarly. PHP file 'run_use_this.php' invokes the class, makes calculations, and displays results.

```php
1  <?php
2  // File run_use_this.php
3  require_once("use_this.php");
4  $list = array(10,20,30);
5  $c = new use_this;
6  echo "Sum is: " . $c->sum($list);
7  echo '<br />';
8  echo "Average is: " . $c->avg();
9  ?>
```

The '//' symbol is a comment that identifies the file name (line 2). As a gentle reminder, I always include the name of the file at the top of each PHP script for clarification. To use the class, include it in the calling script with 'require_once()' (line 3). Variable '$list' (line 4) is assigned an array with three elements. Next, variable '$c' (line 5) is assigned a new instance of class 'use_this' with the 'new' keyword. To invoke a method outside a class, use the name of the object instance (in this case '$c') followed by an arrow and method name. So, the sum of array elements is displayed with '$c->sum($list)' (line 6) and the average of array elements with '$c->avg()' (line 8). Notice that 'echo' (lines 6–8) is used to display output to the screen. Also notice the use of double quotes for displaying character strings and a single dot '.' for concatenation of strings.

Both 'sum()' and 'avg()' methods are accessible because they are defined as 'public' in class 'use_this'. Typically, methods are defined as 'public' to make them available outside a class. The output from 'run_use_this.php' is shown in Figure 2.1.

```
Sum is: 60
Average is: 20
```

Figure 2.1 Output from 'use_this' Class

The next bit of code should help you better understand public, protected, and private visibility. It is not recommended to use 'echo' inside a class, but we do it here to help you visualize the concept at hand.

PHP file 'display.php' contains class 'display' (lines 3–14), which defines 'public', 'protected', and 'private' properties, and assigns values to each (lines 5–7). Method 'displayVals()' (lines 8–13) displays each property to the screen.

```php
1  <?php
2  //File display.php
3  class display
4  {
5  public $dog = 'Spaniel';
6  protected $_cat = 'Persian';
7  private $_bird = 'Parrot';
8  public function displayVals()
9  {
10 echo $this->dog;
```

```
11 echo $this->_cat;
12 echo $this->_bird;
13 }
14 }
15 ?>
```

PHP file 'call_display.php' creates a new instance of class 'display' (line 4) and displays values assigned to the class properties (lines 5–7). Calling script 'call_display.php' produces an error because both 'protected' and 'private' properties are not directly accessible outside the class (Figure 2.2).

```
1  <?php
2  //File call_display.php
3  require_once 'display.php';
4  $see = new display();
5  echo $see->dog; // Works
6  echo $see->_cat; // Fatal Error
7  echo $see->_bird; // Fatal Error
8  ?>
```

Spaniel Fatal error: Cannot access
protected property display::$_cat in
/home/paper/public_html/call_display
on line 6

Figure 2.2 Error Displayed Trying to Access Protected or Private Property

A fatal error occurs whenever you try to access a 'protected' or 'private' class property from the calling environment. To fix the error, modify file 'call_display.php' by calling 'public' method 'displayVals()' (line 5) directly (which works because the method is public). Figure 2.3 shows the desired results, which means that the error was fixed.

```
1  <?php
2  //File call_display.php
3  require_once 'display.php';
4  $see = new display();
5  echo $see->displayVals();
6  ?>
```

SpanielPersianParrot

Figure 2.3 Output from 'display' Class

Inheritance and Polymorphism Example

The next example demonstrates inheritance and polymorphism. Modify the 'display.php' file to include a new class 'poly'. The new class inherits the characteristics of the 'display' class by using the 'extends' keyword.

```php
1  <?php
2  //File display.php
3  class display
4  {
5  public $dog = 'Spaniel';
6  protected $_cat = 'Persian';
7  private $_bird = 'Parrot';
8  public function displayVals()
9  {
10 echo $this->dog;
11 echo $this->_cat;
12 echo $this->_bird;
13 }
14 }
15 class poly extends display
16 {
17 public $dog = 'Terrier';
18 public function displayVals()
19 {
20 $display = parent::displayVals();
21 echo $display;
22 }
23 }
24 ?>
```

Class 'poly' (lines 15–23) *extends* the 'display' class, thereby inheriting all its 'public' and 'protected' properties and methods. Keep in mind that 'private' properties and methods cannot be inherited from the parent class. Also, notice the use of the scope resolution operator '::' preceded by keyword 'parent' in the 'poly' class (line 20), which allows 'poly' to access the 'displayVals()' method from class 'display'. Polymorphism is at play when overriding the value of '$dog' (line 17) and modifying the 'displayVal()' method in 'poly' (lines 18–22). The modified 'call_display.php' script creates a new instance of both 'display' (line 4) and 'poly' (line 7) and displays the results (Figure 2.4).

```php
1  <?php
2  //File call_display.php
3  require_once 'display.php';
4  $see = new display();
5  echo $see->displayVals();
6  echo '<br />';
7  $extend = new poly();
8  echo $extend->displayVals();
9  ?>
```

```
SpanielPersianParrot
TerrierPersianParrot
```

Figure 2.4 Output from 'display' and 'poly' Classes

Setters and Getters

Setters are methods that set the value of a property, while **getters** are methods that get the value of a property (return the value to the calling environment). PHP file 'get_set.php' illustrates both method types.

```php
1  <?php
2  //File get_set.php
3  class get_set
4  {
5  public $testArray = array();
6  public $dog;
7  protected $_cat;
8  private $_bird;
9  public function setVals()
10 {
11 $this->dog = 'Pomeranian';
12 $this->_cat = 'Siamese';
13 $this->_bird = 'Cockatoo';
14 $this->setArray();
15 }
16 public function setArray()
17 {
18 $this->testArray[0] = $this->dog;
19 $this->testArray[1] = $this->_cat;
20 $this->testArray[2] = $this->_bird;
21 }
22 public function getVals()
23 {
24 return $this->testArray;
25 }
26 }
27 ?>
```

PHP file 'get_set.php' contains the 'get_set' class (lines 3–26) with two set methods and one get method. The 'setVals()' method (lines 9–15) sets 'public' property '$dog' (line 11), 'protected' property '$_cat' (line 12), and 'private' property '$_bird' (line 13). The method ends by invoking the 'setArray()' method (line 14). Remember that the characteristics of '$_bird' cannot be inherited because it is defined as 'private'. The 'setArray()' method (lines 16–21) sets the first three elements of array '$testArray' to the values of the three properties respectively (lines 18–20). The 'getVals()' method (lines 22–25) returns (gets) the array back to the calling environment.

PHP file 'call_get_set.php' creates a new instance of 'get_set' (line 4) and invokes the 'setVals()' method (line 5). Once invoked, the last line of the 'setVals()' method invokes the 'setArray()' method (see line 14 in 'get_set').

Next, variable '$see' (line 6) is assigned the populated array. Finally, the 'foreach' loop (lines 7 and 8) iterates through the array elements and displays values one by one (Figure 2.5).

```php
1  <?php
2  //File call_get_set.php
3  require_once 'get_set.php';
4  $animal = new get_set();
5  $animal->setVals();
6  $see = $animal->getVals();
7  foreach($see as $display)
8  { echo $display . '<br />'; }
9  ?>
```

```
Pomeranian
Siamese
Cockatoo
```

Figure 2.5 Output from 'get_set' Class

Constructor Method

When you create a new instance of a class (object), PHP automatically looks for the class constructor first. A ***constructor*** builds the object, sets default values, and assigns values (passed to the class) to properties when an object is initiated. A constructor can also include calls to class methods.

A constructor is designated in a PHP class with keyword 'construct' preceded by *two* consecutive underscores. PHP file 'bear.php' contains class 'bear', which includes a constructor. PHP file 'call_bear.php' instantiates class 'bear' and displays the results. When a new instance of 'bear' is created, the constructor in class 'bear' is automatically run.

```php
1  <?php
2  // File bear.php
3  class bear
4  {
5  public $bearArray = array();
6  public function __construct($tag,$weight,$color)
7  {
8  $this->bearArray['tag'] = $tag;
9  $this->bearArray['weight'] = $weight;
10 $this->bearArray['color'] = $color;
11 }
12 public function getVals()
13 { return $this->bearArray; }
14 }
15 ?>
```

Class 'bear' constructor (lines 6–11) sets '$bearArray' elements with values passed into the class as parameters (lines 8–10). In this case, the constructor obviates the need for a setter. That is, a setter is not needed. The 'getVals()' method (lines 12 and 13) returns (gets) the populated array to the calling environment.

```php
1  <?php
2  // File call_bear.php
3  require_once 'bear.php';
4  $baby = new bear('Baby Bear',100,'brown');
5  $see_it = $baby->getVals();
6  echo 'Tag is ' . $see_it['tag'];
7  echo '<br />Weight is ' . $see_it['weight'];
8  echo '<br />Color is ' . $see_it['color'];
9  ?>
```

PHP file 'call_bear.php' creates a new instance of 'bear' (line 4), assigns the populated array to variable '$see_it' (line 5), and displays the results (lines 6–8). Figure 2.6 shows the results.

```
Tag is Baby Bear
Weight is 100
Color is brown
```

Figure 2.6 Output from 'bear' Class

The next example creates a new class 'polar_bear' in its own file that uses inheritance to access class 'bear' properties and methods. PHP file 'polarbear.php' contains class 'polar_bear' that extends class 'bear'. Class 'polar_bear' thereby inherits all characteristics of class 'bear' with the exception of private elements.

```php
1  <?php
2  // File polar_bear.php
3  class polar_bear extends bear
4  {
5  protected $_cold;
6  public function __construct($tag,$weight,$color)
7  { parent::__construct($tag,$weight,$color); }
8  public function ice()
9  {
10 $this->_cold = 'chilly';
11 return $this->_cold;
12 }
13 }
14 ?>
```

Keyword 'parent' followed by the scope resolution operator (line 7) is used to invoke the constructor from the parent class 'bear'. The scope resolution operator is represented by the '::' symbol (two consecutive colon symbols). Public method 'ice()' (lines 8–12) is a method in 'polar_bear' that is not in 'bear'.

PHP file 'call_polar_bear.php' creates a new instance of 'polar_bear' (line 5), assigns values to variable '$see_it' (line 6) using the 'getVals()' method inherited from 'bear', and displays results (lines 7–9). It also invokes its own method 'ice()', assigns results to '$weather', and displays results (lines 10 and 11). Figure 2.7 shows what is displayed. Notice that you must include both the original file 'bear.php' (since it holds the 'bear' class) and file 'polar_bear.php' for everything to work properly.

```php
1  <?php
2  // File call_polar_bear.php
3  require_once 'bear.php';
4  require_once 'polar_bear.php';
5  $polar = new polar_bear('adult',600,'white');
6  $see_it = $polar->getVals();
7  echo 'Tag is ' . $see_it['tag'];
8  echo '<br />Weight is ' . $see_it['weight'];
9  echo '<br />Color is ' . $see_it['color'];
10 $weather = $polar->ice();
11 echo '<br />Weather is ' . $weather;
12 ?>
```

```
Tag is adult
Weight is 600
Color is white
Weather is chilly
```

Figure 2.7 Output from 'polar_bear' Class

Abstract Class

An *abstract class* defines the basic structure of a class, but *cannot* be instantiated on its own. It must be 'extended' by another class to work. It contains properties and methods, but some methods are incomplete and waiting for some other class to extend them (through inheritance). If a method is defined as 'abstract', it cannot be declared private because inheritance must be used. Remember that only 'public' or 'protected' methods can be extended through inheritance. The advantage is that 'abstract' forces all child classes to define the details of a method so that multiple classes can be created to do different things.

PHP file 'abstract_employee.php' contains abstract class 'abstract_employee' (lines 3–15) with three 'protected' properties (lines 5–7), a 'public' method 'setdata()' (lines 8–13), and an abstract method 'outputData()' (line 14). Keyword 'abstract' (line 3) preceding keyword 'class' defines class 'abstract_ employee' as abstract.

```php
1  <?php
2  // File abstract_employee.php
3  abstract class abstract_employee
4  {
5  protected $_empfirst;
6  protected $_emplast;
```

```
 7  protected $_empage;
 8  public function setdata($empfirst,$emplast,$empage)
 9  {
10  $this->_empfirst = $empfirst;
11  $this->_emplast = $emplast;
12  $this->_empage = $empage;
13  }
14  abstract function outputData();
15  }
16  ?>
```

PHP file 'employee.php' contains class 'employee' (lines 3–21), which extends abstract class 'abstract_employee' (line 3) so that it can use 'setdata()' and 'outputData()' methods from 'abstract_employee'. The constructor invokes the 'setdata()' method (line 8) from the abstract class and its own 'outputData()' method (line 9). The class also contains the 'getVals()' method (lines 17–20). Notice how 'employee' provides its own details for its 'outputData()' method (lines 11–16). Since 'outputData()' is defined as an abstract method in class 'abstract_employee', it *must* be implemented in 'employee' (the class that extended the abstract class).

```
 1  <?php
 2  // File employee.php
 3  class employee extends abstract_employee
 4  {
 5  public $testArray = array();
 6  public function __construct($first,$last,$age)
 7  {
 8  $this->setdata($first,$last,$age);
 9  $this->outputData();
10  }
11  public function outputData()
12  {
13  $this->testArray['first'] = $this->_empfirst;
14  $this->testArray['last'] = $this->_emplast;
15  $this->testArray['age'] = $this->_empage;
16  }
17  public function getVals()
18  {
19  return $this->testArray;
20  }
21  }
22  ?>
```

PHP file 'invoke_abstract_employee.php' creates a new instance of 'employee' (line 5), invokes its 'getVals()' method, places the results in '$see_it' (line 6), and displays the results (lines 7 and 8). Both 'abtract_employee. php' and 'employee.php' files are included (lines 3 and 4). Figure 2.8 shows the results.

```
1  <?php
2  // File invoke_abstract_employee.php
3  require_once 'abstract_employee.php';
4  require_once 'employee.php';
5  $val = new employee('Phil','Collins','50');
6  $see_it = $val->getVals();
7  echo $see_it['first'] . ' ' . $see_it['last'];
8  echo ' ' . $see_it['age'];
9  ?>
```

Phil Collins 50

Figure 2.8 Output from 'employee' Class ('abstract' Class)

Interface

An ***interface*** is a list of methods that *must* be implemented. All methods *must* be 'public'. However, an interface has no properties and cannot define how methods are to be implemented. An advantage is that an interface ensures that all classes that implement it have a common set of functionality.

To illustrate how an interface is implemented, I use the same abstract class 'abstract_employee' in PHP file 'abstract_employee.php', an interface in PHP file 'status.php', a modified 'employee' class in PHP file 'employee.php', and an invocation file 'invoke_status.php'.

Keyword 'interface' in 'interface_status.php' makes 'status' an interface (line 3). Interface 'status' includes public method 'getStatus()' (line 4) with no details.

```
1  <?php
2  // File interface_status.php
3  interface status
4  { public function getStatus(); }
5  ?>
```

Keyword 'implements' in 'employee.php' is *required* to utilize an interface. The 'employee' class (lines 3–26) inherits characteristics of abstract class 'abstract_employee' with keyword 'extends' and utilizes interface 'status' with keyword 'implements' (line 3). The constructor (lines 6–10) invokes methods 'setdata()' and 'outputData()' from abstract class 'abstract_employee'. Method 'outputData()' (lines 11–16) contains details not provided in abstract class 'abstract_employee'. Method 'getVals()' (lines 17 and 18) returns (gets) populated array to the calling environment. Method 'getStatus()' (lines 19–25) includes the details for interface 'status'. Finally, another class 'basic' (lines 27–31) is included in this file and contains different details for interface 'status'. Remember that interface 'status' only includes method 'getStatus()' with no details.

```
1  <?php
2  // File employee.php
3  class employee extends abstract_employee implements status
```

```
 4 {
 5 public $testArray = array();
 6 public function __construct($first,$last,$age)
 7 {
 8 $this->setdata($first,$last,$age);
 9 $this->outputData();
10 }
11 public function outputData()
12 {
13 $this->testArray['first'] = $this->_empfirst;
14 $this->testArray['last'] = $this->_emplast;
15 $this->testArray['age'] = $this->_empage;
16 }
17 public function getVals()
18 { return $this->testArray; }
19 public function getStatus()
20 {
21 if($this->_empage <= '39')
22 { return ' is a young person'; }
23 else
24 { return ' is an old person'; }
25 }
26 }
27 class basic implements status
28 {
29 public function getStatus()
30 { return ', but this is fine!'; }
31 }
32 ?>
```

PHP file 'invoke_interface_status.php' includes 'abstract_employee.php', 'interface_status.php', and 'employee.php' (lines 3–5) to enable access to abstract class 'abstract_employee', interface 'status', and class 'employee'. An instance of 'employee' is created (line 6), which inherits abstract class 'abstract_employee' and implements interface 'status'. An array is set and returned to '$see_it' with method 'getVals()' (line 7). Status is returned to '$status' with method 'getStatus()' (line 8). An instance of 'basic' is created (line 9), which implements interface 'status'. Status is returned to '$stuff' with method 'getStatus()' (line 10) and results are displayed (lines 11 and 12). Figure 2.9 displays the results.

```
1  <?php
2  // File invoke_status.php
3  require_once 'abstract_employee.php';
4  require_once 'interface_status.php';
5  require_once 'employee.php';
6  $val = new employee('Jesse','James','39');
7  $see_it = $val->getVals();
8  $status = $val->getStatus();
9  $more = new basic();
```

```
10 $stuff = $more->getStatus();
11 echo $see_it['first'] . ' ' . $see_it['last'];
12 echo ' ' . $see_it['age'] . ' ' . $status . $stuff;
13 ?>
```

```
Jesse James 39 is a young person, but this is fine!
```

Figure 2.9 Output from 'employee' Class ('abstract' Class and 'status' Interface)

I suggest spending extra time with the abstract class and interface examples because they tend to be two of the harder concepts to digest in OOP.

Aggregation

Aggregation is a technique that allows one object to act as a container for one or more other objects. Aggregation can be thought of as a relationship between two classes that is best described as a 'has-a' and 'whole–part' relationship. The container class is the 'has-a' part, while the contained class is the 'whole–part' of the relationship.

Aggregation can be used as an alternative to inheritance. An advantage of aggregation over inheritance is that it is easier to create cleanly separated classes that are responsible for one task and nothing else. With inheritance, classes are more dependent on one another, given the natural 'parent–child' relationship that is always created. With aggregation, the container class does not pass on its characteristics to the contained class. A disadvantage of aggregation is that you must add large numbers of methods to the interface of the contained class or otherwise expose its instance to the word (which adds complexity to coding). This is because, unlike inheritance, the contained class cannot use properties or methods from the container class. Disadvantages of inheritance include possible bloated class trees that are difficult to change and maintain over time and tight coupling between parent and child, which increases dependencies.

To illustrate aggregation, I first provide a simple inheritance example and then change it to an aggregation example by modifying the files. The example uses three PHP files – 'fruit.php', 'apple.php', and 'invoke_apple.php'.

```
1  <?php
2  // File fruit.php
3  class fruit
4  {
5  public function peel()
6  {
7  return "Peeling is appealing.";
8  }
9  }
10 ?>
```

The 'fruit.php' file contains class 'fruit' (lines 3–9). Class 'fruit' has one method, 'peel()' (lines 5–8), which returns a string to the calling environment.

```
1  <?php
2  // File apple.php
3  class apple extends fruit
4  { }
5  ?>
```

The 'apple.php' file contains class 'apple' (lines 3 and 4). Class 'apple' extends (inherits) class 'fruit'. The class contains nothing else.

```
1  <?php
2  // File invoke_apple.php
3  require_once 'fruit.php';
4  require_once 'apple.php';
5  $apple = new apple();
6  $see = $apple->peel();
7  echo $see;
8  ?>
```

The 'invoke_apple.php' file includes the 'fruit' and 'apple' classes (lines 3 and 4), creates a new instance of 'apple' (line 5), invokes the 'peel()' method (line 6) inherited from the 'fruit' class, and displays results (line 7). Figure 2.10 shows what is displayed in a browser when the URL pointing to 'invoke_apple.php' is loaded.

Peeling is appealing.

Figure 2.10 Output from 'apple' Class ('fruit' Class Inheritance)

Now, let's turn our attention to aggregation. The example uses the same PHP files, but slightly modifies them.

```
1  <?php
2  // File fruit.php
3  class fruit
4  {
5  public $stuff;
6  public function peel()
7  {
8  $this->stuff = 'Yahoo';
9  return "Peeling is appealing.";
10 }
11 }
12 ?>
```

I change class 'fruit' by adding property '$stuff' (line 5) and a setter for the property (line 8).

```
 1  <?php
 2  // File apple.php
 3  class apple
 4  {
 5  private $_fruit;
 6  public function __construct()
 7  {
 8  $this->_fruit = new fruit();
 9  }
10  public function apple_peel()
11  {
12  return $this->_fruit->peel() . " " . $this->_fruit->stuff;
13  }
14  }
15  ?>
```

PHP file 'apple.php' contains a modified class 'apple' (lines 3–14). Changes include adding property '$_fruit' (line 5), a constructor (lines 6–9), and method 'apple_peel()' (lines 10–13).

The constructor assigns a new instance of 'fruit' to '$this->_fruit' (line 8) . The 'apple_peel()' method invokes the 'peel()' method and '$stuff' property from class 'fruit' (line 12), and returns the result to the calling environment.

```
1  <?php
2  // File invoke_apple.php
3  require_once 'fruit.php';
4  require_once 'apple.php';
5  $apple = new apple();
6  $see = $apple->apple_peel();
7  echo $see;
8  ?>
```

File 'invoke_apple.php' creates a new instance of 'apple' (line 5), invokes the 'apple_peel()' method (line 6), and displays results (line 7). Figure 2.11 shows the results.

```
Peeling is appealing. Yahoo
```

Figure 2.11 Output from 'apple' Class ('fruit' Class Aggregation)

In this example, aggregation occurs when class 'apple' creates a new instance of class 'fruit'. All 'public' methods and properties of 'fruit' are accessible to class 'apple'. However, 'protected' and 'private' methods and properties are not available.

Aggregation cleanly separates the two classes, but requires more code and complexity to obtain the same results as inheritance. It is difficult to recommend when to use inheritance or aggregation because it depends on what you are trying to accomplish.

So far in the chapter, I have presented fundamental OOP concepts and reinforced them with coding examples. So, you should possess a basic skill set and understanding of OOP. I now move forward with supplementary OOP concepts, including magic methods, type hinting, constants, static properties and methods, exception handling, and debugging.

Magic Methods

Magic methods are automatically invoked in specific circumstances. The magic methods I cover include constructors, 'toString', and destructors. Since I have already covered constructors, no examples are provided in this section.

PHP magic methods begin with a double underscore. For instance, '__construct()' runs automatically when an object is instantiated with the 'new' keyword. Another useful magic method is '__toString()', which allows you to specify what to display and also runs automatically upon instantiation of a new object.

The next example illustrates how to use the '__toString()' method and uses two PHP files – 'tostring.php' and 'call_tostring.php'.

```php
1  <?php
2  // File tostring.php
3  class person
4  {
5  private $_desc;
6  public function __construct($first_name,$age)
7  {
8  $this->first_name = $first_name;
9  $this->age = $age;
10 }
11 public function getFirstName()
12 {
13 return $this->first_name;
14 }
15 public function getAge()
16 {
17 return $this->age;
18 }
19 public function __toString()
20 {
21 $this->_desc = $this->getFirstName() . ' (age ' .
22 $this->_desc .= $this->getAge() . ')';
23 return $this->_desc;
24 }
25 }
26 ?>
```

PHP file 'tostring.php' contains class 'person' (lines 3–25), a constructor (lines 6–10), method 'getFirst-Name()' (lines 11–14), method 'getAge()' (lines 15–18), and a 'toString()' magic method (lines 19–24). The constructor accepts name and age (line 6) and sets them to properties (lines 8 and 9). When 'person' is instantiated, 'tostring()' is automatically invoked. When invoked, 'tostring()' calls methods 'getFirstName()' and 'getAge()', builds a string, places the string in '$this->_desc' (lines 21 and 22), and returns the result (line 23).

The 'toString()' magic method returns the full description of a person as a string (lines 21–23). To avoid an error, be sure that whatever the 'toString()' method returns is a string. I assign strings to 'private' property '$_desc' (lines 21 and 22), so no errors occur.

```php
1  <?php
2  // File call_tostring.php
3  require_once 'tostring.php';
4  $person = new person('Dave','52');
5  echo $person;
6  ?>
```

PHP file 'call_tostring.php' includes the 'tostring.php' file (line 3), creates a new instance of 'person' (line 4), and displays results (line 5). Figure 2.12 shows the results. The constructor and 'toString()' run automatically upon instantiation of 'person', since they are magic methods. Also notice that object '$person' is displayed directly. This only works because the class contains a 'toString()' method. If you try to display the object of a class directly without a 'toString()' method, an error will occur. So, be careful!

```
Dave (age 52)
```

Figure 2.12 Output from 'person' Class with 'toString' Magic Method

Since 'toString()' automatically builds and returns the final string, less code is needed, which is an advantage of using magic methods. You can also use 'toString()' to help debug since it automatically displays values of your choice.

Two caveats are in order at this point. First, be sure to precede magic methods with two consecutive underscores. Second, be sure that the 'toString()' method returns a character string. If it returns anything else, an error will occur.

I recommend explicitly converting any 'toString()' return values that you are unsure about. Two options are available to accomplish conversion – type casting or the 'strval()' function. Type casting variable '$varname' to a string is accomplished by placing '(string)' before the variable and assigning it to another variable.

```php
$var = (string)$varname;
```

Using the 'strval()' function is accomplished by using the variable as a parameter to the function and assigning it to another variable.

```php
$var = strval($varname);
```

The next example illustrates an improper way to use 'toString()'. The example uses PHP files 'avg.php' and 'call_avg.php'.

```php
1  <?php
2  // File avg.php
3  class avg
4  {
```

```
 5 private $_arr;
 6 private $_avgval;
 7 public function __construct($arr)
 8 {
 9 $this->_arr = $arr;
10 $this->calc_avg();
11 }
12 public function calc_avg()
13 {
14 $this->_avgval = array_sum($this->_arr)/count($this->_arr);
15 return $this->_avgval;
16 }
17 }
18 ?>
```

PHP file 'avg.php' contains class 'avg' (lines 3–17), which returns the average of an array. The constructor (lines 7–11) sets property '$_arr' and invokes the 'calc_avg()' method (lines 12–16). The 'calc_avg()' method uses built-in functions 'array_sum()' and 'count()' (line 14) to calculate the average, and returns the result to the calling environment (line 15).

```
1 <?php
2 // File call_avg.php
3 require_once 'avg.php';
4 $arr = array(10,20,30,40,50);
5 $obj = new avg($arr);
6 echo "Average is: " . $obj;
7 ?>
```

PHP file 'call_avg.php' instantiates class 'avg' (line 5) and attempts (but fails) to display results (Figure 2.13).

```
Catchable fatal error: Object of class avg could not be
converted to string in
/home/paper/public_html/call_avg.php on line 6
```

Figure 2.13 Error Displayed because of Improper Usage of 'toString' Method

The error occurs because the PHP engine expects 'toString()' to set a string value for the object. One solution is to remove the call to the 'calc_avg()' method from the constructor, add an external call to the method, and display results (Figure 2.14). This way, the PHP engine doesn't look for 'toString()' because no attempt was made to display the object as a string.

```
1 <?php
2 // File avg.php
3 class avg
```

```
4 {
5 private $_arr;
6 private $_avgval;
7 public function __construct($arr)
8 {
9 $this->_arr = $arr;
10 }
11 public function calc_avg()
12 {
13 $this->_avgval = array_sum($this->_arr)/count($this->_arr);
14 return $this->_avgval;
15 }
16 }
17 ?>
```

The setter (line 9) is all that remains in the constructor.

```
1 <?php
2 // File call_avg.php
3 require_once 'avg.php';
4 $arr = array(10,20,30,40,50);
5 $obj = new avg($arr);
6 $val = $obj->calc_avg();
7 echo "Average is: " . $val;
8 ?>
```

Notice that I added an explicit call to 'calc_avg()' (line 6).

Average is: 30

Figure 2.14 Output from 'avg' Class with 'toString' Method Removed

Another solution is to add '__toString()' to class 'avg' and modify it accordingly. Be sure to change PHP file 'call_avg.php' back to its original form. Both modified files are shown next for your convenience. Notice that the 'return' statement was removed from method 'calc_avg()' because it is not needed. Also notice that function 'strval()' (line 18) was added to magic method 'toString()' to ensure proper conversion. Figure 2.15 shows the results.

```
1 <?php
2 // File avg.php
3 class avg
4 {
5 private $_arr;
6 private $_avgval;
```

```
 7 public function __construct($arr)
 8 {
 9 $this->_arr = $arr;
10 $this->calc_avg();
11 }
12 public function calc_avg()
13 {
14 $this->_avgval = array_sum($this->_arr)/count($this->_arr);
15 }
16 public function __toString()
17 {
18 $this->_avgval = strval($this->_avgval);
19 return $this->_avgval;
20 }
21 }
22 ?>
```

```
1 <?php
2 // File call_avg.php
3 require_once 'avg.php';
4 $arr = array(10,20,30,40,50);
5 $obj = new avg($arr);
6 echo "Average is: " . $obj;
7 ?>
```

Average is: 30

Figure 2.15 Output from 'avg' Class with 'toString' Method

PHP automatically handles garbage collection, which is removal of variables and objects that are no longer needed once the PHP script has finished processing. However, you can manually delete a resource using magic method '__destruct()'. Like other magic methods, PHP automatically runs '__destruct()'. But unlike others, '__destruct()' is automatically run immediately before the PHP engine removes a defined object from memory. After the destructor is run, the object is released from memory. A destructor cannot take arguments.

An example illustrates how a destructor works. The example uses PHP files 'destruct.php' and 'call_destruct.php'.

```
1 <?php
2 // File destruct.php
3 class destruct
4 {
5 public function __construct()
6 {
```

```
 7  print get_class($this) . ' is defined.' . '<br />';
 8  }
 9  public function __destruct()
10  {
11  print 'Destroying ' . get_class($this);
12  }
13  }
14  ?>
```

Class 'destruct' (lines 3–13) contains a constructor (lines 5–8) and a destructor (lines 9–12). Function 'get_class()' (lines 7 and 11) is built-in and returns the class name of the current instance (because the parameter provided to the function is '$this').

```
1  <?php
2  // File call_destruct.php
3  require_once 'destruct.php';
4  $obj = new destruct();
5  ?>
```

PHP file 'call_destruct.php' invokes class 'destruct'. Figure 2.16 shows the results.

```
destruct is defined.
Destroying destruct
```

Figure 2.16 Output from 'destruct' Class with 'destruct' Magic Method

Type Hinting

PHP *type hinting* allows you to explicitly type cast a value as objects of a class or an array. Type hinting automatically generates an error message if the data type of the actual parameter does not match the data type of the formal parameter. An ***actual parameter*** is the actual value that is passed into a method by the calling program (calling environment). A ***formal parameter*** is the identifier used in a method to stand for the value that is passed into the method by the calling program (calling environment). While an actual parameter is the value itself, a formal parameter acts like a placeholder. When a method is called, the formal parameter is temporarily 'bound' to the actual parameter.

With type hinting, methods can force parameters to be objects or arrays. This is accomplished by preceding the method's parameter with the type of data. For an object type hint, use the name of the class. For an array type hint, use the keyword 'array'.

The next set of examples illustrates how type hinting is implemented, using PHP files 'type_hint.php' and 'call_type_hint.php'. PHP file 'type_hint.php' contains two classes – 'mine' and 'yours'. Class 'mine' (lines 3–13) contains two methods. The first method 'test()' (lines 5–8) includes a type hint for object 'yours' that directly precedes parameter '$yours' (line 5). The second method 'count_array()' (lines 9–12) includes a type hint for an array that directly precedes parameter '$input_array' (line 9). Class 'yours' contains a single public property (lines 14–17).

```php
1  <?php
2  // File type_hint.php
3  class mine
4  {
5  public function test(yours $yours)
6  {
7  return $yours->var;
8  }
9  public function count_array(array $input_array)
10 {
11 return count($input_array);
12 }
13 }
14 class yours
15 {
16 public $var = 'Hello World';
17 }
18 ?>
```

PHP file 'call_type_hint.php' creates new object instances of 'mine' and 'yours' (lines 4 and 5). It then invokes method 'test()' from object 'mine' and passes parameter '$yours' (line 6). Results are displayed (line 7). Finally, method 'count_array()' from object 'mine' is invoked (line 8) and results are displayed (line 9). Figure 2.17 shows the results.

```php
1  <?php
2  // File call_type_hint.php
3  require_once 'type_hint.php';
4  $mine = new mine;
5  $yours = new yours;
6  $see = $mine->test($yours);
7  echo $see . '<br />';
8  $see_count = $mine->count_array(array('a', 'b', 'c'));
9  echo 'Array has ' . $see_count . ' elements.';
10 ?>
```

```
Hello World
Array has 3 elements.
```

Figure 2.17 Output from 'mine' and 'yours' Classes Using Type Hinting

To review, method 'test()' in class 'mine' ensures that parameter '$yours' is of object type 'yours' with type hint 'yours' (line 5, 'type_hint.php'). Method 'count_array()' ensures that parameter '$input_array' is of array type with type hint 'array' (line 9, 'type_hint.php').

For the next four examples, I use the same PHP file 'type_hint.php', but call it with different types of data to illustrate how type hinting works in different contexts. The first example, in file 'call_error1.php', passes a character string to the 'test()' method.

```php
1  <?php
2  // File call_error1.php
3  require_once 'type_hint.php';
4  $mine = new mine;
5  $yours = new yours;
6  $see = $mine->test('hello');
7  ?>
```

PHP file 'call_error1.php' creates an instance of both classes (lines 4 and 5) and then passes string 'hello' as a parameter to method 'test' (line 6). An error occurs because method 'test()' includes a type hint that restricts the parameter to object type 'yours'. Since, we passed string 'hello' (which is not an object of type 'yours') to the 'test()' method, PHP automatically returns an error (Figure 2.18).

Catchable fatal error: Argument 1 passed to mine::test() must be an instance of yours, string given, called in /home/paper/public_html/call_error1.php on line 6 and defined in /home/paper/public_html/type_hint.php on line 5

Figure 2.18 Error Displayed Trying to Pass a String Type Hinted for an Object

The second example in PHP file 'call_error2.php' passes an object of class 'mine' to the 'test()' method.

```php
1  <?php
2  // File call_error2.php
3  require_once 'type_hint.php';
4  $mine = new mine;
5  $yours = new yours;
6  $see = $mine->test($mine);
7  ?>
```

PHP file 'call_error2.php' creates an instance of both classes (lines 4 and 5) and then passes an instance of 'mine' as a parameter to method 'test' (line 6). An error occurs because the 'test()' method includes a type hint that restricts the parameter to object type 'yours'. Since, we passed an instance of 'mine' (which is an object of type 'mine', not an object of type 'yours') to the 'test()' method, PHP automatically returns an error (Figure 2.19).

Catchable fatal error: Argument 1 passed to mine::test() must be an instance of yours, instance of mine given, called in /home/paper/public_html/call_error2.php on line 6 and defined in /home/paper/public_html/type_hint.php on line 5

Figure 2.19 Error Displayed Trying to Pass 'mine' Type Hinted for 'yours' Object

The third example in PHP file 'call_error3.php' passes 'null' to the 'test()' method.

```php
1  <?php
2  // File call_error3.php
3  require_once 'type_hint.php';
4  $mine = new mine;
5  $yours = new yours;
6  $see = $mine->test(null);
7  ?>
```

PHP file 'call_error3.php' creates an instance of both classes (lines 4 and 5) and then passes 'null' as a parameter to method 'test' (line 6). An error occurs because the 'test()' method includes a type hint that restricts the parameter to type 'yours'. Since, we passed 'null' to the 'test' method, PHP automatically returns an error (Figure 2.20).

Catchable fatal error: Argument 1 passed to mine::test() must be an instance of yours, null given, called in /home/paper/public_html/call_error3.php on line 6 and defined in /home/paper/public_html/type_hint.php on line 5

Figure 2.20 Error Displayed Trying to Pass 'null' Type Hinted for 'yours' Object

The fourth example in PHP file 'call_error4.php' passes a string to the 'count_array()' method.

```php
1  <?php
2  // File call_error4.php
3  require_once 'type_hint.php';
4  $mine = new mine;
5  $yours = new yours;
6  $see_array = $mine->count_array('a string');
7  ?>
```

PHP file 'call_error4.php' creates an instance of both classes (lines 4 and 5) and then passes a string as a parameter to method 'count_array()' (line 6). An error occurs because the 'count_array' method includes a type hint that restricts the parameter to type 'array'. Since, we passed a string to the 'count_array()' method, PHP automatically returns an error (Figure 2.21).

Catchable fatal error: Argument 1 passed to mine::count_array() must be of the type array, string given, called in /home/paper/public_html/call_error4.php on line 6 and defined in /home/paper/public_html/type_hint.php on line 9

Figure 2.21 Error Displayed Trying to Pass String Type Hinted for an Array

The final example uses an 'array' type hint for parameter '$a' in a constructor. PHP file 'avg_hint.php' contains class 'avg_hint' (lines 3–25), which contains a public and private property (lines 5 and 6), a constructor (lines 7–11), and two methods. Public property '$arr' (line 5) is cast as an array type. The constructor accepts one parameter that is protected with an 'array' type hint (line 7), which means that only an array type can be passed to the constructor. The method 'dynamic()' (lines 12–20) totals all elements of the array passed to the class (lines 14–18) and assigns the average to '$this->_avg' (line 19). Method 'getAvg()' (lines 21–24) returns the array average (line 23).

```php
1  <?php
2  // File avg_hint.php
3  class avg_hint
4  {
5  public $arr = array();
6  private $_avg;
7  public function __construct(array $a)
8  {
9  $this->arr = $a;
10 $this->dynamic();
11 }
12 public function dynamic()
13 {
14 $total = 0;
15 foreach ($this->arr as $avg)
16 {
17 $total = $total + $avg;
18 }
19 $this->_avg = $total/count($this->arr);
20 }
21 public function getAvg()
22 {
23 return $this->_avg;
24 }
25 }
26 ?>
```

PHP file 'call_avg_hint.php' creates an array (line 4), a new instance of 'avg_hint' (line 5), calls method 'getAvg()' (line 6), and displays the results (line 7). Figure 2.22 shows the results.

```php
1  <?php
2  // File call_avg_hint.php
3  require_once 'avg_hint.php';
4  $array = array(10,20,30,20,20);
5  $total = new avg_hint($array);
6  $see_it = $total->getAvg();
7  echo $see_it;
8  ?>
```

20

Figure 2.22 Output from 'avg_hint' Class Type Hinted for an Array

Type hinting is a useful technique for limiting the types of acceptable data passed to a class method. Although limited to objects and arrays, it strengthens the ability to protect websites from what comes in from the outside world.

Constants

Constants are values that never change. Unlike properties, constants do not begin with '$'. Constants are normally written in uppercase letters. You do not need to instantiate an object to access a constant, but you do need to instantiate an object if you want to access a method that uses a constant.

To access a constant inside a class, use the 'self' keyword with the scope resolution operator followed by the name of the constant. To access a constant externally, use the class name with the scope resolution operator followed by the name of the constant.

I now illustrate constants with an example. The example uses two PHP files – 'lbs_to_kilos.php' and 'call_lbs_to_kilos.php'.

```php
1  <?php
2  // File lbs_to_kilos.php
3  class lbs_to_kilos
4  {
5  const POUNDS_TO_KILOGRAMS = 0.45359237;
6  private $_val;
7  function displayInfo()
8  {
9  $this->_val = self::POUNDS_TO_KILOGRAMS;
10 return $this->_val;
11 }
12 }
13 ?>
```

PHP file 'lbs_to_kilos.php' contains a class 'lbs_to_kilos' (lines 3–12) with a constant (line 5), private property (line 6), and method that refers to the constant (lines 7–11). Method 'displayInfo()' (lines 7–11) assigns the constant to '$this_val' (line 9), and returns it to the calling environment. Notice that the 'self' keyword followed by the scope resolution operator and constant name are required to access the constant inside the class (line 9).

```php
1  <?php
2  // File call_lbs_to_kilos.php
3  require_once 'lbs_to_kilos.php';
4  echo lbs_to_kilos::POUNDS_TO_KILOGRAMS;
5  $val = new lbs_to_kilos();
6  $hold = $val->displayInfo();
7  echo '<br />' . $hold;
8  ?>
```

PHP file 'call_lbs_to_kilos.php' displays the constant without instantiating a new object (line 4), creates a new object so the constant within the method can be accessed externally (line 5), invokes 'displayInfo()' method and assigns result to '$hold' (line 6), and displays results (line 7). Figure 2.23 shows what is displayed. Notice that the class name, scope resolution operator, and constant name are needed to access the constant outside the class (line 4).

```
0.45359237
0.45359237
```

Figure 2.23 Output from Constant and 'lbs_to_kilos' Class

To review, object instantiation is not needed to display the constant, but object instantiation is needed to use the method that contains the constant. Also, remember to use the keyword 'self' with the scope resolution operator and constant name to access the constant inside the class method, and use the class name with the scope resolution operator and constant name to access the constant outside the class.

Static Properties and Methods

A *static property* is accessible without needing instantiation of a class, but, unlike a constant, *cannot* be accessed with an instantiated class object. To access a static property, place it in a 'public' static method and return its value. An example should help clarify how to use static properties and methods.

The example uses two PHP files – 'count.php' and 'call_count.php'. PHP file 'count.php' includes class 'count' (lines 3–11) with static property '$count' (line 5) and static method 'keep_track()' (lines 6–10), and class 'see_count' (lines 12–18) with static method 'see_result()' (lines 14–18).

In class 'count', static method 'keep_track()' uses the 'self' keyword with scope resolution operator and name of static property to access static property '$count'. So, 'self::$count++;' (line 8) increments static property '$count' by one and 'return self::$count;' (line 9) gets (returns) the value of '$count' to the calling environment with each call to 'keep_track()'.

Class 'see_count' extends 'count' (line 12), thereby inheriting the characteristics of class 'count'. Static method 'see_result()' uses the 'parent' keyword with scope resolution operator and name of static property (line 16) to access the value of static property '$count', which is returned. Since static property '$count' cannot be accessed with an instantiated class object, pseudo-variable '$this' is not available.

```php
 1  <?php
 2  // File count.php
 3  class count
 4  {
 5  public static $count = 0;
 6  public static function keep_track()
 7  {
 8  self::$count++;
 9  return self::$count;
10  }
11  }
12  class see_count extends count
13  {
```

```
14  public static function see_result()
15  {
16  return parent::$count;
17  }
18  }
19  ?>
```

PHP file 'call_count.php' displays the value of static property '$count' without instantiating a new object with class name, scope resolution operator, and static property name (line 4). To access and display the value of static property '$count' with a method, a new object instance is created (line 5) and public static method 'keep_track()' is invoked three times (lines 6–8). A new instance of 'see_count' is then created (line 9) and public static method 'see_result()' is invoked once (line 10). Figure 2.24 shows the results.

```
1   <?php
2   // call_count.php
3   require_once 'count.php';
4   echo count::$count . '<br />';
5   $obj = new count();
6   echo $obj->keep_track() . '<br />';
7   echo $obj->keep_track() . '<br />';
8   echo $obj->keep_track() . '<br />';
9   $obj = new see_count();
10  echo $obj->see_result() . '<br />';
11  ?>
```

```
0
1
2
3
3
```

Figure 2.24 Output from Static Variable, and 'count' and 'see_count' Classes

Static properties are valuable because they retain previously assigned values. In our example, we were able to build a counter with the help of a static property and a static method.

The next example converts pounds to kilograms and vice versa using static properties and methods. The example uses two files – 'convert_static.php' and 'call_convert_static.php'.

PHP file 'convert_static.php' contains the 'convert_static' class (lines 3–17). The class contains two static properties (lines 5 and 6), two private properties (lines 7 and 8), and two static methods. Static method 'convertLbToKg()' (lines 9–12) converts pounds to kilograms and static method 'convertKgToLb()' (lines 13–16) converts kilograms to pounds.

```
1   <?php
2   // File convert_static.php
3   class convert_static
```

```
 4 {
 5 protected static $_lbToKg = 0.45359237;
 6 protected static $_KgToIb = 2.20462262;
 7 private $_pounds;
 8 private $_kilograms;
 9 public static function convertLbToKg($_pounds)
10 {
11 return $_pounds * self::$_lbToKg;
12 }
13 public static function convertKgToLb($_kilograms)
14 {
15 return $_kilograms * self::$_KgToIb;
16 }
17 }
18 ?>
```

PHP file 'call_convert_static.php' uses the static methods from class 'call_convert' for conversions. First, a new instance of 'convert_static' is created (line 4). Static properties '$_lbToKg' and '$_KgToIb' are accessed indirectly by public static methods 'convertLbToKg' (line 5) and 'convertKgToLb' (line 7), which return (get) the appropriate values. Figure 2.25 shows the results.

```
1  <?php
2  // File call_convert_static.php
3  require_once 'convert_static.php';
4  $val = new convert_static();
5  $weight_in_kilo = $val->convertLbToKg(100);
6  echo 'Weight in Kilograms is: ' . $weight_in_kilo;
7  $weight_in_pounds = $val->convertKgToLb(100);
8  echo '<br />Weight in Pounds is: ' . $weight_in_pounds;
9  ?>
```

```
Weight in Kilograms is: 45.359237
Weight in Pounds is: 220.462262
```

Figure 2.25 Output from 'convert_static' Class

Exception Handling

An *exception* is when something goes wrong in a block of code. Instead of handling the error when it occurs in the script, you can throw an exception and catch it in a special block. One advantage is that you can keep all error handling in a single place rather than scattering it throughout your script. Another advantage is that you can display what you wish to the screen rather than letting PHP display a generic and typically nasty looking error message. This is a big advantage because anyone seeing the message will only see what you wish them to see.

Within a customized message, you can instruct users what to do next instead of having them see a nasty PHP error message. PHP has a built-in 'Exception' class that utilizes a 'Try' block, a 'Throw', and a 'Catch' block. The 'Try' block contains code that is being tested for errors. The 'Throw' is a mechanism for triggering an exception. Each 'Throw' must have at least one 'Catch' block. The 'Catch' block retrieves the exception and creates an object containing exception information.

If an exception is not triggered, code processing continues as normal. If an exception is triggered, an exception is thrown (triggered). Since the 'Exception' class has a built-in 'toString()' method, details can be displayed to the calling environment. An example is provided to help understanding.

The example uses two PHP files – 'checknum.php' and 'call_check_num.php'. PHP file 'checknum.php' includes class 'checknum' (lines 3–14) with 'private' property '$_num' (line 5) and 'public' method 'chk()' (lines 6–13).

Method 'chk()' accepts a number as parameter (line 6). If the number is not numeric (line 9), an exception is triggered (line 10). PHP built-in function 'is_numeric()' checks for numeric values. Placing '!' before the function does the opposite. That is, it checks for nonnumeric values. Although a custom message is included (line 10), a nasty message is displayed because the method does not include a 'try–catch' block.

```
1  <?php
2  // File checknum.php
3  class checknum
4  {
5  private $_num;
6  public function chk($number)
7  {
8  $this->_num = $number;
9  if(!is_numeric($this->_num))
10 { throw new Exception("Value '$this->_num' is nonnumeric!"); }
11 else
12 { return true; }
13 }
14 }
15 ?>
```

PHP file 'call_checknum.php' creates an instance of 'checknum' (line 5), invokes 'chk()' (line 6) with a non-numeric value from line 4, and displays a nasty result (line 7) (because no 'try–catch' block is present). Figure 2.26 shows the results.

```
1  <?php
2  // File call_checknum.php
3  require_once 'checknum.php';
4  $var = 'chicken';
5  $obj = new checknum();
6  $result = $obj->chk($var);
7  echo $result;
8  ?>
```

Fatal error: Uncaught exception 'Exception' with
message 'Value 'chicken' is nonnumeric!' in
/home/paper/public_html/checknum.php:10 Stack trace:
#0 /home/paper/public_html/call_checknum.php(6):
checknum->chk('chicken') #1 {main} thrown in
/home/paper/public_html/checknum.php on line 10

Figure 2.26 Nasty Error Displayed from Uncaught Exception

To rectify the problem, modify class 'checknum' by adding a 'try–catch' block.

```php
1  <?php
2  // File checknum.php
3  class checknum
4  {
5  private $_num;
6  public function chk($number)
7  {
8  $this->_num = $number;
9  try
10 {
11 if(!is_numeric($this->_num))
12 { throw new Exception("Value '$this->_num' is nonnumeric!"); }
13 else
14 { return true; }
15 }
16 catch(Exception $e)
17 { echo $e->getMessage(); }
18 }
19 }
20 ?>
```

Reload 'call_checknum.php' in a browser to see results (Figure 2.27).

Value 'chicken' is nonnumeric!

Figure 2.27 Nice Message Displayed from Trapped Exception

Now, the error message is clean and informative. The 'catch' block uses the 'Exception' class built into the PHP engine. Two parameters – 'Exception' and '$e' – are passed to 'catch' (line 16). Parameter 'Exception' tells PHP to use the 'Exception' class. Parameter '$e' tells PHP to create a new instance of 'Exception' and place the object into variable '$e'. The message to users is retrieved by invoking method 'getMessage()' (line 17) from the 'Exception' class and displayed with the 'echo' statement (line 17).

The 'Exception' class can be extended to create custom error messages. PHP file 'custom_exception.php' contains class 'custom_exception' (lines 3–12) that extends 'Exception'. The class includes method 'errorMessage()'

(lines 5–11) that builds a customized error message. Built-in methods 'getLine()' (line 7), 'getFile()' (line 8), and 'getMessage()' (line 8) are used to build the error message.

```php
1  <?php
2  // File custom_exception.php
3  class custom_exception extends Exception
4  {
5  public function errorMessage()
6  {
7  $errorMsg = 'Error on line '. $this->getLine().
8  ' in '.$this->getFile() .': <b>'.$this->getMessage().
9  '</b> is not a valid E-Mail address';
10 return $errorMsg;
11 }
12 }
13 ?>
```

PHP file 'call_custom_exception.php' validates an email address with a built-in validate function and flag (lines 7 and 8). If the email address is invalid, an exception is triggered (line 10) and the 'catch' block (lines 13–16) displays the custom error message. Figure 2.28 shows the results.

```php
1  <?php
2  // File call_custom_exception.php
3  require_once 'custom_exception.php';
4  $email = "someone@example...com";
5  try
6  {
7  if(filter_var($email,
8  FILTER_VALIDATE_EMAIL) == FALSE)
9  {
10 throw new custom_exception ($email);
11 }
12 }
13 catch (custom_exception $e)
14 {
15 echo $e->errorMessage();
16 }
17 ?>
```

```
Error on line 9 in
/home/paper/public_html/call_custom_exception.php:
someone@example...com is not a valid E-Mail address
```

Figure 2.28 Nice Message Displayed from Custom Exception

A custom exception class can be used with the built-in 'Exception' class. PHP file 'call_multiple.php' uses the custom class we created (line 9) to test for a valid email address. If valid, a test is made (line 10) to see if the word 'example' is in the valid email.

```
 1  <?php
 2  // File call_multiple.php
 3  require_once 'custom_exception.php';
 4  $email = "someone@example...com";
 5  try
 6  {
 7  if(filter_var($email,
 8  FILTER_VALIDATE_EMAIL) == FALSE)
 9  { throw new custom_exception($email); }
10  if(strpos($email, "example") == FALSE)
11  { throw new Exception
12  ("$email is not an example e-mail"); }
13  }
14  catch (custom_exception $e)
15  { echo $e->errorMessage(); }
16  catch(Exception $e)
17  { echo $e->getMessage(); }
18  ?>
```

Since email 'someone@example...com' is invalid, 'custom_exception' is triggered and the appropriate error message is displayed (Figure 2.29).

```
Error on line 8 in
/home/paper/public_html/call_multiple.php:
someone@example...com is not a valid E-Mail address
```

Figure 2.29 Nice Message Displayed from Custom and Built-In Exceptions

Modify PHP file 'call_multiple.php' to use a valid email address – 'someone@exampe.com' (line 4). The email is valid, so class 'custom_exception' is not triggered. However, the email address does not include the word 'example', so built-in class 'Exception' is triggered (Figure 2.30).

```
 1  <?php
 2  // File call_multiple.php
 3  require_once 'custom_exception.php';
 4  $email = "someone@exampe.com";
 5  try
 6  {
 7  if(filter_var($email,
 8  FILTER_VALIDATE_EMAIL) == FALSE)
```

```
 9 { throw new custom_exception($email); }
10 if(strpos($email, "example") == FALSE)
11 { throw new Exception
12 ("$email is not an example e-mail"); }
13 }
14 catch (custom_exception $e)
15 { echo $e->errorMessage(); }
16 catch(Exception $e)
17 { echo $e->getMessage(); }
18 ?>
```

```
someone@exampe.com is not an example e-mail
```

Figure 2.30 Nice Message Displayed from Custom and Built-In Exceptions

Debugging

In this section, some simple techniques to aid in debugging are discussed. First, build classes that have a single theme whenever possible. That is, build classes that focus on one idea or task. The classes built in this chapter adhere to the notion of 'one idea or task' per OOP class. Single-theme classes mitigate (reduce) potential errors and are easier to debug. Second, use magic method 'toString()' to display values of properties. Third, use 'foreach()' to display the contents of an array or object. Extensive use of 'foreach()' is covered in later chapters. Fourth, use 'var_dump()' or 'print_r' to display information about a variable, including 'protected' and 'private' properties of an object. Use 'print_r()' to display more human-readable information. Finally, display contents of an array or property by getting values set in a class. An example should help.

The example uses two PHP files – 'dim.php' and 'call_dim.php'. PHP file 'dim.php' contains class 'dim' (lines 3–16) with a constructor (lines 6–11) that sets array elements (lines 8–10) from three incoming parameters (line 6) and a method 'getVals()' (lines 12–15) that gets the array.

```
 1 <?php
 2 // File dim.php
 3 class dim
 4 {
 5 public $dim = array();
 6 public function __construct($l,$w,$h)
 7 {
 8 $this->dim['length'] = $l;
 9 $this->dim['width'] = $w;
10 $this->dim['height'] = $h;
11 }
12 public function getVals()
13 {
14 return $this->dim;
```

```
15 }
16 }
17 ?>
```

PHP file 'call_dim.php' creates a new instance of 'dim' with the parameters length, width, and height (line 4). It then invokes 'getVals()' (line 5), and displays array contents (lines 7–11). Figure 2.31 shows the results.

```php
1  <?php
2  // File call_dim.php
3  require_once 'dim.php';
4  $dim = new dim('20','5','12');
5  $see_it = $dim->getVals();
6  echo 'Length is ' .
7  $see_it['length'] . ' inches ';
8  echo '<br />Width is ' .
9  $see_it['width'] . ' inches';
10 echo '<br />Height is ' .
11 $see_it['height'] . ' inches';
12 ?>
```

```
Length is 20 inches
Width is 5 inches
Height is 12 inches
```

Figure 2.31 Output from 'dim' Class that Displays Returned Array

Modify 'call_dim.php' to display contents of the array with 'foreach()' (lines 6 and 7), 'var_dump()' (line 9), and 'print_r' (line 11). With 'foreach()', display the index and corresponding element. With 'var_dump()', all array information is displayed, but can be difficult for an untrained programmer to decipher. With 'print_r()', less information is displayed but it is easier to understand. Figure 2.32 shows the results.

```php
1  <?php
2  // File call_dim.php
3  require_once 'dim.php';
4  $dim = new dim('20','5','12');
5  $see_it = $dim->getVals();
6  foreach($see_it as $key=>$value)
7  { echo "$key  $value<br />"; }
8  echo "<p>";
9  var_dump($see_it);
10 echo "<p>";
11 print_r($see_it);
12 ?>
```

```
length  20
width  5
height  12

array(3) { ["length"]=> string(2) "20" ["width"]=>
string(1) "5" ["height"]=> string(2) "12" }

Array ( [length] => 20 [width] => 5 [height] => 12 )
```

Figure 2.32 Output from 'dim' Class Using 'foreach', 'var_dump', and 'print_r'

Now, modify class 'dim' in PHP file 'dim.php' by adding a 'toString()' magic method (lines 13–22). Be sure to include two consecutive underscores before the 'toString()' magic method. Notice how concatenation is used with the '.=' symbol to add to '$this->desc' property (lines 17–20).

```php
1  <?php
2  // File dim.php
3  class dim
4  {
5  public $dim = array();
6  public $desc;
7  public function __construct($l,$w,$h)
8  {
9  $this->dim['length'] = $l;
10 $this->dim['width'] = $w;
11 $this->dim['height'] = $h;
12 }
13 public function __toString()
14 {
15 $this->desc = "Length is " .
16 $this->dim['length'];
17 $this->desc .= "<br />Width is " .
18 $this->dim['width'];
19 $this->desc .= "<br />Height is " .
20 $this->dim['height'];
21 return $this->desc;
22 }
23 }
24 ?>
```

Modify PHP file 'call_dim.php'. Notice that the code is simplified because the 'toString()' magic method is automatically invoked when the instance is created. All that is needed is to display object instance '$dim' (Figure 2.33).

```php
1  <?php
2  // File call_dim.php
3  require_once 'dim.php';
```

```
4  $dim = new dim('20','5','12');
5  echo $dim;
6  ?>
```

```
Length is 20 inches
Width is 5 inches
Height is 12 inches
```

Figure 2.33 Output from 'dim' Class Using 'toString'

OOP Concepts Revisited

In this chapter, OOP advantages, fundamentals, and supplements with applicable code examples were introduced to reinforce and deepen knowledge. To further deepen understanding of OOP, a discussion of three important concepts – encapsulation, visibility, and extensibility – ends the chapter.

The idea of encapsulation is to create self-contained classes. As such, encapsulation facilitates modularity, reusability, information-hiding, and debugging. Independent classes promote modularity. Modular classes are easy to access from the outside world and to use in different contexts; this promotes reusability. Self-contained classes allow you to easily hide the details of the class from the outside world, thus promoting information-hiding. Finally, modular classes promote debugging ease because the code is simple and changing the code does not impact other classes.

If you create methods encapsulated in a class that are as mutually exclusive as possible, this further enhances modularity, reusability, information-hiding, and debugging ease. For instance, if you add a new method that is mutually exclusive from the existing methods, existing methods will work as before. So, even if the new method doesn't work properly, the other methods still work. Therefore, encapsulation not only facilitates modularity, reusability, information-hiding, and debugging ease, it also stabilizes a class by allowing addition or modification of methods without impacting the usability of the class.

Visibility determines whether a property or method can be accessed directly by any part of a script that uses a class or if it remains internal to the class. So, visibility promotes information-hiding. Visibility is determined by the keywords 'public', 'protected', and 'private', which were introduced as part of encapsulation at the beginning of the chapter. Visibility is therefore a term used to describe how to hide information as we attempt to encapsulate class methods and properties from the outside world.

Since methods often serve as the interface to the functionality of a class, they usually need to be 'public'. Properties, however, should almost always be hidden away as 'protected' or 'private', to prevent them from being accidently changed. If you ever intend to extend a class, you should use 'protected' visibility. Use 'private' visibility only if you do not want a method or property to be accessed outside the class. When you need to expose or change the value of a property, the normal way to do so is through a getter (expose) or setter (change) method.

Extensibility refers to the ability to extend a class through inheritance. To use inheritance, notice that we always use the keyword 'extends'. Extensibility is therefore the ability to implement inheritance principles in OOP.

Summary

The goal of this chapter was to facilitate a fundamental understanding of OOP concepts. I believe this goal was met by introducing fundamental OOP concepts and including coding examples (with explanation) to enrich practical application.

3   Login Security

Overview

Web security is critical to building a robust website. To help you build a secure website, several techniques are introduced, including login authentication, cleansing login data, encryption, strong password creation, SQL injection protection, session protection, and CAPTCHA. The security techniques introduced in this chapter are concerned with securing interactions with the Oracle database. Another form of web security, input validation, is introduced in the next chapter.

Learning Objectives

After you complete this chapter, you will gain a fundamental understanding of web security techniques that mitigate improper interactions with the Oracle database. The following objectives summarize the skills the chapter will help you develop:

1   Learn how to create an Oracle login table.
2   Learn how to cleanse login-related data.
3   Learn how to encrypt passwords.
4   Learn how to create a login page.
5   Learn how to implement login authentication.
6   Learn how to create a strong password.
7   Learn how to protect against SQL injection attacks.
8   Learn how to use session variables for *added* login security.
9   Learn how to implement CAPTCHA for *added* login security.

Login Data

Before you can learn about website security, you need data to secure. So, I start by showing you how to create an Oracle database table with valid usernames and passwords. Next, I show you how to create an Oracle database connection class. Finally, I show you how to test the connection class to ensure that it is working properly.

To interact with Oracle, I highly recommend using 'Oracle SQL Developer' (see Chapter 1 for installation guidance). Not only is this tool very widely used, it is user friendly.

Now, open an 'Oracle SQL Developer' session. On the top menu, click 'View', and choose 'Connections'. Click on the 'green' button (top left, directly under 'Connections' tab) and a login window appears. Enter 'Connection Name', 'Username', 'Password', 'Hostname', 'Port', and 'SID'.

'Connection Name' is your choice (I use 'test'). 'Username' and 'Password' are for the Oracle database (not for your Linux account). However, I use the same usernames and passwords for both Oracle and Linux accounts when I teach. 'Hostname' is the name of the host server where Oracle is installed. 'Port' is where Oracle listens for user requests. 'SID' is the system identifier for your Oracle instance. Ask your IT expert for appropriate login information. Click the 'Test' button. If successful, click the 'Connect' button to start a new session. Figure 3.1 shows the connection information that I use to access Oracle.

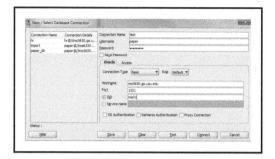

Figure 3.1 Display of Login Information from Oracle SQL Developer (http://www.oracle.com/technetwork/developer-tools/sql-developer/downloads/index.html)

Once connected, icon 'test' (or whatever name you entered for 'Connection Name') appears because this is the name you provided for 'Connection Name'. Click the small '+' button to the left of the 'Connection Name'. You see a multitude of object types from 'Tables' to 'Other Users'. Figure 3.2 shows the available Oracle objects.

Figure 3.2 Display of Available Oracle Objects (http://www.oracle.com/technetwork/developer-tools/sql-developer/downloads/index.html)

Click on the small '+' to the left of 'Tables' to see table objects. Since no table objects have been created, none are displayed. To the right, there should be a 'Worksheet' window. This window is where you type Structured Query Language (SQL) commands. ***SQL*** is the language of choice for interacting with relational databases like Oracle. If the worksheet is not displayed, click the 'Tools' tab and choose 'SQL Worksheet'. Now you are ready to create your first Oracle database table. Type (or copy) the SQL code into the worksheet window as follows:

```
CREATE TABLE web_site
( vid CHAR(3),
vuser VARCHAR2(15),
pswd VARCHAR2(50),
lvl NUMBER(1)
);
```

Figure 3.3 shows how the code should look in the worksheet window.

Figure 3.3 Output from SQL Worksheet of Table Creation Code (http://www.oracle.com/technetwork/developer-tools/
          sql-developer/downloads/index.html)

Remove any blank lines or spaces from the beginning or end of code. To run code, click the second button from the left (directly above the 'Worksheet' tab). The button looks like a document with a small green triangle (on its side). Don't click the first button (green triangle on its side) because it does not run SQL scripts. A message stating that the table was created properly should appear in a new window below the worksheet window, labeled 'Script Output' (see Figure 3.4).

Figure 3.4 Output from SQL Worksheet, Showing that Table Was Created (http://www.oracle.com/technetwork/
          developer-tools/sql-developer/downloads/index.html)

The next step is to add data. First, clear the 'Worksheet' and 'Script Output' windows by pressing the eraser buttons that look like the end of a pencil. Type (or copy) the SQL code into the worksheet window.

```
INSERT INTO web_site VALUES ('001','ben','dover',1);
INSERT INTO web_site VALUES ('002','dandy','lion',2);
INSERT INTO web_site VALUES ('003','sally','forth',2);
INSERT INTO web_site VALUES ('004','oliver','clozoff',2);
INSERT INTO web_site VALUES ('005','betty','wont',2);
```

Run the code by pressing the little document button with the green triangle. You should see that five rows have been inserted (see Figure 3.5).

Figure 3.5 Output from SQL Worksheet, Showing that Data Was Added to Table (http://www.oracle.com/technetwork/developer-tools/sql-developer/downloads/index.html)

Clear both windows again by pressing the pencil eraser buttons. To save changes to the database, type (or copy) 'COMMIT;' in the worksheet window and run.

COMMIT;

Clear both windows once again. To verify that data was added, type (or copy) the code in the worksheet window and run.

SELECT * FROM web_site;

The 'Script Output' window should show data from 'web_site' (Figure 3.6).

VID	VUSER	PSWD	LVL
001	ben	dover	1
002	dandy	lion	2
003	sally	forth	2
004	oliver	closoff	2
005	betty	wont	2

Figure 3.6 Output from SQL Worksheet, Showing Data from Table (http://www.oracle.com/technetwork/developer-tools/sql-developer/downloads/index.html)

Let's review. To create a new table, use SQL command 'CREATE TABLE' with table name, field names, and data types for each field. The 'vid' field is defined as a fixed-length string of three characters. The 'vuser' field is defined as a variable-length string of up to 15 characters. The 'pswd' field is defined as a variable-length string of up to 50 characters. The 'lvl' field is defined as a number with a size of one digit. Use SQL command 'INSERT' to add data to the 'web_site' table with values for each field. Use SQL command 'COMMIT' to save changes to the database (to undo changes, use SQL command 'ROLLBACK'). Use SQL command 'SELECT' to retrieve all records from the table. The '*' symbol retrieves all records and all fields from a table.

Connection Class

In this chapter, I use application programming interfaces (APIs) to communicate with Oracle. An *API* enables a software program to interact with other software programs.

PHP includes a set of Oracle APIs to enable interaction with Oracle. The database connection class needs four APIs – three to connect, parse, and execute an SQL statement, and one to fetch a result set of data. The API to connect to Oracle is 'OCI_CONNECT'. The API to parse (prepare) an Oracle statement for execution is 'OCI_PARSE'. The API to execute an Oracle statement is 'OCI_EXECUTE'. The API to return the next row from a result set of data as an associative array is 'OCI_FETCH_ASSOC'. An example is now presented.

The example uses two PHP files – 'dbGeneral.php' and 'call_dbGeneral.php'. PHP file 'dbGeneral.php' includes an Oracle connection class 'dbGeneral' (lines 3–44). The class connects to Oracle, parses an SQL query, and executes the SQL query. PHP file 'call_dbGeneral.php' creates a new instance of class 'dbGeneral' (line 5) and verifies that it works properly.

In the 'dbGeneral' class, the Oracle username, password, and host server are not included (left empty) in the 'setParms()' method (lines 17–22) for two reasons. First, you must supply your own Oracle connection information in the 'setParms()' method. Second, I am protecting my database information. Be careful to surround your user (schema), password, and host server information with *single* quotes. In my Oracle installation, the host is composed of two forward slashes, the host server where Oracle resides followed by a forward slash, and the system identifier (SID) – *//host_server/SID*. As an example, my host information is:

//dbase.brigham.usu.edu:1521/orcl/doracle

The 'dbGeneral' class contains five 'private' properties (lines 5–9) and one 'public' property (line 10). The class also contains a constructor (lines 11–16) that sets the SQL query to a property and automatically invokes 'setParms()' (lines 17–22) and 'connDB()' (lines 23–28) methods. Methods 'parse()' (lines 29–35) and 'exe()' (lines 40–43) are invoked by the calling environment when needed. Since binding is introduced later in the chapter, ignore the 'bind()' method (lines 36–39) for now.

The 'private' properties are used to hold the username, password, host string, SQL query, and connection information. The 'public' property is used to hold the result set generated by the SQL query. The constructor sets the incoming query to a property (line 13), and invokes the 'setParms()' (line 14) and 'connDB()' (line 15) methods. The 'setParms()' method sets the username (line 19), password (line 20), and host string (line 21).

```php
1  <?php
2  // File dbGeneral.php
3  class dbGeneral
4  {
5  private $_schema;
6  private $_password;
7  private $_host;
8  private $_query;
9  private $_conn;
10 public $result;
11 function __construct($sql)
12 {
13 $this->_query = $sql;
14 $this->setParms();
15 $this->connDB();
16 }
17 function setParms()
18 {
19 $this->_schema = '';
20 $this->_password = '';
21 $this->_host = '';
22 }
23 function connDB()
24 {
25 if(!$this->_conn = oci_connect($this->_schema,
```

```
26  $this->_password, $this->_host))
27  { echo 'error connecting'; }
28  }
29  function parse()
30  {
31  if(!$parse = oci_parse($this->_conn, $this->_query))
32  { echo 'error parsing'; }
33  else
34  { $this->result = $parse; }
35  }
36  function bind($bind,$choice,$length)
37  {
38  oci_bind_by_name($this->result, $bind, $choice,$length);
39  }
40  function exe()
41  {
42  oci_execute($this->result);
43  }
44  }
45  ?>
```

The 'connDB()' method uses API 'oci_connect()' with username, password, and host string as parameters to connect to Oracle (lines 25 and 26). If the connection is unsuccessful an error message is displayed (line 27). The 'parse()' method uses API 'oci_parse()' with connection and query information to parse the SQL query (line 31). If the parse is unsuccessful an error message is displayed (line 32). Otherwise, parse information is set to '$this->_result' (line 34). The 'exe()' method uses API 'oci_execute()' with '$this->_result' as parameter to run the query (line 42).

```
1   <?php
2   // File call_dbGeneral.php
3   require_once 'dbGeneral.php';
4   $query = "SELECT * FROM web_site ORDER BY vid";
5   $connect = new dbGeneral($query);
6   $connect->parse();
7   $stmt = $connect->result;
8   $connect->exe();
9   while($row = oci_fetch_assoc($stmt))
10  {
11  echo $row['VID'] . ' ' . $row['VUSER'];
12  echo ' ' . $row['PSWD'] . $row['LVL'];
13  echo '<br />';
14  }
15  ?>
```

PHP file 'call_dbGeneral.php' sets the query (line 4), creates a new instance of 'dbGeneral()' (line 5), parses the SQL query (line 6), sets the parse result to '$stmt' (line 7), runs the parsed query (line 8), and displays results (lines 9–14).

The 'oci_fetch_assoc()' API (line 9) grabs one row at a time from the Oracle result set as an associative array. Using an associative array is very practical because you can use the field names from the 'web_site' table to access their corresponding values. That is, you can associatively retrieve the field value with it corresponding field name. For instance, '$row['VID']' is the field value of the database field 'VID' for a particular row from the result set. Be sure to use *capital* letters when retrieving field names because Oracle only recognizes capital letters for field names in database tables.

Load 'call_dbGeneral.php' in a browser to verify that the connection class is working properly. If you encounter difficulties, consult your IT expert. Figure 3.7 shows the results.

```
001 ben dover1
002 dandy lion2
003 sally forth2
004 oliver clozoff2
005 betty wont2
```

Figure 3.7 Output from 'dbGeneral' Class, Showing Data from Table

Cleansing Login Data

Login implements user authentication, but does not protect against unauthorized injection of spurious (bad) data. In this section, I build a simple class to prevent unauthorized injection of 'DOCTYPE' declarations, HTML and PHP tags, HTML entities, and select special characters. Hackers inject such information to trick the web browser and PHP engine into carrying out nefarious activities.

Usernames and passwords should *never* contain 'DOCTYPE' declarations, HTML or PHP tags, or HTML entities. It is therefore prudent to remove any such material. Depending on the application, you may or may not want to allow special characters. The example illustrates how to cleanse login information.

The example uses two PHP files – 'clean.php' and 'call_clean.php'. The 'clean' class (lines 3–26) in PHP file 'clean.php' uses PHP built-in functions to remove any such nefarious material from input data. The class adds flexibility with the addition of a method for dealing with special characters and a method for reducing the size of a string. You can use either method or both depending on your needs. You can also allow or disallow special characters by modifying the first parameter string (line 18) of the 'preg_replace' function in the 'clean_special()' method. If you do not wish to change the size of a string, do not use the 'reduce_size()' method.

```php
1  <?php
2  // File clean.php
3  class clean
4  {
5  function cleanse($data)
6  {
7  $clean = str_replace('<!DOCTYPE','<DOCTYPE',$data);
8  $clean = strip_tags($clean);
9  $clean = htmlentities(trim($clean));
10 $clean = html_entity_decode($clean);
11 $clean = str_replace(' ','',$clean);
12 $clean = str_replace(' ','',$clean);
13 return $clean;
```

```
14 }
15 function clean_special($data)
16 {
17 $clean_special = preg_replace
18 ('#[.\\\/*\#$?!=@%,\'\"]#s','',$data);
19 return $clean_special;
20 }
21 function reduce_size($data)
22 {
23 $reduced = substr($data,0,20);
24 return $reduced;
25 }
26 }
27 ?>
```

In the 'cleanse()' method (lines 5–14), the 'str_replace()' function (line 7) deals with 'DOCTYPE' declaration injections. The '<!DOCTYPE>' declaration tells the web browser the version of the HTML document. The '<!DOCTYPE>' declaration is not HTML. It is supported in all browsers and must be the very first item in an HTML document, before the <html> tag. The 'strip_tags()' function (line 8) strips HTML and PHP tags from a string. The 'htmlentities()' function (line 9) converts applicable characters to HTML entities. The 'trim()' function removes any leading and following blank spaces from a string. The 'html_entity_decode()' function (line 10) converts all HTML entities to their applicable characters. Finally, two 'str_replace()' functions are provided. The first one (line 11) removes any ' ' HTML entities. The second one (line 12) removes all spaces by replacing ' ' with ".

The result is robust because you normally do not want any spaces in a username or password. In the 'clean_special()' method (lines 15–20), the 'preg_replace()' function (lines 17 and 18) replaces special characters (first parameter) with " (second parameter) for string '$data' (third parameter). The string provided in the first parameter is a regular expression. A *regular expression* is a way to recognize strings of text. Regular expressions are discussed in detail in the next chapter.

In the 'reduce_size()' method (lines 21–25), the 'substr()' function (line 23) ensures that input data is no longer than 20 characters. You can modify this length depending on your needs. However, keep this number as low as possible because hackers like to use long strings of characters to inject nefarious instructions into the web browser or PHP engine.

PHP file 'call_clean.php' creates a new instance of 'clean' (line 6), invokes 'cleanse()' (line 7), and outputs the cleansed string (line 8). Next, 'clean_special()' is invoked (line 9) and results are displayed (line 10). Finally, 'reduce_size()' is invoked (line 11) and results are displayed (line 12). Figure 3.8 shows the results.

```
1  <?php
2  // File call_clean.php
3  require_once 'clean.php';
4  $data = ' "hey"/\*<html><div>#%=@!?$  ';
5  $data .= '..</html>dudes, how\'s it hanging? ';
6  $clean = new clean();
7  $clean_tags = $clean->cleanse($data);
8  echo $clean_tags;
9  $clean_special = $clean->clean_special($clean_tags);
```

```
10  echo '<br />' . $clean_special;
11  $reduced = $clean->reduce_size($clean_special);
12  echo '<br>' . $reduced
13  ?>
```

```
"hey"/\*#%=@!?$..dudes,how'sithanging?
heydudeshowsithanging
heydudeshowsithangin
```

Figure 3.8 Output from 'clean' Class

The 'cleanse()' method removes HTML tags and the ' ' HTML entity. The 'clean_special()' method removes all special characters. The 'reduce_size()' method reduces the size of the string to 20 characters. I recommend that you study class 'clean' and the resultant output very carefully before moving on to the next section because the class looks pretty simple but it is quite complex.

Encryption

Encryption is the conversion of data into a form that cannot be easily understood (deciphered) by unauthorized users. To encrypt passwords, I use 'SHA1', which is a cryptographic hash algorithm developed by the National Security Agency (NSA). This algorithm is the successor to the earlier 'MD5' algorithm. I add a double-salt algorithm for enhanced security. A *salt* is a random string of data used to modify a password hash. A *hash* is the digital footprint of a piece of data. The next example illustrates how to encrypt passwords.

The example uses two PHP files – 'salt.php' and 'encrypt.php'. PHP file 'salt.php' contains a 'salt' class (lines 3–16) that uses two salts to modify the password hash. The password hash is created with the 'SHA1' algorithm.

```
1  <?php
2  // File salt.php
3  class salt
4  {
5  function doubleSalt($toHash,$password)
6  {
7  if(strlen($password) < 40)
8  {
9  $arr_pass = str_split($toHash,
10  (strlen($toHash)/2)+1);
11  $hash = hash('sha1', $password.$arr_pass[0] .
12  'centerSalt'.$arr_pass[1]);
13  return $hash;
14  }
15  }
16  }
17  ?>
```

Class 'salt' includes the 'doubleSalt()' method (lines 5–15), which takes a salt string and password hash as parameters (line 5). The double salt is accomplished by rearranging the salt and feeding the 'SHA1' algorithm the password hash and different pieces of the revised salt as a single concatenated string.

Specifically, function 'str_split()' (lines 9 and 10) converts the salt into an array '$arr_pass' with the number of elements determined by the length of salt divided by two, plus one (first salt). For instance, a salt of six characters is converted to an array of index 4 ((6/2)+1). Remember, PHP arrays start at index zero, so an array with index four contains five elements. Function 'hash' (lines 11 and 12) uses 'SHA1' to encrypt a string composed of the password hash, the first element of '$arr_pass', the string 'centerSalt', and the second element of '$arr_pass' concatenated together (second salt). PHP file 'encrypt.php' contains the code that encrypts a string (typically a password).

```php
1  <?php
2  // File encrypt.php
3  require_once 'dbGeneral.php';
4  require_once 'salt.php';
5  $query = "SELECT * FROM web_site
6  WHERE vid = '001'";
7  $connect = new dbGeneral($query);
8  $connect->parse();
9  $stmt = $connect->result;
10 $connect->exe();
11 $row = oci_fetch_assoc($stmt);
12 $name = $row['PSWD'];
13 $name = trim($name);
14 if(strlen($name) >= 40)
15 { $flag = FALSE; }
16 elseif(strlen($name) < 40)
17 { $flag = TRUE; }
18 $vid = $row['VID'];
19 $toHash = 'tiger';
20 $salt = new Salt();
21 if($flag)
22 {
23 $pass = $salt->doubleSalt($toHash,$name);
24 $sql = "UPDATE web_site SET
25 pswd = '$pass' WHERE vid = '$vid'";
26 $connect = new dbGeneral($sql);
27 $connect->parse();
28 $stmt = $connect->result;
29 $connect->exe();
30 echo 'Password <strong style="color: indianred;">';
31 echo $name . '</strong> encrypted!';
32 }
33 else
34 { echo 'Password already encrypted!'; }
35 ?>
```

I include 'dbGeneral.php' and 'salt.php' (lines 3 and 4) so the script can access the 'dbGeneral' and 'salt' classes. The query (lines 5 and 6) access a row from the 'web_site' table. Next, the result set is obtained by creating a new instance of 'dbGeneral' (line 7), using 'parse()' (line 8) to parse the query, placing the parsed result in '$stmt' (line 9), using 'exe()' (line 10) to run the parsed result, and using 'oci_fetch_assoc()' (line 11) to fetch the result into '$row'.

The password value is then placed in '$name' by referencing the password with '$row['PSWD']' (line 12). The password length is checked to see if it is already encrypted (lines 14–17). If the length is greater than or equal to '40', I know it has been encrypted because 'SHA1' creates a string of 40 characters, and most unencrypted passwords are much shorter than that. Line 19 is the hash string used in the 'salt' class. If the password has not been encrypted (line 21), run 'doubleSalt()' method (line 23) and update the table with the new password (lines 24–29). If the password is already encrypted, pass an appropriate message back to the calling environment (lines 33 and 34). Load 'encrypt.php' to encrypt the password for the first record (Figure 3.9). Run 'encrypt.php' again and see what happens (Figure 3.10).

Password **dover** encrypted!

Figure 3.9 Output from 'dbGeneral' Class, Showing Encrypted Data

Password already encrypted!

Figure 3.10 Output from 'dbGeneral' Class, Attempting to Encrypt Same Data

Since the code tests for length, it does not encrypt an already encrypted password. To verify encryption, open 'Oracle SQL Developer' and login. Click '+' to left of 'Tables' and click '+' to left of 'WEB_SITE' table. Click 'Data' tab to see results. The first username 'ben' should now have an encrypted password. Now, change the 'vid' field value (line 6) and run 'encrypt.php' (once for each record) to encrypt the remaining passwords. The remaining queries should look like this:

```
$query = "SELECT * FROM web_site WHERE vid = '002'";
$query = "SELECT * FROM web_site WHERE vid = '003'";
$query = "SELECT * FROM web_site WHERE vid = '004'";
$query = "SELECT * FROM web_site WHERE vid = '005'";
```

Be sure to run 'encrypt.php' *one time* for each of the four queries. Load 'call_dbGeneral.php' to see data with encrypted passwords (Figure 3.11).

```
001 ben 1649869de3d29daab675ad252b9bd02248fd9ea71
002 dandy 85aa14a772c00238f44f5a2b4edee7b9602aee2d2
003 sally ae79c3ab02ccd046df6f0ba809c753fef7b1d44f2
004 oliver 82008b43682796ae6255c402eec2e49bea6904ad2
005 betty f11d88e5c0ca93d109c9c4af63a3155bd749f0e52
```

Figure 3.11 Output from 'dbGeneral' Class, Showing Five Encrypted Passwords

Before you move to the next section, study 'encrypt.php' carefully to make sure that you understand how the entire piece of code works.

Create Login Page and Authenticate

The login page example authenticates usernames and passwords. Three PHP files are used to demonstrate login authentication. First, 'login.php' contains HTML for login. Second, 'verify.php' authenticates usernames and passwords. Third, 'onward.php' is activated if login is successful.

```php
1  <?php
2  // File login.php
3  ?>
4  <html><head>
5  <style type="text/css">
6  table.center {
7  margin-left:auto;
8  margin-right:auto;
9  }
10 </style></head>
11 <body style="background-color:burlywood;">
12 <div style="text-align:center;">
13 <h1 style="color:indigo;">Sign On Page</h1>
14 <form method="post" action="verify.php">
15 <table class="center">
16 <tr><td>User:</td>
17 <td><input type="text"
18 name="user"></td></tr>
19 <tr><td>Password:</td>
20 <td><input type="password"
21 name="password"></td></tr>
22 <tr><td></td><td></td></tr>
23 <tr><td></td>
24 <td><input type="submit"
25 value="Log In"></td></tr>
26 <tr><td></td>
27 </table></form></div>
28 </html>
```

PHP file 'login.php' uses the more secure 'post' method (line 14) to send data placed in 'user' (lines 16–18) and 'password' (lines 19–21). It includes a 'submit' button (lines 24 and 25) to allow manual submission of the form. Once submitted, action moves to 'verify.php' (line 14). The form is contained in an HTML table (lines 15–27).

PHP file 'verify.php' cleans 'user' and 'password' data posted from the form (lines 9–14), encrypts the password (15–17), queries the database (lines 18–23) to see if the passwords match (line 24), and takes appropriate action. If the passwords match, three session variables are created to hold the values (lines 26–28) for use in PHP file 'onward.php'. A PHP *session* provides a way to preserve certain data across subsequent accesses. PHP function 'session_start()' should be at the beginning of a script (line 3) and starts a new session or resumes an existing one. A PHP *session variable* is the mechanism used to preserve data.

```
 1  <?php
 2  // File verify.php
 3  session_start();
 4  require_once 'clean.php';
 5  require_once 'dbGeneral.php';
 6  require_once 'salt.php';
 7  $user = $_POST['user'];
 8  $pass = $_POST['password'];
 9  $clean = new clean();
10  $clean_tags = $clean->cleanse($user);
11  $clean_special = $clean->clean_special($clean_tags);
12  $user = $clean->reduce_size($clean_special);
13  $clean_tags = $clean->cleanse($pass);
14  $pass = $clean->clean_special($clean_tags);
15  $toHash = 'tiger';
16  $salt = new Salt();
17  $pass = $salt->doubleSalt($toHash,$pass);
18  $query = "SELECT * FROM web_site WHERE";
19  $query = $query . " vuser='$user' AND pswd='$pass'";
20  $connect = new dbGeneral($query);
21  $connect->parse();
22  $stmt = $connect->result;
23  $connect->exe();
24  if ($row = oci_fetch_assoc($stmt))
25  {
26  $_SESSION['VID'] = $row['VID'];
27  $_SESSION['VUSER'] = $row['VUSER'];
28  $_SESSION['VPSWD'] = $row['PSWD'];
29  header ("location: onward.php");
30  }
31  else
32  { header ("location: login.php"); }
33  ?>
```

Session variables are created with '$_SESSION['*varname*']' (lines 26–28). Notice how 'verify.php' directs the browser to a PHP file with the 'header()' function (lines 29 and 32). Don't forget to turn on a session with 'session_start()' (to create and use session variables). So, both 'verify.php' and 'onward.php' start new sessions.

```
 1  <?php
 2  // File onward.php
 3  session_start();
 4  $vid = $_SESSION['VID'];
 5  $vuser = $_SESSION['VUSER'];
 6  $vpswd = $_SESSION['VPSWD'];
 7  ?>
 8  <html>
 9  <head><style type="text/css">
```

```
10  table.center {
11  margin-left:auto;
12  margin-right:auto;
13  }
14  </style></head>
15  <body style="background-color:burlywood;">
16  <div style="text-align:center;">
17  <h1 style="color:indigo">Successful Login</h1>
18  <table class="center">
19  <tr><td><?php echo $vid . ' ' . $vuser . ' ' .
20  $vpswd; ?></td></tr>
21  </table></div></body>
22  </html>
```

PHP file 'onward.php' retrieves and outputs session variables created in 'verify.php'. Session variables are retrieved (lines 4–6) and their values are displayed (lines 19 and 20). Load 'login.php' in a browser. Figure 3.12 shows the login page with username 'sally' and password 'forth'. Click the 'Log In' button. Figure 3.13 show the results.

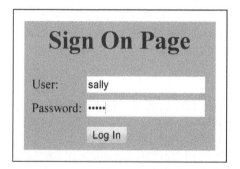

Figure 3.12 Display of Login Page with Username and Password

Figure 3.13 Display of Successful Login

Strong Passwords

I intentionally created simple (weak) passwords to ease testing. However, you should create stronger passwords for added security. First, make your passwords at least eight characters long. Second, mix together uppercase letters, lowercase letters, and numbers. Although including special characters creates a stronger password, it is not recommended. The reason is that special characters have meaning in PHP, HTML, Oracle, Linux, JavaScript, and web browsers. For instance, two tags have meaning in multiple contexts. Symbol '>' is part of a PHP tag, part of an HTML tag, and signals output redirection in Linux. Symbol '?' is used to append content to a URL in a web browser, is part of a PHP tag, and can be used as a placeholder for binding variables in Oracle.

Many special characters have meaning in multiple contexts, so be careful if you allow such characters in passwords. For even more security, change passwords often, don't use the same password for everything, store your passwords off site so that others cannot access them, and be sure that no one is watching when you type in your password.

SQL Injection Protection

SQL injection is a technique often used to attack databases through a website. Specifically, it involves creating or altering existing SQL commands to expose hidden data, override valuable data or even execute dangerous system-level commands on the database host. Your website can actually enable SQL injection by allowing spurious user input and unknowingly combining it with static parameters to build an unauthorized SQL query. For instance, a culprit can send spurious SQL to your website and use his or her knowledge of PHP (in this case your PHP code) to inject.

SQL injection can be dealt with. First, never trust any kind of input coming into your website, especially that which comes from the client (user) side. Even input that comes from a 'select' box, hidden input field, or cookie is suspect. Second, never connect to the database as a super user, database administrator (DBA) user, or database owner. Third, allow only customized users with very limited privileges (i.e., the 'web_site' table I built in this chapter holds only the users authorized to access the website). Fourth, check whether the given input has the expected data type. Fifth, always use bind variables (covered in the next section) with SQL statements for security and performance reasons. Sixth, do not print out any database-specific information, especially information about your schema. A *schema* is synonymous with an Oracle user account. Seventh, use stored procedures and previously defined cursors (discussed later in the chapter) to abstract data access so that users do not directly access tables or views.

Bind Variables

Oracle uses the value of a bind variable exclusively and does not interpret the contents of the variable in any way, which drastically mitigates SQL injection problems. A *bind variable* is a placeholder variable in an SQL statement that must be replaced with a valid value before the statement can successfully execute.

Binding allows the database to reuse statement context and caches from previous executions of the statement, even if another user or process originally executed it. Binding also reduces SQL injection concerns because data associated with a bind variable is never treated as part of the SQL statement. Bound PHP variables can be changed and the SQL statement re-executed without needing to re-parse or re-bind the SQL statement.

To implement SQL injection protection, prepare the SQL statement with the 'OCI_BIND_BY_NAME' API. The API serves two purposes. First, it enhances performance because you can use the same SQL statement with different bind values without changing the database (query) execution plan. A *database execution plan* is an ordered set of steps used to access or modify information in an Oracle database management system (DBMS). Second, it protects against SQL injection if the SQL statement is properly prepared.

The 'dbGeneral' class I built earlier includes a 'bind()' method. The 'bind()' method uses the Oracle API 'OCI_BIND_BY_NAME' to bind a PHP placeholder to an Oracle placeholder by name. The 'bind()' method accepts a bind variable, the variable being bound, and the maximum length of the variable being bound. Replace the original 'verify.php' with the following code.

```
1  <?php
2  // File verify.php
3  session_start();
4  require_once 'clean.php';
5  require_once 'dbGeneral.php';
6  require_once 'salt.php';
7  $user = $_POST['user'];
```

```
 8  $pass = $_POST['password'];
 9  $clean = new clean();
10  $clean_tags = $clean->cleanse($user);
11  $clean_special = $clean->clean_special($clean_tags);
12  $user = $clean->reduce_size($clean_special);
13  $clean_tags = $clean->cleanse($pass);
14  $pass = $clean->clean_special($clean_tags);
15  $toHash = 'tiger';
16  $salt = new Salt();
17  $pass = $salt->doubleSalt($toHash,$pass);
18  $query = "SELECT * FROM web_site
19  WHERE vuser=:a AND pswd=:b";
20  $connect = new dbGeneral($query);
21  $connect->parse();
22  $connect->bind(':a',$user,20);
23  $connect->bind(':b',$pass,50);
24  $stmt = $connect->result;
25  $connect->exe();
26  if ($row = oci_fetch_assoc($stmt))
27  {
28  $_SESSION['VID'] = $row['VID'];
29  $_SESSION['VUSER'] = $row['VUSER'];
30  $_SESSION['VPSWD'] = $row['PSWD'];
31  header ("location: onward.php");
32  }
33  else
34  { header ("location: login.php"); }
35  ?>
```

Only a few changes have been made to the original file. First, the SQL 'SELECT' statement uses placeholders ':a' and ':b' (lines 18 and 19) respectively instead of '$user' and '$pass' values. Second, the 'bind()' method is called twice (once for each bind variable) to bind PHP placeholders '$user' and '$pass' to Oracle placeholders (lines 22 and 23).

Now, let's test login with bind variables. Clear all browser information because earlier login information might still be in the browser's cache. Next, load 'login.php' in a browser. Figure 3.14 shows the login page with username 'sally' and password 'forth'. Click the 'Log In' button. Figure 3.15 shows the results.

Figure 3.14 Display of Login Page with Username and Password

Figure 3.15 Display of Successful Login Based on Strict Security

Although the results look the same, the variables in SQL query were bound properly, which greatly mitigates SQL injection. To this point, I built a secure login page with login authentication, cleansed data, encrypted passwords, and illustrated SQL injection protection (for the 'SELECT' SQL statement). SQL can also be injected through the 'INSERT', 'UPDATE', and 'DELETE' SQL statements. An 'INSERT' SQL statement is used to add data to the database. PHP file 'bind_ins.php' prepares (protects) an 'INSERT' statement from SQL injection.

```php
1  <?php
2  // File bind_ins.php
3  require_once 'dbGeneral.php';
4  $query = "INSERT INTO web_site VALUES ";
5  $query = $query . "(:a, :b, :c, :d)";
6  $connect = new dbGeneral($query);
7  $connect->parse();
8  $connect->bind(':a','006',3);
9  $connect->bind(':b','eileen',15);
10 $connect->bind(':c','downe',50);
11 $connect->bind(':d',2,1);
12 $stmt = $connect->result;
13 $connect->exe();
14 ?>
```

Lines 4 and 5 represent the 'insert' query with four bind variables – ':a', ':b', ':c', and ':d'. A new 'dbGeneral' object is created (line 6), the query is parsed (line 7), bind variables are given proper values (lines 8–11), and the query is run (lines 12 and 13).

Load the file in a browser. To verify that the code worked as intended, load 'call_dbGeneral.php' (created earlier in the chapter) in a browser. Figure 3.16 shows that a record with 'VID' of '006' was added to the table.

```
001 ben 1649869de3d29daab675ad252b9bd02248fd9ea71
002 dandy 85aa14a772c00238f44f5a2b4edee7b9602aee2d2
003 sally ae79c3ab02ccd046df6f0ba809c753fef7b1d44f2
004 oliver 82008b43682796ae6255c402eec2e49bea6904ad2
005 betty f11d88e5c0ca93d109c9c4af63a3155bd749f0e52
006 eileen downe2
```

Figure 3.16 Output from 'dbGeneral' Class, Showing Added Bound Record

The 'UPDATE' SQL statement is used to modify database data. PHP file 'bind_upd.php' prepares (protects) an 'UPDATE' statement against SQL injection. It also encrypts the password of the newly added record.

Lines 5 and 6 establish the 'vid' and 'password' (to be encrypted). Line 7 is the hash string fed to the 'salt' class. Lines 8 and 9 encrypt the password. Lines 10 and 11 represent the query. Lines 12–17 run the update. Load the file in a browser.

```php
1  <?php
2  // File bind_upd.php
3  require_once 'dbGeneral.php';
4  require_once 'salt.php';
5  $name = 'downe';
6  $vid = '006';
7  $toHash = 'tiger';
8  $salt = new Salt();
9  $pass = $salt->doubleSalt($toHash,$name);
10 $sql = "UPDATE web_site SET
11 pswd = :a WHERE vid = :b";
12 $connect = new dbGeneral($sql);
13 $connect->parse();
14 $connect->bind(':a',$pass,50);
15 $connect->bind(':b',$vid,3);
16 $stmt = $connect->result;
17 $connect->exe();
18 ?>
```

Notice that the script encrypts the new user's password and updates the database with this new information. Load 'call_dbGeneral.php' in a browser to verify. Figure 3.17 shows that the new record's password was encrypted.

```
001 ben 1649869de3d29daab675ad252b9bd02248fd9ea71
002 dandy 85aa14a772c00238f44f5a2b4edee7b9602aee2d2
003 sally ae79c3ab02ccd046df6f0ba809c753fef7b1d44f2
004 oliver 82008b43682796ae6255c402eec2e49bea6904ad2
005 betty f11d88e5c0ca93d109c9c4af63a3155bd749f0e52
006 eileen d7a43df7783b9e22ccd0fa03b6e68f430557358d2
```

Figure 3.17 Output from 'dbGeneral' Class, Showing Updated Bound Record

The 'DELETE' SQL statement is used to delete database data. PHP file 'bind_del.php' prepares (protects) a 'DELETE' statement from SQL injection. Lines 4 and 5 represent the record to be deleted and the query. Lines 6–10 connect to the database, parse, bind, and run the query. Load the file in a browser.

```php
1  <?php
2  // File bind_del.php
3  require_once 'dbGeneral.php';
4  $vid = '006';
5  $sql = "DELETE FROM web_site WHERE vid = :a";
6  $connect = new dbGeneral($sql);
7  $connect->parse();
```

```
 8 $connect->bind(':a',$vid,3);
 9 $stmt = $connect->result;
10 $connect->exe();
11 ?>
```

Notice that the script deletes the most recently added user. Again, load 'call_dbGeneral.php' in a browser. Figure 3.18 shows that the most recently added record is no longer in the table.

```
001 ben 1649869de3d29daab675ad252b9bd02248fd9ea71
002 dandy 85aa14a772c00238f44f5a2b4edee7b9602aee2d2
003 sally ae79c3ab02ccd046df6f0ba809c753fef7b1d44f2
004 oliver 82008b43682796ae6255c402eec2e49bea6904ad2
005 betty f11d88e5c0ca93d109c9c4af63a3155bd749f0e52
```

Figure 3.18 Output from 'dbGeneral' Class, Showing Deleted Bound Record

Before I add, modify or delete data, I always prepare (protect) the statement from SQL injection. I also prepare any 'SELECT' SQL when appropriate.

PL/SQL Binding

In the 'Bind Variable' section, seven ways to mitigate SQL injection were introduced. The seventh advocates stored procedures and previously defined cursors. Oracle has an embedded procedural language (PL/SQL) that enables such activity. **PL/SQL** is an extension to SQL embedded in the Oracle database. It has an advantage in that every reference to a variable is automatically a bind variable.

PL/SQL can be compiled and executed in 'Oracle SQL Developer' in the same window as SQL. In the following examples, I illustrate how to use PL/SQL to protect input data from SQL injection. Be sure to *remove* all line numbers before running the PL/SQL scripts. Line numbers are only included to explain the code.

The first example is presented in two parts. Part one shows you how to create a stored PL/SQL procedure using 'SELECT' to place data in a result set. Part two shows you how to run the procedure.

Compile the code for part one in 'Oracle SQL Developer'. To accomplish this, open an 'SQL Worksheet', place the PL/SQL code in the window, and press the button that looks like a document with a green triangle on its side. Be careful to remove the line numbers and any leading or following blank lines and spaces from the code. The button is second from the left. Do not press the button that looks like a green triangle on its side because this one is for single-line SQL statements only.

```
 1 CREATE OR REPLACE PROCEDURE rpt(p_id IN CHAR)
 2 AS
 3 v_data web_site%ROWTYPE;
 4 v_stmt VARCHAR2(100);
 5 BEGIN
 6 v_stmt := 'SELECT * FROM web_site WHERE vid = :vid';
 7 EXECUTE IMMEDIATE v_stmt INTO v_data USING p_id;
 8 DBMS_OUTPUT.PUT(v_data.vid || ' ' || v_data.vuser || ' ');
 9 DBMS_OUTPUT.PUT_LINE(v_data.pswd || ' ' || v_data.lvl);
10 END rpt;
```

Create the PL/SQL procedure (line 1). Define variables (lines 3 and 4). The 'v_data' variable is defined as '%ROWTYPE', which means that it mirrors a record in the 'web_site' table. So, 'v_data' is really a record with all fields in the 'web_site' table. The 'v_stmt' variable is defined to hold a variable-length character string of up to 100 characters. PL/SQL procedures begin logic with a 'BEGIN' (line 5) and end logic with an 'END' (line 10). 'v_stmt' (line 6) is assigned an SQL statement. Notice that assignment in PL/SQL is ':='. So, be careful because this is different from other programming languages. Next SQL is run with 'EXECUTE IMMEDIATE' (line 7), which reconciles the bind variable ':vid' from the SQL statement.

'EXECUTE IMMEDIATE' is dynamic SQL, which is an advanced topic in PL/SQL. So, I will not discuss it in any more depth. 'DMBS_OUTPUT.PUT' (line 8) and 'DBMS_OUTPUT.PUT_LINE' (line 9) display results to the Oracle SQL Developer console.

Figure 3.19 shows the results displayed in the 'Script Output' window when the PL/SQL code is run. You should see 'PROCEDURE rpt compiled', which means that the code executed properly.

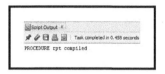

Figure 3.19 Output from SQL Worksheet, Showing Compiled 'rpt' Procedure

To review, procedure 'rpt' has a 'CHAR' parameter 'p_id' (line 1), which is the 'VID' from the 'web_site' table that you wish to display. Variable 'v_data' is a '%ROWTYPE' record, which means that it takes on the field characteristics of an entire row in the 'web_site' table. Variable 'v_stmt' is a variable-length variable that holds the 'SELECT' statement. The 'EXECUTE_IMMEDIATE' statement places the data from the query into 'v_data'. The 'DBMS_OUTPUT' statements display each piece of 'v_data' by database field names.

Once compiled, PL/SQL procedure 'rpt' is stored in the Oracle database. The following anonymous block of code runs 'rpt'. An *anonymous block* is code that is not named. Notice that the procedure compiled earlier was named 'rpt', so it is not anonymous. Run the anonymous block in an 'SQL worksheet'.

```
1 SET SERVEROUTPUT ON
2 DECLARE
3 v_id CHAR(3) := '001';
4 BEGIN
5 rpt(v_id);
6 END;
```

Line 1 turns the Oracle display on. If this is not turned on, nothing will be displayed. Line 2 defines a 'DECLARE' block, where variables are declared in an anonymous block. Line 3 defines 'v_id' as a fixed character with length of '3' and assigns '001' to it. Lines 4 and 6 define a 'BEGIN–END' block. Line 5 runs the 'rpt' procedure. Figure 3.20 shows the results from the 'Script Output' window. This is expected, since the anonymous block called procedure 'rpt' with parameter '001'.

Figure 3.20 Output from SQL Worksheet, Showing Results from 'rpt' Procedure

The next three examples are also in two parts – compile and run – for 'INSERT', 'UPDATE', and 'DELETE' SQL injection protection. The 'add_dynamic' procedure prepares an 'INSERT' statement. I suggest using the button that looks like a little pencil with an eraser to clean up the windows for each example and corresponding output.

```
1  CREATE OR REPLACE PROCEDURE add_dynamic(
2  p_id web_site.vid%TYPE,
3  p_user web_site.vuser%TYPE,
4  p_pswd web_site.pswd%TYPE,
5  p_lvl web_site.lvl%TYPE)
6  AS
7  v_stmt VARCHAR2(100);
8  BEGIN
9  v_stmt := 'INSERT INTO web_site VALUES(:vid,:vuser,:pswd,:lvl)';
10 EXECUTE IMMEDIATE v_stmt USING p_id,p_user,p_pswd,p_lvl;
11 COMMIT;
12 END add_dynamic;
```

Line 1 creates the procedure with four parameters (lines 2–5). The '%TYPE' keyword defines a variable or parameter as the corresponding field type of a table. For instance, 'p_id' is defined the same as the 'vid' field in the 'web_site' table. Both '%TYPE' and '%ROWTYPE' are very convenient! Line 7 defines 'v_stmt' as a variable-length string of up to 100 characters. Lines 8 and 12 define the 'BEGIN–END' block. Line 9 assigns an 'insert' query to 'v_stmt'. Line 10 runs the query. Line 11 saves query results to the database. Be sure to commit any 'insert', 'update', or 'delete' queries. Otherwise, the changes will not be saved to the database!

First, compile 'add_dynamic' (same as 'rpt'). Next, run the following anonymous block of code.

```
1  SET SERVEROUTPUT ON
2  BEGIN
3  add_dynamic('007','ivan','tohumpalot',2);
4  END;
```

Figure 3.21 shows the results of compiling the 'add_dynamic' procedure. You should see 'PROCEDURE add_dynamic compiled'. Figure 3.22 shows the results from running the anonymous block.

Figure 3.21 Output from SQL Worksheet, Showing Compiled 'add_dynamic'

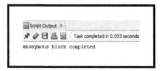

Figure 3.22 Output from SQL Worksheet, Showing Results from 'add_dynamic'

Load 'call_dbGeneral.php' in a browser. Figure 3.23 shows that a record with 'VID' of '007' was added.

```
001 ben 1649869de3d29daab675ad252b9bd02248fd9ea71
002 dandy 85aa14a772c00238f44f5a2b4edee7b9602aee2d2
003 sally ae79c3ab02ccd046df6f0ba809c753fef7b1d44f2
004 oliver 82008b43682796ae6255c402eec2e49bea6904ad2
005 betty f11d88e5c0ca93d109c9c4af63a3155bd749f0e52
007 ivan tohumpalot2
```

Figure 3.23 Output from 'dbGeneral' Class, Showing that Record Was Added

The 'update_dynamic' procedure uses similar logic to 'add_dynamic', but prepares an 'UPDATE' SQL statement instead. Line 1 creates the procedure. Lines 2–5 define the parameters. Line 7 defines a variable. Lines 8–13 represent the logic of the procedure.

```
1 CREATE OR REPLACE PROCEDURE update_dynamic(
2 p_id web_site.vid%TYPE,
3 p_user web_site.vuser%TYPE,
4 p_pswd web_site.pswd%TYPE,
5 p_lvl web_site.lvl%TYPE)
6 AS
7 v_stmt VARCHAR2(200);
8 BEGIN
9 v_stmt := 'UPDATE web_site
10 SET vuser = :vuser, pswd = :pswd,
11 lvl = :lvl WHERE vid = :vid';
12 EXECUTE IMMEDIATE v_stmt USING p_user,
13 p_pswd,p_lvl,p_id;
14 COMMIT;
15 END update_dynamic;
```

Compile 'update_dynamic' and run the following anonymous block to invoke it.

```
1 SET SERVEROUTPUT ON
2 BEGIN update_dynamic('007','ivan','tohumpalot',1);
3 END;
```

Check the 'web_site' table to ensure that 'LVL' changed from '2' to '1'.

The 'del_dynamic' procedure allows you to delete a record of your choice. Compile the procedure. Line 1 creates the procedure. Line 2 defines the parameter. Line 4 defines the variable that holds the SQL statement. Line 7 runs the query and line 8 saves results to the Oracle database.

```
1  CREATE OR REPLACE PROCEDURE del_dynamic(
2  p_id web_site.vid%TYPE)
3  AS
4  v_stmt VARCHAR2(100);
5  BEGIN
6  v_stmt := 'DELETE FROM web_site WHERE vid = :vid';
7  EXECUTE IMMEDIATE v_stmt USING p_id;
8  COMMIT;
9  END del_dynamic;
```

Run the anonymous block to delete record with 'VID' of '007'.

```
1  SET SERVEROUTPUT ON
2  BEGIN
3  del_dynamic('007');
4  END;
```

Check the 'web_site' table to see that the record was deleted. Now, I will show you how to run PL/SQL stored procedures from PHP scripts. In the first example, I add data with the 'add_dynamic' procedure. In the second, I modify data with the 'update_dynamic' procedure. Finally, I delete data with the 'del_dynamic' procedure. Login to your Linux account using 'PuTTY', change to the 'public_html' directory, and create and save the PHP file 'add_plsql.php'.

```
1  <?php
2  // File add_plsql.php
3  require_once 'dbGeneral.php';
4  $a = '008';
5  $b = 'mark';
6  $c = 'deespot';
7  $d = '2';
8  $sql = "BEGIN add_dynamic(:a,:b,:c,:d); END;";
9  $connect = new dbGeneral($sql);
10 $connect->parse();
11 $connect->bind(':a',$a,3);
12 $connect->bind(':b',$b,15);
13 $connect->bind(':c',$c,50);
14 $connect->bind(':d',$d,1);
15 $stmt = $connect->result;
16 $connect->exe();
17 ?>
```

Lines 4–7 define the values for each field. Line 8 assigns PL/SQL to '$sql'. Instead of an SQL query, a 'BEGIN–END' block is used to run the procedure. Line 9 creates a new 'dbGeneral' object. Line 10 parses the 'BEGIN–END' block. Lines 11–14 bind values to variables. Finally, lines 15 and 16 complete the run.

Load 'add_plsql.php' in a web browser to add the new record. Load 'call_dbGeneral.php' in a browser to see what happened. Figure 3.24 shows that a record with 'VID' of '008' was added.

```
001 ben 1649869de3d29daab675ad252b9bd02248fd9ea71
002 dandy 85aa14a772c00238f44f5a2b4edee7b9602aee2d2
003 sally ae79c3ab02ccd046df6f0ba809c753fef7b1d44f2
004 oliver 82008b43682796ae6255c402eec2e49bea6904ad2
005 betty f11d88e5c0ca93d109c9c4af63a3155bd749f0e52
008 mark deespot2
```

Figure 3.24 Output from 'dbGeneral' Class, Showing Another Record Added

Create and save PHP file 'mod_plsql.php'.

```php
1  <?php
2  // File mod_plsql.php
3  require_once 'dbGeneral.php';
4  $a = '008';
5  $b = 'mark';
6  $c = 'deespot';
7  $d = '1';
8  $sql = "BEGIN update_dynamic(:a,:b,:c,:d); end;";
9  $connect = new dbGeneral($sql);
10 $connect->parse();
11 $connect->bind(':a',$a,3);
12 $connect->bind(':b',$b,15);
13 $connect->bind(':c',$c,50);
14 $connect->bind(':d',$d,1);
15 $stmt = $connect->result;
16 $connect->exe();
17 ?>
```

Lines 4–7 assign field values. Line 8 builds the 'BEGIN–END' block. Line 9 creates a new 'dbGeneral' object. Line 10 parses the PL/SQL block. Lines 11–14 bind values to variables. Lines 15 and 16 complete the run. Load the file in a browser. The 'LVL' for the record should now be '1'.

Create and save the PHP file 'del_plsql.php'.

```php
1  <?php
2  // File del_plsql.php
3  require_once 'dbGeneral.php';
4  $vid = '008';
5  $sql = "BEGIN del_dynamic(:vid); end;";
6  $connect = new dbGeneral($sql);
7  $connect->parse();
8  $connect->bind(':vid',$vid,3);
9  $stmt = $connect->result;
10 $connect->exe();
11 ?>
```

Line 4 assigns the field value. Line 5 builds the 'BEGIN–END' block. Line 6 creates a new 'dbGeneral' object. Line 7 parses the PL/SQL block. Line 8 binds a value to a variable. Lines 9 and 10 complete the run. Load the file in a browser. The record with 'VID' of '008' should be deleted.

To this point in the chapter, several techniques have been introduced to enhance the security of a website, with the focus on securing login. The remaining two sections delve even deeper by offering advanced techniques for securing login and protecting other web pages from unauthorized access.

Session Variables (Redirect Unauthorized Access)

Session variables are used for two purposes. First, the values of input data can be saved for as long as the session is active. This allows the use of these values on any web page during an active session. Second, unauthorized users can be kept away from a web page by testing whether a session variable was set.

In 'verify.php', I set a session variable for 'VID' with '$_SESSION['VID'] = $row['VID'];' if login was successful. So, I have modified 'onward.php' to redirect users to the login page ('login.php') if login was unsuccessful. I also added a JavaScript event handler. A *JavaScript event handler* executes JavaScript when an event occurs (like pressing a button). Replace the original 'onward.php' with the following code.

```php
 1  <?php
 2  // File onward.php
 3  session_start();
 4  if(!IsSet($_SESSION['VID']))
 5  { header ("location: login.php"); }
 6  $vid = $_SESSION['VID'];
 7  $vuser = $_SESSION['VUSER'];
 8  ?>
 9  <html><head><style type="text/css">
10  table.center {
11  margin-left:auto;
12  margin-right:auto;
13  }
14  </style></head>
15  <body style="background-color:burlywood;">
16  <script src="destroy.js"></script>
17  <div style="text-align:center;">
18  <h1 style="color:indigo">Successful Login</h1>
19  <table class="center">
20  <tr><td><input type=button onClick="killSession();"
21  value="destroy"</td></tr>
22  </table></div>
23  <div style="text-align:center;" id="txtHint">
24  <?php
25  echo "<h5 style='text-align:center;'";
26  print_r($_SESSION);
27  ?>
28  </div></body></html>
```

At the beginning of 'onward.php', I start a new session with 'session_start()' (line 3). Next, an 'if' statement checks if session variable 'VID' is set (or not) (line 4). If not set, the page is redirected to 'login.php' (line 5).

If set, processing continues normally. Values of session variables 'VID' and 'VUSER' are captured from the session array set in the 'verify.php' script (lines 6 and 7). In line 20, I added a JavaScript event handler 'onClick' (inactive at this time). I also added a 'print_r[$_SESSION]' statement (line 26) to display session variables.

Test what we have so far by reloading 'login.php' into a browser and submitting with username 'sally' and password 'forth'. Figure 3.25 shows the login page and Figure 3.26 shows the result. The 'destroy' button does not work yet, but don't worry. I will show you how to make this work in the next section.

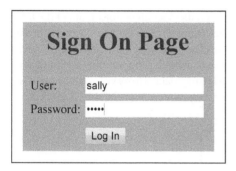

Figure 3.25 Display of Login Page with Username and Password

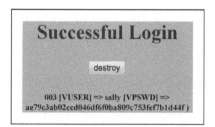

Figure 3.26 Display of Successful Login with Simple AJAX Functionality

To test the redirect logic, clear the browser cache and load 'onward.php' directly into a browser. Figure 3.27 shows that the page was automatically redirected to 'login.php', which means that the web page is protected!

Figure 3.27 Display of Login Page, Verifying that Page Was Redirected

AJAX

Asynchronous JavaScript and XML (AJAX) allows web pages to be updated asynchronously by exchanging small amounts of data with the server without reloading the whole page. ***Asynchronous*** describes communications in data that can be transmitted intermittently rather than in a steady stream. For instance, a telephone conversation is asynchronous because both parties can talk whenever they like. If it were synchronous, each party would have to wait a specified interval before speaking. AJAX therefore allows content on web pages to update immediately when a user performs an action. In contrast, with a synchronous HTTP request (i.e., HTML form submission) the user must wait for a whole new page to load.

AJAX uses a combination of an 'XMLHttpRequest' object, JavaScript, the document object model (DOM), CSS (optional), and XML (optional). The 'XMLHttpRequest' object enables asynchronous data exchange with a server. The 'JavaScript/DOM' allows display and interaction of information on a web page. 'CSS' allows styling of the data for refined web design. Since this book focuses on web programming, I do not present design principles. 'XML' is often used as the format for transferring data. However, AJAX can also transfer text, images, and database data. Figure 3.28 offers a graphical representation of the AJAX process.

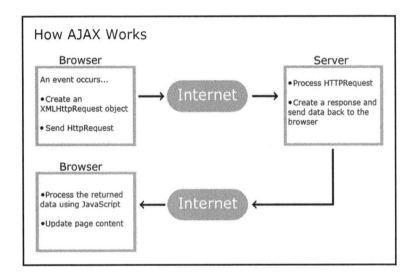

Figure 3.28 Graphical Representation of the AJAX Process (http://www.w3schools.com/ajax/ajax_intro.asp)

AJAX works with a JavaScript file that creates an 'XMLHttpRequest' object and sends it to the server. The user can load this file through a JavaScript event handler (i.e., by clicking a button). Once the file is loaded, the web browser sends the request to the server. The server processes the 'HTTPRequest', creates a response, and sends data back to the browser. The browser processes the returned data using JavaScript (in the JavaScript file), and updates web page content.

To implement JavaScript event hander 'onClick()' in 'onward.php', a JavaScript file that implements AJAX is required. I created JavaScript file 'destroy.js' for this purpose. Be careful to use file extension 'js' to inform the PHP engine that the file is JavaScript.

```
1  /* File destroy.js */
2  var xhr;
3  xhr = new XMLHttpRequest();
4  function killSession(str)
```

```
 5 {
 6 var url="logout.php";
 7 xhr.open("POST",url,true);
 8 xhr.setRequestHeader('Content-Type',
 9 'application/x-www-form-urlencoded; charset=iso-8859-1');
10 xhr.send("q="+str+"&sid="+Math.random());
11 xhr.onreadystatechange=function()
12 {
13 if (xhr.readyState==4)
14 { document.getElementById("txtHint").innerHTML =
15 xhr.responseText; }
16 }
17 }
```

I create an instance of 'XMLHttpRequest' and place it in variable 'xhr' (line 3). In function 'killSession()' (lines 4–17), 'logout.php' is placed in variable 'url' (line 6). With method 'open' (line 7) the browser is informed to 'POST' file 'logout.php'. With 'POST', header information must be manually sent with method 'setRequestHeader()' (lines 8 and 9). The request is sent with method 'send()' (line 10). The response from the server is checked with method 'onreadystatechange()' (line 11). Once the response is verified (line 13), it is then sent to the web page with method 'responseText' (line 15) and placed in document 'onward.php' with 'document.getElementById("txtHint").innerHTML' (line 14).

The identifier of one of the HTML 'div' tags in 'onward.php' is 'txtHint', which appropriately directs the response. That is, the response is added directly after the 'div' tag.

Next, I create PHP file 'logout.php'. This file is invoked when the JavaScript event handler ('destroy' button) is pressed. The file contains a 'logout' class (lines 3–11) that destroys all session information (lines 8 and 9). It also contains a statement that creates a new instance of the 'logout' class (line 12) and displays that the session was destroyed (line 13).

```
 1 <?php
 2 //File logout.php
 3 class logout
 4 {
 5 public function __construct()
 6 {
 7 session_start();
 8 unset($_SESSION);
 9 session_destroy();
10 }
11 }
12 $logout = new logout();
13 echo "<h5>Session Destroyed</h5>";
14 ?>
```

Now, let's test the latest 'login' incarnation. Reload 'login.php' into a web browser with username 'sally' and password 'forth', and press the 'Log In' button.

Figure 3.29 displays the results. Now press the 'destroy' button, which is now active because we implemented AJAX. Figure 3.30 displays that the session was destroyed.

Figure 3.29 Display of Successful Login with 'destroy' Button

Figure 3.30 Display after 'destroy' Button Is Pressed

CAPTCHA

A completely automated public Turing test to tell computers and humans apart (CAPTCHA) is a type of challenge–response test used to ensure that a response is not generated by a computer. The challenge–response is typically a distorted image of letters and numbers that (hopefully) only a human being can decipher. The process usually involves one computer (server) asking a user to complete a simple test that the computer is able to generate and grade. For websites, CAPTCHA is used to verify a form or other login. To implement CAPTCHA, I use 'Securimage'.

Securimage

Securimage is an open-source free PHP CAPTCHA script for generating complex images and CAPTCHA codes to protect forms from spam and abuse. To install, go to www.phpcaptcha.org and click the 'Download' link. Click the 'zip download' link in the green window for version 3.5.4 (this is the latest stable version as of writing). Keep in mind that the version and download instructions may change at the discretion of 'Securimage' administration. This version assumes that you are running PHP 5 or higher.

Click the arrow to the right of 'securimage.zip' on the bottom left of the display and choose 'Show in folder'. Right click the 'securimage' icon in your 'Downloads' directory and choose 'Extract All'. Click the 'Extract' button (use the default destination provided). A new 'securimage' directory should now appear in your 'Downloads' directory.

Open and log into 'WinSCP' and you should see a left and right window. The left window is the local computer and the right window is the Linux file structure. On the left window, open the 'Downloads' directory. On the right window, open 'public_html' directory. Next, copy the contents of the 'securimage' directory to the right window (into a 'securimage' directory that you must create), and copy (be careful to put it within your 'public_html'). Now, you should have the 'securimage' directory in your 'public_html' directory. If you have any difficulty running the software, consult your IT expert.

PHP file 'login_captcha.php' shows the code for the CAPTCHA-protected login script.

```
1  <?php
2  // File login_captcha.php
3  session_start();
4  if(!isSet($_SESSION['captcha']) )
5  { $_SESSION['captcha'] = 0; }
6  ?>
7  <html><head><style type="text/css">
8  table.center {
9  margin-left:auto;
10 margin-right:auto;
11 }
12 </style></head>
13 <body style="background-color:lightgreen";>
14 <h1 style="text-align:center";>Sign On Page</h1>
15 <form method=post action='verify_captcha.php'>
16 <table class="center";>
17 <tr><td>User:</font></td>
18 <td><input type=text name=user></td></tr>
19 <tr><td>Password:</font></td>
20 <td><input type=password name=password></td></tr>
21 <tr><td colspan=2>
22 <tr><td></td><td></td></tr>
23 <tr><td></td>
24 <td><input type=submit value="Log In"></td></tr>
25 <tr><td></td>
26 <?php
27 if($_SESSION['captcha']>= 5)
28 {
29 echo "<td><img id=\"captcha\"
30 src=\"securimage/securimage_show.php\"
31 alt=\"CAPTCHA Image\" /></td></tr>";
32 echo "<tr><td></td>";
33 echo "<td><input type=\"text\" name=\"captcha_code\"
34 size=\"10\" maxlength=\"6\" /></td></tr> <tr><td></td>";
35 echo "<td><a href=\"#\"
36 onclick=\"document.getElementById('captcha').src =
37 'securimage/securimage_show.php?' + Math.random();
38 return false\">Reload Image</a></td></tr>";
39 }
40 ?>
41 </table></form></html>
```

The 'login_captcha.php' file is modified (from 'login.php') in three ways. First, a new session is started at the beginning of the script (line 3). Second, logic is added to check if login has been attempted. If not, the session variable 'captcha' is set to zero (lines 4 and 5). Otherwise, processing continues normally. Third, logic is added to check if session variable 'captcha' is greater than or equal to five (five or more login attempts) (line 27). If so, CAPTCHA code is executed (lines 29–38). Don't be too concerned if you don't understand the new logic because it was adapted from logic provided on the 'Securimage' website. Go to the 'Quickstart Guide' on the 'Securimage' website to see details or just use the code provided.

PHP file 'verify_captcha.php' has two additions. First, it checks if 'captcha' is greater than or equal to five (number of login attempts) (line 7). If so, it loads the CAPTCHA code (line 9), creates a new instance of the 'Securimage' class (line 10), and checks if the user typed the CAPTCHA text correctly (line 11). Second, it iterates 'captcha' by one each time login fails (line 42). So, 'login_captcha.php' and 'verify_captcha.php' scripts work together to show the CAPTCHA image if more than five login attempts are made.

```php
1  <?php
2  // File verify_captcha.php
3  session_start();
4  require_once 'clean.php';
5  require_once 'dbGeneral.php';
6  require_once 'salt.php';
7  if($_SESSION['captcha'] >= 5)
8  {
9  include_once ('securimage/securimage.php');
10 $securimage = new Securimage();
11 if($securimage->check($_POST['captcha_code']) == false)
12 { die('The code you entered was incorrect.
13 Go back and try again.'); }
14 }
15 $user = $_POST['user'];
16 $pass = $_POST['password'];
17 $clean = new clean();
18 $clean_tags = $clean->cleanse($user);
19 $clean_special = $clean->clean_special($clean_tags);
20 $user = $clean->reduce_size($clean_special);
21 $clean_tags = $clean->cleanse($pass);
22 $pass = $clean->clean_special($clean_tags);
23 $toHash = 'tiger';
24 $salt = new Salt();
25 $pass = $salt->doubleSalt($toHash,$pass);
26 $query = "SELECT * FROM web_site
27 WHERE vuser=:a AND pswd=:b";
28 $connect = new dbGeneral($query);
29 $connect->parse();
30 $connect->bind(':a',$user,20);
31 $connect->bind(':b',$pass,50);
32 $stmt = $connect->result;
33 $connect->exe();
34 if ($row = oci_fetch_assoc($stmt))
35 {
36 $_SESSION['VID'] = $row['VID'];
37 $_SESSION['VUSER'] = $row['VUSER'];
```

```
38 header ("location: onward_captcha.php");
39 }
40 else
41 {
42 $_SESSION['captcha'] += 1;
43 header ("location: login_captcha.php");
44 }
45 ?>
```

PHP file 'onward_captcha.php' has the same logic as the most recently modified 'onward.php', except that it redirects to 'login_captcha.php' (line 5).

```
1  <?php
2  // File onward_captcha.php
3  session_start();
4  if(!IsSet($_SESSION['VID']))
5  { header ("location: login_captcha.php"); }
6  $vid = $_SESSION['VID'];
7  $vuser = $_SESSION['VUSER'];
8  ?>
9  <html><body style="background-color:lightgreen";>
10 <script src="destroy_captcha.js"></script>
11 <h1 style="text-align:center";>Successful Login</h1>
12 <div style="text-align:center"; id="txtHint">
13 <table align=center>
14 <tr><td><input type=button onClick="killSession();
15 clearInnerHTML();" value="destroy"</td></tr>
16 </table>
17 </body>
18 <?php
19 echo "<br />Session array: ";
20 print_r($_SESSION);
21 ?>
22 </div><html>
```

JavaScript file 'destroy_captcha.js' includes the same logic as 'destroy.js'. Be sure to use extension 'js' to tell PHP that the file is JavaScript.

```
1 /* File destroy_captcha.js */
2 var xhr;
3 xhr = new XMLHttpRequest();
4 function killSession(str)
5 {
```

```
 6 var url="logout_captcha.php";
 7 xhr.open("POST",url,true);
 8 xhr.setRequestHeader('Content-Type',
 9 'application/x-www-form-urlencoded; charset=iso-8859-1');
10 xhr.send("q="+str+"&sid="+Math.random());
11 xhr.onreadystatechange=function()
12 {
13 if (xhr.readyState==4)
14 {
15 document.getElementById("txtHint").innerHTML =
16 xhr.responseText;
17 }
18 }
19 }
```

PHP file 'logout_captcha.php' adds a bit of HTML for a different look than the earlier 'logout.php' file.

```
 1 <?php
 2 //File: logout_captcha.php
 3 class logout
 4 {
 5 public function __construct()
 6 {
 7 session_start();
 8 unset($_SESSION);
 9 session_destroy();
10 }
11 }
12 $logout = new logout();
13 ?>
14 <html style="align-text:center";>
15 <form method="post" action="login_captcha.php">
16 <input type="submit" value="Return">
17 </form>
18 </html>
19 <?php
20 echo '<strong style="color:yellow;">
21 Session Destroyed!</strong>';
22 ?>
```

Allowing only five attempts at login before CAPTCHA is enacted mitigates the chances of unauthorized access. Load 'login_captcha.php' into a browser and click the 'Log In' button five times. Type in an authorized username and password (in this case username 'ben' and password 'dover'), and type the required text underneath the CAPTCHA image. Figure 3.31 shows the page at this point. Now, click 'Log In' to enter. Figure 3.32 shows a successful login.

Figure 3.31 Display of 'CAPTCHA' Login Page with Login Information

Figure 3.32 Display of Successful 'CAPTCHA' Login

Click the 'destroy' button. The session is now destroyed, as shown in Figure 3.33. Click 'Return' to go back to the login page. In this section, I showed you how to rethink earlier login logic to incorporate added security with CAPTCHA. I strongly recommend using this added feature to protect your website from unauthorized access.

Successful Login

Return

Session Destroyed!

Figure 3.33 Display after 'destroy' Button Is Pressed, Showing 'Return' Button

Summary

The goal of this chapter was to help you gain a fundamental understanding of web security techniques that mitigate improper interactions with Oracle. I introduced ways to 'cleanse' data, encrypt data, protect web pages from unauthorized access, and use CAPTCHA for added login security.

4   Input Validation and Report Generation

Overview

Any form of data entering a website is potentially harmful. Input validation is therefore very important. Two techniques for input validation are presented. First, Perl Compatible Regular Expressions (PCRE) are introduced, explained, and implemented as a means to verify input form data. PCRE closely resembles Perl in terms of pattern-matching functionality. Second, PHP includes a set of built-in filter functions for input validation. The chapter concludes by introducing two small applications for safe report generation.

Learning Objectives

After completing this chapter, you will gain a fundamental understanding of input validation to mitigate potentially harmful form data from entering your website. You will also learn how to create safe report generation using drop-down menus. Understanding is enhanced through explanation and code examples. The following objectives summarize the skills the chapter will help you develop:

1 Learn the definition of a regular expression.
2 Learn the definition of PCRE.
3 Learn how to use PCRE to validate form data.
4 Learn how to build a PCRE form data validation application.
5 Learn how to use PHP built-in validation functions.
6 Learn how to build an application with PCRE and built-in functions.
7 Learn the advantages and disadvantages of PCRE and built-in functions.
8 Learn how to build a simple report generation application.
9 Learn how to build a sophisticated report generation application.
10 Learn how to build a report generation application with PL/SQL cursors.

Regular Expressions

A *regular expression* is a pattern describing a certain amount of text; abbreviated as 'regex'. The idea is to test for a match between the regex and the form data input. A **match** is the piece of text that the pattern was found to correspond to by the regex processing software.

PCRE

Perl Compatible Regular Expressions (*PCRE*) is a set of PHP functions that implement regular expression pattern-matching using the same syntax and semantics as Perl 5. PCRE uses special symbols to facilitate pattern-matching. PCRE allows many special symbols, but I cover the ones that I use most often to enable form input validation.

To make it easier, I start by introducing a small set of special characters and then provide a corresponding example to facilitate learning. I continue by introducing another set of special characters and a corresponding example, and so on. After the symbols are introduced, I provide examples of regexes that I use for form input validation. I end the 'regex' sections with an application that validates form data.

Special Symbols

The '^' indicates the start of a string. The '$' indicates the end of a string. The '?' indicates that the previous token is optional. A *token* is a tangible way to represent a piece of a regex. The '|' is a Boolean OR. Braces '{}' are used to match the number of occurrences. Parentheses '()' are used to quantify a sequence of characters. *Delimiters* are used to mark the beginning and end of a pattern. A delimiter can be any nonalphanumeric, nonbackslash, nonwhitespace character.

I use the '#' symbol as a delimiter because it is then easier for me to discern the regex. Often-used delimiters are '/', '#', and '~'. PCRE can quickly become complex, so let's look at an example.

PHP file 'pcre1.php' includes five regexes (lines 4–8) that match against the string 'hello world' (line 3). The 'preg_match()' function (lines 9, 12, 15, 18, and 21) is used to perform a regex match. Each regex is compared to '$string'. The results are displayed as 'Match' or 'No Match'.

```php
1  <?php
2  // File pcre1.php
3  $string = 'hello world';
4  $regex1 = '#^hello#';
5  $regex2 = '#world$#';
6  $regex3 = '#^(he(l{2})o)#';
7  $regex4 = '#(hello)|(world)#';
8  $regex5 = '#^hello world$#';
9  if(preg_match($regex1,$string))
10 { echo "Match<br />"; }
11 else { echo "No Match<br />"; }
12 if(preg_match($regex2,$string))
13 { echo "Match<br />"; }
14 else { echo "No Match<br />"; }
15 if(preg_match($regex3,$string))
16 { echo "Match<br />"; }
17 else { echo "No Match<br />"; }
18 if(preg_match($regex4,$string))
19 { echo "Match<br />"; }
20 else { echo "No Match<br />"; }
21 if(preg_match($regex5,$string))
22 { echo "Match"; }
23 else { echo "No Match"; }
24 ?>
```

```
Match
Match
Match
Match
Match
```

Figure 4.1 Display of Matching 'hello world' with Regexes

Figure 4.1 illustrates that each regex matched string 'hello world'. '$regex1' (line 4) matches a string that starts with 'hello'. '$regex2' (line 5) matches a string that ends with 'world'. '$regex3' (line 6) matches a string that begins with 'he', followed by exactly two 'l's, and ends with 'o'. '$regex4' (line 7) matches either 'hello' or 'world'. '$regex5' (line 8) matches a string that begins with 'hello' and ends with 'world'.

To include special symbols as part of a regex, escape them with a backslash '\'. So, to be taken literally, special characters '!@#$%^&*()_-+=:;"'<>,.?/' must be escaped because they have special meaning. You must escape the backslash character itself if you need to use it as part of a regex.

Let's look at another example that uses two additional special symbols – '[]' and '\s'. Brackets '[]' contain characters allowed in a single position of a string. The '\s' indicates a space. PHP file 'pcre2.php' illustrates how these symbols can be used as part of a regex.

```php
 1  <?php
 2  // File pcre2.php
 3  $string1 = 'My phone is: ';
 4  $string2 = '(290)444-3333';
 5  $string3 = 'My phone is: (290)444-3333';
 6  $regex1 = '#^[a-zA-Z]{2}\s[a-z]{5}\s[a-z]{2}\:\s#';
 7  $regex2 = '#^\([0-9]{3}\)[0-9]{3}\-[0-9]{4}#';
 8  $regex3 = '#^[a-zA-Z]{2}\s[a-z]{5}\s[a-z]{2}\:\s\([0-9]{3}\)[0-9]{3}\-[0-9]{4}#';
 9  if(preg_match($regex1,$string1))
10  { echo "Match<br />"; }
11  else { echo "No Match<br />"; }
12  if(preg_match($regex2,$string2))
13  { echo "Match<br />"; }
14  else { echo "No Match<br />"; }
15  if(preg_match($regex3,$string3))
16  { echo "Match<br />"; }
17  else { echo "No Match<br />"; }
18  ?>
```

```
Match
Match
Match
```

Figure 4.2 Display of Matching Various Strings with Regexes

Figure 4.2 illustrates that each regex (lines 6–8) matched its corresponding string (lines 3–5). '$regex1' (line 6) matches a string that starts with exactly two letters that can be upper- or lowercase, continues with exactly one space, followed by exactly five lowercase letters, then exactly one space, followed by exactly two lowercase letters, a single colon (notice that the colon was escaped with a backslash), and ends with exactly one space. '$regex2' (line 7) matches a string that starts with a single left parenthesis, continues with exactly three digits between zero and nine, followed by a single right parenthesis, then exactly three digits from zero to nine, followed by a dash, and ends with exactly four digits between zero and nine. '$regex3' (combines regexes from '$regex1' and '$regex2') (line 8) matches the full string ('$string3' combines '$string1' and '$string2').

In 'pcre2.php', you learned how to validate a US phone number with area code. If you want to validate a phone number with an optional area code, the regex must be modified.

PHP file 'pcre3.php' validates a phone number with or without an area code. I leave out validation of text to concentrate on phone number validation with optional area code.

```php
1  <?php
2  // File pcre3.php
3  $string1 = '(801)787-1234';
4  $string2 = '787-1234';
5  $regex = '#^\(?([0-9]{3})?\)?[0-9]{3}\-[0-9]{4}$#';
6  if(preg_match($regex,$string1))
7  { echo "Match<br />"; }
8  else { echo "No Match<br />"; }
9  if(preg_match($regex,$string2))
10 { echo "Match<br />"; }
11 else { echo "No Match<br />"; }
12 ?>
```

```
Match
Match
```

Figure 4.3 Display of Matching Phone Numbers with Regex

'$regex' (line 5) matches a pattern that optionally begins with an area code in parentheses, continues with three digits followed by the '-' symbol, and ends with four digits. Notice the use of the '?' symbol to indicate an optional pattern. At the beginning of the regex, the '(' symbol is optional, the next three digits are optional, and the closing ')' is optional (the '?' symbol identifies the *previous* token as optional). I added a '$' symbol at the end of the regex to ensure that the patterns ends with four digits. If you adopt this regex, you must inform the user to use the proper format.

An easier way to force phone number format is to build an input form that accepts up to ten digits and then use PHP to cleanse the data. The following example shows you how to build a simple form and validate the data. The example uses two files – one for the HTML form, 'phone.php', and another for processing form data, 'verify_phone.php'.

PHP file 'phone.php' includes an HTML data form (lines 14–22) that accepts a phone number of up to ten digits by including the 'maxlength' attribute inside the 'input' tag (line 17). It also includes a submit button (line 19) that sends user input to PHP file 'verify_phone.php' for processing and a reset button (line 20) to clear the contents of the text box.

```
1  <?php
2  // File phone.php
3  ?>
4  <html><head>
5  <style type="text/css">
6  table.center {
7  margin-left:auto;
8  margin-right:auto;
9  }
10 </style></head>
11 <body style="background-color:burlywood;">
12 <div style="text-align:center;">
13 <h1 style="color:indigo;">Enter Phone Number</h1>
14 <form method="post" action="verify_phone.php">
15 <table class="center">
16 <tr><td>Phone:</td>
17 <td><input type="text" name="phone" maxlength="10"></td>
18 </tr>
19 <td><input type="submit" value="Enter"></td>
20 <td><input type="reset" value="Reset"></td>
21 </tr>
22 </table></form></div>
23 </html>
```

PHP file 'verify_phone.php' checks the length of the phone number (line 4). Based on length, the phone number is translated into a phone number without area code (lines 6 and 7) or with area code (lines 12–14) or an error message is generated (lines 17 and 18).

```
1  <?php
2  // File verify_phone.php
3  $phone = $_POST["phone"];
4  if(strlen($phone)==7)
5  {
6  $phone = substr($phone,0,3) .
7  '-' . substr($phone,3,4);
8  echo 'Translated phone number is: ' . $phone;
9  }
10 elseif(strlen($phone)==10)
11 {
12 $p1 = '(' . substr($phone,0,3) . ')' .
13 substr($phone,3,3);
14 $phone = $p1 . '-' . substr($phone,6,4);
15 echo 'Translated phone number is: ' . $phone;
16 }
17 else { echo 'Enter a valid phone number
18 of 7 or 10 digits'; }
19 ?>
```

Let's try a seven-digit number and see what happens. Load 'phone.php' into a browser. Figure 4.4 shows the seven-digit number before submission of the form. Be sure to enter only digits without a '-'. Figure 4.5 shows what happens after submission of the seven-digit number.

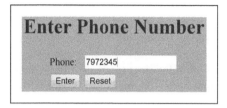

Figure 4.4 Display of Form with Valid Seven-Digit String

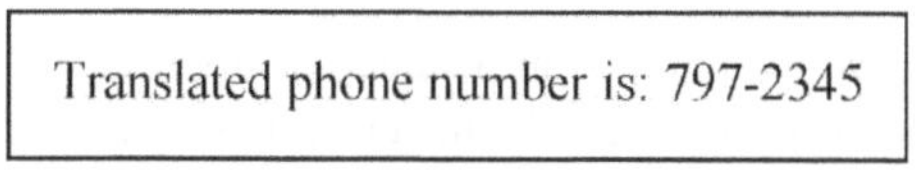

Figure 4.5 Display of Translated Seven-Digit String

Let's try a ten-digit number and see what happens. Figure 4.6 shows the ten-digit number before submission of the form. Be sure to enter only digits. Figure 4.7 shows what happens after submission of the ten-digit number.

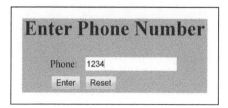

Figure 4.6 Display of Form with Valid Ten-Digit String

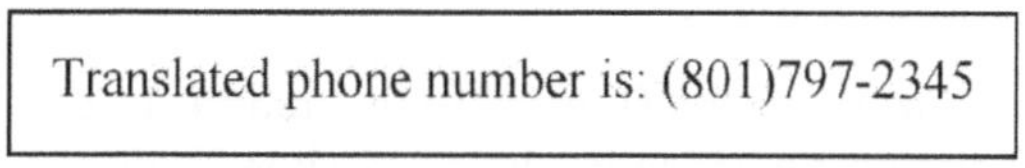

Translated phone number is: (801)797-2345

Figure 4.7 Display of Translated Ten-Digit String

Let's try a four-digit number and see what happens. Figure 4.8 shows the four-digit number before submission of the form. Figure 4.9 shows what happens after submission of the four-digit number.

Figure 4.8 Display of Form with Invalid Four-Digit String

Enter a valid phone number of 7 or 10 digits

Figure 4.9 Display of Message with Acceptable Strings

The seven- and ten-digit numbers were processed properly by the 'verify_phone.php' file. The four-digit number generated an error message.

However, if the user inputs data other than numbers, trouble ensues. A solution is to create a regex that works with the form. Since the form accepts data up to a maximum length of ten, the regex can be simplified to search for numbers only.

Object-Oriented Validation

To encapsulate the phone regex, I create a class with a method. I can then create an instance of the class to validate phone numbers. I always test a new class before using it in an application. The next example tests the new class.

The example uses two PHP files – 'validate_regex.php' and 'call_validate_regex.php'. PHP file 'validate_regex.php' holds the class. PHP file 'call_validate_regex.php' tests the class.

```
1  <?php
2  // File validate_regex.php
3  class validate_regex
4  {
5  function get_valid_phone($phone)
6  {
7  $regex = '#^[0-9]{7}$|^[0-9]{10}$#';
8  return preg_match($regex,trim($phone));
9  }
10 }
11 ?>
```

Class 'validate_regex' (lines 3–10) includes the get_valid_phone()' method (lines 5–9) that returns true if the number is either seven or ten digits and returns false otherwise. Specifically, the regex (line 7) checks if the input is a seven- or ten-digit number. Notice the use of the '^' symbol at the beginning of the regex and the '$' symbol at the end of the regex to ensure compliance. Also notice the 'preg_match()' function (line 8), which performs a regex match. The function matches the regex (line 7) with the (trimmed) phone number coming in as a parameter to the method (line 5).

```
1  <?php
2  // File call_validate_regex.php
3  require_once 'validate_regex.php';
4  $phones = array(
5  '1234567', 'abc', '123', '8017972456',
6  '7972456', '1m2j4k1', '88822234',
7  '6186872121', '1112223334444',
8  );
```

```
 9  $validate = new validate_regex();
10  foreach($phones as $phone)
11  {
12  if($validate->get_valid_phone($phone))
13  { echo "Valid Phone: " . $phone; }
14  else
15  { echo "Invalid Phone: " . $phone; }
16  echo "<br />";
17  }
18  ?>
```

PHP file 'call_validate_regex.php' instantiates the class (line 9) and validates a set of phone numbers. Using array '$phones' (lines 4–8) to hold a set of phone numbers is convenient because a 'foreach' loop (lines 10–17) can then be used to easily traverse the array to test each phone number for compliance with the 'get_valid_phone()' method (line 12).

Load 'call_validate_regex.php' into a browser. Figure 4.10 shows the results. Strings of seven or ten digits are the only ones shown as valid.

```
Valid Phone: 1234567
Invalid Phone: abc
Invalid Phone: 123
Valid Phone: 8017972456
Valid Phone: 7972456
Invalid Phone: 1m2j4k1
Invalid Phone: 88822234
Valid Phone: 6186872121
Invalid Phone: 1112223334444
```

Figure 4.10 Output from 'validate_regex' Class Showing Valid and Invalid Phone Numbers

Since the 'validate_regex' class is tested, it can now be used in the form built earlier. For this example, I use the 'phone.php', 'validate_regex.php', and 'verify_phone.php' files. The form logic in 'phone.php' remains the same. The class in 'validate_regex.php' remains the same. I include the logic for 'phone.php' again here for your convenience.

```
1  <?php
2  // File phone.php
3  ?>
4  <html><head>
5  <style type="text/css">
6  table.center {
7  margin-left:auto;
8  margin-right:auto;
9  }
```

```
10  </style></head>
11  <body style="background-color:burlywood;">
12  <div style="text-align:center;">
13  <h1 style="color:indigo;">Enter Phone Number</h1>
14  <form method="post" action="verify_phone.php">
15  <table class="center">
16  <tr><td>Phone:</td>
17  <td><input type="text" name="phone" maxlength="10"></td>
18  </tr>
19  <td><input type="submit" value="Enter"></td>
20  <td><input type="reset" value="Reset"></td>
21  </tr>
22  </table></form></div>
23  </html>
```

I had to modify the logic in 'verify_phone.php'. First, I included 'validate_regex.php' (line 3) to enable use of the class. Second, I created a new instance of the class (line 4). Third, I invoked method 'get_valid_phone()' (line 6) to test if the number contains seven or ten digits. The remaining logic is the same as before. The phone number still has to be checked to determine whether it has either seven or ten digits so it can be formatted properly (lines 8–14). If the phone number is not valid, an error message is generated, as before (line 7). Actually, the logic is a bit simpler with the use of the class instance.

```php
1   <?php
2   // File verify_phone.php
3   require_once 'validate_regex.php';
4   $validate = new validate_regex();
5   $phone = $_POST["phone"];
6   if($validate->get_valid_phone($phone))
7   {
8   if(strlen($phone)==7)
9   { $phone = substr($phone,0,3) . '-' . substr($phone,3,4); }
10  elseif(strlen($phone)==10)
11  {
12  $p1 = '(' . substr($phone,0,3) . ')' . substr($phone,3,3);
13  $phone = $p1 . '-' . substr($phone,6,4);
14  }
15  echo 'Translated phone number is: ' . $phone;
16  }
17  else { echo 'Enter a valid phone number of 7 or 10 digits'; }
18  ?>
```

Load 'phone.php' into a browser. Figure 4.11 shows the form prior to submission with a seven-digit phone number. Figure 4.12 shows what happens after submission of the seven-digit number. Figure 4.13 shows the form prior to submission with a ten-digit phone number. Figure 4.14 shows what happens after submission of the ten-digit number. Figure 4.15 shows the form prior to submission with an invalid entry. Figure 4.16 shows what happens after submission of the invalid entry.

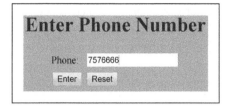

Figure 4.11 Display of Form with Valid Seven-Digit String

Translated phone number is: 757-6666

Figure 4.12 Display of Translated Seven-Digit String Using 'validate_regex' Class

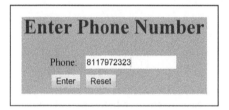

Figure 4.13 Display of Form with Valid Ten-Digit String

Translated phone number is: (811)797-2323

Figure 4.14 Display of Translated Ten-Digit String Using 'validate_regex' Class

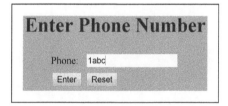

Figure 4.15 Display of Form with Invalid Four-Digit String

Enter a valid phone number of 7 or 10 digits

Figure 4.16 Display of Message with Acceptable Strings Using 'validate_regex' Class

Now, let's create a simple regex to validate email. We need two additional symbols – '+' matches one or more of a pattern, and '.' matches any single character. Modify PHP file 'validate_regex.php' to include a new method for email validation (lines 10–14). The regex (line 12) tests if the email is valid.

```php
 1  <?php
 2  // File validate_regex.php
 3  class validate_regex
 4  {
 5  function get_valid_phone($phone)
 6  {
 7  $regex = '#^[0-9]{7}$|^[0-9]{10}$#';
 8  return preg_match($regex,trim($phone));
 9  }
10  function get_valid_email($email)
11  {
12  $regex = '#^[0-9A-Za-z._%+-]{2,}@[0-9A-Za-z.-]+\.[A-Za-z]{2,6}$#';
13  return preg_match($regex,trim($email));
14  }
15  }
16  ?>
```

The email regex must begin with two or more of the following (number, case insensitive letter, period, underscore, percent, plus or minus). It must continue with the '@' symbol, one or more of the following (number, case insensitive letter, period or minus), a period, and end with two to six case insensitive letters.

Again, I always test a new method independently of the form application. So, modify PHP file 'call_validate_regex.php' to validate emails.

```php
 1  <?php
 2  // File call_validate_regex.php
 3  require_once 'validate_regex.php';
 4  $emails = array(
 5  'my.name@gmail.com',
 6  'another@gmail.co.uk',
 7  'best@yahoo',
 8  'hellomsn.net',
 9  'long@123.org',
10  '123.me.you@ymail.com',
11  'miss@yahoo.',
12  'Miss@Yahoo.com',
13  '.@yahoo.com'
14  );
15  $validate = new validate_regex();
16  foreach($emails as $email)
17  {
18  if($validate->get_valid_email($email))
```

```
19 { echo "Valid Email: " . $email; }
20 else
21 { echo "Invalid Email: " . $email; }
22 echo "<br />";
23 }
24 ?>
```

The '$emails' array (lines 4–14) includes various emails to test. The class is instantiated in line 15. A 'foreach' loop (lines 16–23) iterates the email array. Each email is tested with 'get_valid_email()' (line 18) and the appropriate message is returned (lines 19 and 21). Load the modified 'call_validate.php' to see the results shown in Figure 4.17.

```
Valid Email: my.name@gmail.com
Valid Email: another@gmail.co.uk
Invalid Email: best@yahoo
Invalid Email: hellomsn.net
Valid Email: long@123.org
Valid Email: 123.me.you@ymail.com
Invalid Email: miss@yahoo.
Valid Email: Miss@Yahoo.com
Invalid Email: .@yahoo.com
```

Figure 4.17 Output from 'validate_regex' Class Showing Valid and Invalid Email Addresses

To finalize the 'validate' class, I create four new methods with a regex to validate first name, last name, address, and ZIP code. Modify PHP file 'validate_regex.php' as follows:

```
 1 <?php
 2 // File validate_regex.php
 3 class validate_regex
 4 {
 5 function get_valid_first($first)
 6 {
 7 $regex = '#^[a-zA-Z]{2,10}$#';
 8 return preg_match($regex,trim($first));
 9 }
10 function get_valid_last($last)
11 {
12 $regex = '#^[a-zA-Z]{1}\'?[a-zA-Z]{2,20}$#';
13 return preg_match($regex,trim($last));
14 }
15 function get_valid_address($address)
16 {
17 $regex = '#^[a-zA-Z-0-9]{1,}\s[a-zA-Z0-9]{1,}+#';
```

```
18 return preg_match($regex,trim($address));
19 }
20 function get_valid_zip($zip)
21 {
22 $regex = '#^([0-9]{5})(-[0-9]{4})?$#';
23 return preg_match($regex,trim($zip));
24 }
25 function get_valid_phone($phone)
26 {
27 $regex = '#^[0-9]{7}$|^[0-9]{10}$#';
28 return preg_match($regex,trim($phone));
29 }
30 function get_valid_email($email)
31 {
32 $regex = '#^[0-9A-Za-z._%+-]{2,}@[0-9A-Za-z.-]+\.[A-Za-z]{2,6}$#';
33 return preg_match($regex,trim($email));
34 }
35 }
36 ?>
```

The regex for the first name must start with two (or more) case insensitive letters (line 7). The length of the first name is limited to ten letters, but you can change this value. The regex for the last name (line 12) can optionally start with one case insensitive letter followed by an apostrophe and continue with up to 20 letters. The regex for address (line 17) must start with one or more case insensitive letters or numbers followed by a space and continue with one or more letters or numbers. The address regex is very general because addresses can take on so many combinations. The regex for the ZIP code (line 22) can take only two forms – five digits or optionally five digits, a '-', and end with four digits. Modify 'call_validate_regex.php' to test each method.

Begin by validating first names (line 10) (Figure 4.18).

```
1  <?php
2  // File call_validate_regex.php
3  require_once 'validate_regex.php';
4  $firsts = array(
5  'Dave', '1234_jim?', 'J', 'McN\'Nay',
6  'Susan', 'Ahmed', '.John.');
7  $validate = new validate_regex();
8  foreach($firsts as $first)
9  {
10 if($validate->get_valid_first($first))
11 { echo "Valid First Name: " . $first; }
12 else
13 { echo "Invalid First Name: " . $first; }
14 echo "<br />";
15 }
16 ?>
```

```
Valid First Name: Dave
Invalid First Name: 1234_jim?
Invalid First Name: J
Invalid First Name: McN'Nay
Valid First Name: Susan
Valid First Name: Ahmed
Invalid First Name: .John.
```

Figure 4.18 Output from 'validate_regex' Class Showing Valid and Invalid First Names

Continue by validating last names (line 10) (Figure 4.19).

```php
1  <?php
2  // File call_validate_regex.php
3  require_once 'validate_regex.php';
4  $lasts = array (
5  'Jones', '_1234?', 'O\'Reilly',
6  'McN\'Nay', 'McKay');
7  $validate = new validate_regex();
8  foreach($lasts as $last)
9  {
10 if($validate->get_valid_last($last))
11 { echo "Valid Last Name: " . $last; }
12 else
13 { echo "Invalid Last Name: " . $last; }
14 echo "<br />";
15 }
16 ?>
```

```
Valid Last Name: Jones
Invalid Last Name: _1234?
Valid Last Name: O'Reilly
Invalid Last Name: McN'Nay
Valid Last Name: McKay
```

Figure 4.19 Output from 'validate_regex' Class Showing Valid and Invalid Last Names

Continue by validating addresses (line 10) (Figure 4.20).

```php
1  <?php
2  // File call_validate_regex.php
3  require_once 'validate_regex.php';
4  $addrs = array(
5  '665 W. North # 5', '_1234?',
```

```
 6  '987 North Pine, Ste. 7', '_622 444 7');
 7  $validate = new validate_regex();
 8  foreach($addrs as $address)
 9  {
10  if($validate->get_valid_address($address))
11  { echo "Valid Address: " . $address; }
12  else
13  { echo "Invalid Address: " . $address; }
14  echo "<br />";
15  }
16  ?>
```

```
Valid Address: 665 W. North # 5
Invalid Address: _1234?
Valid Address: 987 North Pine, Ste. 7
Invalid Address: _622 444 7
```

Figure 4.20 Output from 'validate_regex' Class Showing Valid and Invalid Addresses

Finish by validating ZIP codes (line 10) (Figure 4.21).

```
 1  <?php
 2  // File call_validate_regex.php
 3  require_once 'validate_regex.php';
 4  $zips = array(
 5  '84321', '84321-3515', '8sjj3',
 6  'Sssss-8888');
 7  $validate = new validate_regex();
 8  foreach($zips as $zip)
 9  {
10  if($validate->get_valid_zip($zip))
11  { echo "Valid Zip Code: " . $zip; }
12  else
13  { echo "Invalid Zip Code: " . $zip; }
14  echo "<br />";
15  }
16  ?>
```

```
Valid Zip Code: 84321
Valid Zip Code: 84321-3515
Invalid Zip Code: 8sjj3
Invalid Zip Code: Sssss-8888
```

Figure 4.21 Output from 'validate_regex' Class Showing Valid and Invalid ZIP Codes

I deliberately built the 'validate_regex' class by beginning with one method and testing it. I continued by adding methods and testing them, one by one, until all methods had been tested. This technique is how I build all classes. In my many years of programming, I have found this methodology to work perfectly. That is, it drastically reduces coding errors, produces modular code, and adheres to OOP principles.

PCRE Form Validation Application

The 'validate_regex' class is now complete ('validate_regex.php') and tested ('call_validate_regex.php' for each method). So, we have the tools to build a simple PCRE form data validation application.

The application uses three PHP files – 'validate_regex.php' (just completed in the previous section), 'form.php', and 'validate_form.php'. The input form is in 'form.php' and the validation of form data is handled in 'validate_form.php'.

```
1  <?php
2  // File form.php
3  ?>
4  <html><head>
5  <style type="text/css">
6  table.center{margin-left:auto;margin-right:auto;}
7  </style></head>
8  <body style="background-color:lightgreen;">
9  <div style="text-align:center;">
10 <h1 style="color:indigo;">Enter Input Data</h1>
11 <form method="post" action="validate_form.php">
12 <table class="center">
13 <tr><td>First Name:</td>
14 <td><input type="text" name="first" maxlength="10"></td>
15 </tr>
16 <tr><td>Last Name:</td>
17 <td><input type="text" name="last" maxlength="20"></td>
18 </tr>
19 <tr><td>Address:</td>
20 <td><input type="text" name="address" maxlength="30"></td>
21 </tr>
22 <tr><td>Zip Code:</td>
23 <td><input type="text" name="zip" maxlength="10"></td>
24 </tr>
25 <tr><td>Phone:</td>
26 <td><input type="text" name="phone" maxlength="10"></td>
27 </tr>
28 <tr><td>Email:</td>
29 <td><input type="text" name="email" maxlength="30"></td>
30 </tr>
31 <tr>
32 <td><input type="submit" value="Enter"></td>
33 <td><input type="reset" value="Reset"></td>
34 </tr>
35 </table></form></div>
36 </html>
```

PHP file 'form.php' includes an input tag for each type of data (lines 14, 17, 20, 23, 26, and 29). The final two input tags (lines 32 and 33) are for form submission and form reset. The form attributes 'method' and 'action' (line 11) are 'post' and 'validate_form.php' respectively. Upon submission, the browser 'posts' data to the redirection file 'validate_form.php'.

```php
1  <?php
2  // File validate_form.php
3  require_once 'validate_regex.php';
4  $validate = new validate_regex();
5  $first = $_POST["first"];
6  $last = $_POST["last"];
7  $address = $_POST["address"];
8  $zip = $_POST["zip"];
9  $phone = $_POST["phone"];
10 $email = $_POST["email"];
11 $good_data = array();
12 $bad_data = array();
13 $i = 0;
14 $j = 0;
15 if($validate->get_valid_first($first))
16 { $good_data[$i] = $first;
17 $i++; }
18 else
19 { $bad_data[$j] = 'Enter a valid first name';
20 $j++; }
21 if($validate->get_valid_last($last))
22 { $good_data[$i] = $last;
23 $i++; }
24 else
25 { $bad_data[$j] = 'Enter a valid last name';
26 $j++; }
27 if($validate->get_valid_address($address))
28 { $good_data[$i] = $address;
29 $i++; }
30 else
31 { $bad_data[$j] = 'Enter a valid address';
32 $j++; }
33 if($validate->get_valid_zip($zip))
34 { $good_data[$i] = $zip;
35 $i++; }
36 else
37 { $bad_data[$j] = 'Enter a valid zip code';
38 $j++; }
39 if($validate->get_valid_phone($phone))
40 {
41 if(strlen($phone)==7)
42 { $phone = substr($phone,0,3) . '-' . substr($phone,3,4); }
43 elseif(strlen($phone)==10)
44 { $p1 = '(' . substr($phone,0,3) . ')' . substr($phone,3,3);
```

```
45  $phone = $p1 . '-' . substr($phone,6,4); }
46  $good_data[$i] = $phone;
47  $i++;
48  }
49  else
50  { $bad_data[$j] =
51  'Enter a valid phone number of 7 or 10 digits';
52  $j++; }
53  if($validate->get_valid_email($email))
54  { $good_data[$i] = $email;
55  $i++; }
56  else
57  { $bad_data[$j] = 'Enter a valid email';
58  $j++; }
59  echo '<h3>Good Data Report</h3>';
60  foreach($good_data as $good)
61  { echo $good . '<br />'; }
62  echo '<h3>Bad Data Report</h3>';
63  foreach($bad_data as $bad)
64  { echo $bad . '<br />'; }
65  ?>
```

PHP file 'validate_form.php' posts input data from the form (lines 5–10). A new instance of 'validate_regex' is created in line 4. Two arrays are created and initialized (lines 11 and 12). One array ($good_data) stores the validated form data and the other ($bad_data) stores the error messages. These arrays are used to create a report for valid and invalid form data. Each input data item is validated by invoking the corresponding method from class 'validate_regex' (lines 15, 21, 27, 33, 39, and 53).Valid data are stored in the '$good_data' array indexed with '$i' (lines 16, 22, 28, 34, 46, and 54). Invalid data are stored in the '$bad_data' array indexed with '$j' (lines 19, 25, 31, 37, 50, and 57). Data are reported by traversing both arrays (lines 60–64).

Load 'form.php' and enter some data. Figure 4.22 shows the form before submission.

Figure 4.22 Display of Form with Various Information Included

Click 'Enter'. The results are shown in Figure 4.23. The report shows that the first name, last name, and phone number are correct, but the address, ZIP code, and email are not correct.

Good Data Report

David
Paper
797-2457

Bad Data Report

Enter a valid address
Enter a valid zip code
Enter a valid email

Figure 4.23 Display of Good and Bad Data from Form

Built-in Validation Functions

PHP has built-in filter functions that validate form data. One such function is 'filter_var()', which filters a single piece of data. The next example illustrates how to use this function to filter email data. Load PHP file 'filter_email.php' to validate emails using built-in function 'filter_var()' (Figure 4.24).

```php
1  <?php
2  // File filter_email.php
3  $emails = array(
4  'my.name@gmail.com', 'another@gmail.co.uk',
5  'best@yahoo', 'hellomsn.net', 'long@123.org',
6  '123.me.you@ymail.com', 'miss@yahoo.',
7  'Miss@Yahoo.com', '.@yahoo.com');
8  foreach($emails as $email)
9  {
10 if(filter_var($email,FILTER_VALIDATE_EMAIL))
11 { echo "Valid Email: " . $email; }
12 else
13 { echo "Invalid Email: " . $email; }
14 echo "<br />";
15 }
16 ?>
```

Valid Email: my.name@gmail.com
Valid Email: another@gmail.co.uk
Invalid Email: best@yahoo
Invalid Email: hellomsn.net
Valid Email: long@123.org
Valid Email: 123.me.you@ymail.com
Invalid Email: miss@yahoo.
Valid Email: Miss@Yahoo.com
Invalid Email: .@yahoo.com

Figure 4.24 Display of Valid and Invalid Emails Using Built-In Validate Functions

The 'filter_var()' function uses the 'FILTER_VALIDATE_EMAIL' filter (line 10). The results shown in Figure 4.24 are exactly the same as those in Figure 4.17, which used a regex for email validation.

PHP file 'filter_age.php' uses 'filter_var()' to validate numbers between 18 and 65 (inclusive) with filter 'FILTER_VALIDATE_INT' (line 10) and the '$options' array (lines 5 and 6). The 'filter_var()' function has added flexibility by allowing an associative array of options to be included as a parameter. In this example, I specified the minimum and maximum age ranges ('min_range'=>18 & 'max_range'=>65) (line 6) as options.

```
1  <?php
2  // File filter_age.php
3  $ages = array(
4  '17', '0', '18', '65', '-10', '66');
5  $options = array(
6  'options'=>array('min_range'=>18, 'max_range'=>65));
7  foreach($ages as $age)
8  {
9  $filtered = filter_var($age,
10 FILTER_VALIDATE_INT, $options);
11 if($filtered)
12 { echo "Valid Age: " . $age; }
13 else
14 { echo "Invalid Age: " . $age; }
15 echo "<br />";
16 }
17 ?>
```

```
Invalid Age: 17
Invalid Age: 0
Valid Age: 18
Valid Age: 65
Invalid Age: -10
Invalid Age: 66
```

Figure 4.25 Display of Valid and Invalid Ages Using Built-In Validate Functions

As shown in Figure 4.25, only 18 and 65 are valid ages. I use this filter to allow people between the ages of 18 and 65 inclusive (lines 9 and 10) to access a web page. Of course, you can vary this range to your requirements.

PHP file 'filter_url.php' validates a URL. I prefer to use a built-in function to validate a URL because the regex required is very complex.

```
1  <?php
2  // File filter_url.php
3  $urls = array(
4  'http://www.whodunit.com', 'www.whodunnit.com',
5  'https://www.hello.org', 'ww.whodunnit.com');
6  foreach($urls as $url)
```

```
 7 {
 8 if(filter_var($url,
 9 FILTER_VALIDATE_URL,FILTER_FLAG_HOST_REQUIRED))
10 { echo "Valid URL: " . $url; }
11 else
12 { echo "Invalid URL: " . $url; }
13 echo "<br />";
14 }
15 ?>
```

```
Valid URL: http://www.whodunit.com
Invalid URL: www.whodunnit.com
Valid URL: https://www.hello.org
Invalid URL: ww.whodunnit.com
```

Figure 4.26 Display of Valid and Invalid URLs Using Built-In Validate Functions

The results are shown in Figure 4.26. The 'FILTER_VALIDATE_URL' filter (line 9) validates a URL. The flag 'FLAG_HOST_REQUIRED' (line 9) restricts a valid URL to one that includes the host name – either 'http://' or 'https://'. The second URL is invalid because it does not contain a host string. The fourth URL is invalid because it is not properly formed.

Multiple Variable Validation Functions

While 'filter_var()' function filters a single variable, 'filter_var_array()' filters multiple variables. This function is useful for retrieving many values without repetitively calling 'filter_var()'. However, I am not sure it is worth the trouble because of the added programming complexity. PHP file 'filter_multiple.php' validates email, age, and URL using the 'filter_var_array()' function. Figure 4.27 shows the results.

```
 1 <?php
 2 // File filter_multiple.php
 3 $data = array(
 4 'email'=>'david.paper@usu.edu', 'age'=>'21',
 5 'url'=>'https://www.okay.com');
 6 $args = array(
 7 'email'=>FILTER_VALIDATE_EMAIL,
 8 'age'=>array('filter'=>FILTER_VALIDATE_INT,
 9 'options'=>array('min_range'=>18,'max_range'=>65)),
10 'url'=>array('filter'=>FILTER_VALIDATE_URL,
11 'flags'=>FILTER_FLAG_HOST_REQUIRED));
12 $inputs = filter_var_array($data,$args);
13 if($inputs['email'])
14 { echo "Valid Email: " . $data['email']; }
15 else
16 { echo "Invalid Email: " . $data['email']; }
17 echo "<br />";
18 if($inputs['age'])
```

```
19  { echo "Valid Age: " . $data['age']; }
20  else
21  { echo "Invalid Age: " . $data['age']; }
22  echo "<br />";
23  if($inputs['url'])
24  { echo "Valid URL: " . $data['url']; }
25  else
26  { echo "Invalid URL: " . $data['url']; }
27  ?>
```

```
Valid Email: david.paper@usu.edu
Valid Age: 21
Valid URL: https://www.okay.com
```

Figure 4.27 Display of Valid and Invalid Entries Using Built-In Validate Functions

Lines 3–5 provide the data to be filtered in the '$data' array. Lines 6–11 provide the filters for each piece of data from '$data' in array '$args'. Email is filtered with 'FILTER_VALIDATE_EMAIL' (line 7). Age is filtered with 'FILTER_VALIDATE_INT' (line 8) and the age range provided in '$options' (line 9). URL is filtered with 'FILTER_VALIDATE_URL' (line 10) and 'FILTER_FLAG_HOST_REQUIRED' (line 11). The 'filter_var_array()' function (line 12) uses '$data' and '$args' as parameters. The rest of the code (lines 13–26) display the resulting messages about the data being filtered.

The advantage of using built-in filter functions is ease of use. The disadvantage is that they are severely limited in flexibility. That is, they can only be used specifically as prescribed. They cannot be adjusted. Also, you cannot see how they filter the data. Regexes, in contrast, are not easy to build, but they can be built to meet your needs. You can build regexes to match virtually any kind of text string or number.

Form Validation Application with PCRE and Built-In Functions

We now have all the knowledge we need to build a robust and sophisticated application by pulling together PCRE and built-in function validation. The application uses four PHP files 'validate_app_regex.php', 'app_form.php', 'validate_app_form.php', and 'success.php'.

I modified 'validate_regex' by adding two new validation methods – one for age (lines 36–41) and one for URL (lines 42–47). Both of these methods use built-in PHP functions for validation. I also changed the name of the class to 'validate_app_regex'.

```
1  <?php
2  // File validate_app_regex.php
3  class validate_app_regex
4  {
5  function get_valid_first($first)
6  {
7  $regex = '#^[a-zA-Z]{2,10}$#';
8  return preg_match($regex,trim($first));
9  }
```

```
10  function get_valid_last($last)
11  {
12  $regex = '#^[a-zA-Z]{1}\'?[a-zA-Z]{2,20}$#';
13  return preg_match($regex,trim($last));
14  }
15  function get_valid_address($address)
16  {
17  $regex = '#^[a-zA-Z-0-9]{1,}\s[a-zA-Z0-9]{1,}+#';
18  return preg_match($regex,trim($address));
19  }
20  function get_valid_zip($zip)
21  {
22  $regex = '#^([0-9]{5})(-[0-9]{4})?$#';
23  return preg_match($regex,trim($zip));
24  }
25  function get_valid_phone($phone)
26  {
27  $regex = '#^[0-9]{7}$|^[0-9]{10}$#';
28  return preg_match($regex,trim($phone));
29  }
30  function get_valid_email($email)
31  {
32  $regex =
33  '#^[0-9A-Za-z._%+-]{2,}@[0-9A-Za-z.-]+\.[A-Za-z]{2,6}$#';
34  return preg_match($regex,trim($email));
35  }
36  function get_valid_age($age)
37  {
38  $filtered = filter_var($age,FILTER_VALIDATE_INT,
39  array('options'=>array('min_range'=>18, 'max_range'=>65)));
40  return $filtered;
41  }
42  function get_valid_url($url)
43  {
44  $filtered = filter_var
45  ($url,FILTER_VALIDATE_URL, FILTER_FLAG_HOST_REQUIRED);
46  return $filtered;
47  }
48  }
49  ?>
```

The 'app_form.php' file holds the form used for data entry. Since we are building a robust application, the form requires quite a bit of code.

```
1  <?php
2  // File app_form.php
3  session_start();
```

```
 4  ?>
 5  <html><head>
 6  <style type="text/css">
 7  table.center {
 8  margin-left:auto;
 9  margin-right:auto;
10  }
11  </style></head>
12  <body style="background-color:lightgreen;">
13  <div style="text-align:center;">
14  <h1 style="color:indigo;">Enter Input Data</h1>
15  <form method="post" action="validate_app_form.php">
16  <table class="center">
17  <tr><td>First Name:</td>
18  <td><input type="text" name="first" maxlength="10"
19  value=<?php if(isset($_SESSION['first']))
20  { echo $_SESSION['first']; } ?> >
21  </td>
22  </tr>
23  <tr><td>Last Name:</td>
24  <td><input type="text" name="last" maxlength="20"
25  value=<?php if(isset($_SESSION['last']))
26  { echo $_SESSION['last']; } ?> >
27  </td>
28  </tr>
29  <tr><td>Address:</td>
30  <td><input type="text" name="address" maxlength="30"
31  value=<?php if(isset($_SESSION['address']))
32  { echo $_SESSION['address']; } ?> >
33  </td>
34  </tr>
35  <tr><td>Zip Code:</td>
36  <td><input type="text" name="zip" maxlength="10"
37  value=<?php if(isset($_SESSION['zip']))
38  { echo $_SESSION['zip']; } ?> >
39  </td>
40  </tr>
41  <tr><td>Phone:</td>
42  <td><input type="text" name="phone" maxlength="10"
43  value=<?php if(isset($_SESSION['phone']))
44  { echo $_SESSION['phone']; } ?> > </td>
45  </tr>
46  <tr><td>Email:</td>
47  <td><input type="text" name="email" maxlength="30"
48  value=<?php if(isset($_SESSION['email']))
49  { echo $_SESSION['email']; } ?> >
50  </td>
51  </tr>
52  <tr><td>Age:</td>
53  <td><input type="text" name="age" maxlength="3"
```

```
54 value=<?php if(isset($_SESSION['age']))
55 { echo $_SESSION['age']; } ?> >
56 </td>
57 </tr>
58 <tr><td>URL:</td>
59 <td><input type="text" name="url"
60 value=<?php if(isset($_SESSION['url']))
61 { echo $_SESSION['url']; } ?> >
62 </td>
63 </tr>
64 <tr>
65 <td><input type="submit" value="Enter"></td>
66 <td><input type="reset" value="Reset"></td>
67 </tr>
68 </table></form></div>
69 <table class="center">
70 <tr><td>
71 <?php
72 if(isset($_SESSION['err_first']))
73 { echo $_SESSION['err_first'] . '<br />'; }
74 if(isset($_SESSION['err_last']))
75 { echo $_SESSION['err_last'] . '<br />'; }
76 if(isset($_SESSION['err_address']))
77 { echo $_SESSION['err_address'] . '<br />'; }
78 if(isset($_SESSION['err_zip']))
79 { echo $_SESSION['err_zip'] . '<br />'; }
80 if(isset($_SESSION['err_phone']))
81 { echo $_SESSION['err_phone'] . '<br />'; }
82 if(isset($_SESSION['err_email']))
83 { echo $_SESSION['err_email'] . '<br />'; }
84 if(isset($_SESSION['err_age']))
85 { echo $_SESSION['err_age'] . '<br />'; }
86 if(isset($_SESSION['err_url']))
87 { echo $_SESSION['err_url']; }
88 ?>
89 </td></tr>
90 </table>
91 </html>
```

The form begins by starting a new session with 'session_start()' (line 3) because we need to check and set session variables. The form 'method' is 'post' and 'action' is a redirect to 'validate_app_form.php' (line 15). The input tags allow text data to be entered on a web page. All input tags (for data) follow the same logic. A session variable is checked. If set, its value is displayed inside the tag. The ability to display data inside an 'input' tag is very convenient. In this case, I ensure that what was typed doesn't have to be retyped when the page is reloaded.

The first tag is for first name (lines 18–20). The 'value' attribute (lines 19 and 20) includes a bit of PHP code that checks if the session variable 'first' is set (line 19). If set, the value of session variable 'first' is placed inside the input tag (line 20). The second input tag is for last name (lines 24–26). The 'value' attribute (lines 25 and 26) uses PHP code to display session variable 'last' if set. The third input tag is for address (lines 30–32). The 'value' attribute (lines 31 and 32) uses PHP code to display session variable 'address' if set. The fourth input tag is for ZIP code (lines 36–38). The 'value' attribute (lines 37 and 38) uses PHP code to display session variable 'zip' if set.

The fifth input tag is for phone (lines 42–44). The 'value' attribute (lines 43 and 44) uses PHP code to display session variable 'phone' if set. The sixth input tag is for email (lines 47–49). The 'value' attribute (lines 48 and 49) uses PHP code to display session variable 'email' if set. The seventh input tag is for age (lines 53–55). The 'value' attribute (lines 54 and 55) uses PHP code to display session variable 'age' if set. The eighth input tag is for URL (lines 59–61). The 'value' attribute (lines 60 and 61) uses PHP code to display session variable 'url' if set.

The final two input tags are for 'submit' (line 65) and 'reset' (line 66) buttons. The form ends in line 68.

A new table begins (line 69) that includes PHP code (lines 71–88) to check for error messages set in 'validate_app_form.php' (I will show and explain this code momentarily). Each error message is checked. If set, the error message is displayed. For instance, 'err_first' is checked (line 72). If set, it is displayed (line 73).

```
 1  <?php
 2  // File validate_app_form.php
 3  session_start();
 4  require_once 'validate_app_regex.php';
 5  $validate = new validate_app_regex();
 6  $first = $_POST["first"];
 7  $last = $_POST["last"];
 8  $address = $_POST["address"];
 9  $zip = $_POST["zip"];
10  $phone = $_POST["phone"];
11  $email = $_POST["email"];
12  $age = $_POST["age"];
13  $url = $_POST["url"];
14  if($validate->get_valid_first($first))
15  { $_SESSION['first'] = $first;
16  unset($_SESSION['err_first']); }
17  else
18  { $_SESSION['err_first'] = 'Enter a valid first name'; }
19  if($validate->get_valid_last($last))
20  { $_SESSION['last'] = $last;
21  unset($_SESSION['err_last']); }
22  else
23  { $_SESSION['err_last'] = 'Enter a valid last name'; }
24  if($validate->get_valid_address($address))
25  { $_SESSION['address'] = '"' . $address . '"';
26  unset($_SESSION['err_address']); }
27  else
28  { $_SESSION['err_address'] = 'Enter a valid address'; }
29  if($validate->get_valid_zip($zip))
30  { $_SESSION['zip'] = $zip;
31  unset($_SESSION['err_zip']); }
32  else
33  { $_SESSION['err_zip'] = 'Enter a valid zip code'; }
34  if($validate->get_valid_phone($phone))
35  {
36  if(strlen($phone)==7)
37  { $phones = substr($phone,0,3) . '-' . substr($phone,3,4); }
38  elseif(strlen($phone)==10)
39  { $p1 = '(' . substr($phone,0,3) . ')' . substr($phone,3,3);
```

```
40 $phones = $p1 . '-' . substr($phone,6,4); }
41 $_SESSION['phone'] = $phone;
42 unset($_SESSION['err_phone']);
43 }
44 else
45 { $_SESSION['err_phone'] =
46 'Enter a valid phone number of 7 or 10 digits'; }
47 if($validate->get_valid_email($email))
48 { $_SESSION['email'] = $email;
49 unset($_SESSION['err_email']); }
50 else
51 { $_SESSION['err_email'] = 'Enter a valid email'; }
52 if($validate->get_valid_age($age))
53 { $_SESSION['age'] = $age;
54 unset($_SESSION['err_age']); }
55 else
56 { $_SESSION['err_age'] = 'Enter a valid age'; }
57 if($validate->get_valid_url($url))
58 { $_SESSION['url'] = $url;
59 unset($_SESSION['err_url']); }
60 else
61 { $_SESSION['err_url'] = 'Enter a valid url'; }
62 if( isSet($_SESSION['err_first'])| isSet($_SESSION['err_last'])|
63 isSet($_SESSION['err_address'])| isSet($_SESSION['err_zip'])|
64 isSet($_SESSION['err_phone'])| isSet($_SESSION['err_email'])|
65 isSet($_SESSION['err_age'])| isSet($_SESSION['err_url']) )
66 { header('Location: app_form.php'); }
67 else
68 { header('Location: success.php'); }
69 ?>
```

The 'validate_app_form.php' file holds the validation logic. Logic begins by starting a new session (line 3). A new instance of 'validate_app_regex' is created (line 5). Lines 6–13 assign 'post' values from the form to their respective variables. The first 'if' (lines 14–16) uses the 'get_valid_first()' to validate '$first'. If valid, session variable '$_SESSION['first']' is created (line 15). I also unset the error message so that it won't be displayed on the form (line 16). If '$first' is invalid, error message '$_SESSION['err_first']' is set. For each input value from the form, the logic is the same. That is, each input value is validated, and either the session variable for that value is set (valid) or the error message for that value is set (invalid) (lines 19–61). Lines 62–65 check if any error message has been set. If so, logic is redirected to form 'app_form.php' (line 66). If no errors are set, all form values are valid and logic is redirected to 'success.php' (line 68).

Although this file has a lot of code, the logic is rather simple. All form values are 'posted' and set to variables. Next, variables are validated with their corresponding methods from the 'validate_app_regex' class. Finally, if any error messages have been set, logic is redirected to the form 'app_form.php'. Otherwise, logic is redirected to 'success.php'.

```
1 <?php
2 // File success.php
3 session_start();
4 $first = $_SESSION['first'];
```

```
 5 $last = $_SESSION['last'];
 6 $address = $_SESSION['address'];
 7 $zip = $_SESSION['zip'];
 8 $phone = $_SESSION['phone'];
 9 $email = $_SESSION['email'];
10 $age = $_SESSION['age'];
11 $url = $_SESSION['url'];
12 ?>
13 <html>
14 <body style="background-color:lightgreen;">
15 <div style="text-align:center;">
16 <h1 style="color:indigo;">Success</h1>
17 <?php
18 echo $first . '<br />';
19 echo $last . '<br />';
20 echo $address . '<br />';
21 echo $zip . '<br />';
22 echo $phone . '<br />';
23 echo $email . '<br />';
24 echo $age . '<br />';
25 echo $url;
26 ?>
27 </div></html>
```

The 'success.php' file holds simple logic to indicate that the form was completed properly. It starts a new session (line 3), assigns session variable values to PHP variables (lines 4–11) and displays the values (lines 18–25). Session variables are very useful because once set they are available until the session is closed.

Whew! That's a lot of code. Let's test the application. Load PHP file 'app_form.php' into a browser. Enter 'David' in the 'First Name' text box, 'Paper' in the 'Last Name' text box, '84321' in the 'ZIP code' text box, and '21' in the 'Age' text box. Press the 'Enter' button. Figure 4.28 shows the results.

Figure 4.28 Display of Form Application with Some Information Included

The entries you made are valid because they appear in their respective text boxes. Four messages appear after the form indicating data that must be entered. The text boxes with invalid data are blank. Enter '666 E 100 S' in the 'Address' text box, '7872121' in the 'Phone' textbox, 'john.doe@usu.edu' in the 'Email' text box, and 'https://www.usu.edu' in the 'URL' text box and press the 'Enter' button. Figure 4.29 shows the results. The data you entered is valid and is displayed on this page.

Figure 4.29 Display with Successful Entries

Advantages and Disadvantages of PCRE and Built-In Functions

The main advantage of PCRE is its flexibility. PCRE enables you to build a regex to validate any pattern. The main disadvantage of PCRE is that it requires a sharp learning curve to master. PCRE is also embraced because it is based on Perl. Perl is widely used in industry, so Perl-related knowledge can only increase your marketability in the world of technology. Another advantage is that someone with PCRE or Perl skills can look at your regex and readily see its value.

The main advantage of built-in validation functions is their ease of use. To use them, no PCRE knowledge is required. The main disadvantage is that built-in functions are inflexible. You can only validate data that fits with the available functions.

Report Generation Application

It is possible to obtain directives from users without having to validate. An example is report generation with drop-down menus. With such menus, users can safely generate a variety of reports.

To build a report generation application, start by creating sequences and tables, continue by populating the tables, and 'commit' the work. An Oracle ***sequence*** is a database object that allows a user to generate unique integers. A typical application uses a sequence to automatically generate primary key values. The '***COMMIT***' statement makes permanent any changes made to the database during the current transaction.

Open an 'Oracle SQL Developer' connection. In the 'SQL Worksheet', create the 'customer_sequence' sequence with the following SQL. The 'Script Output' window should indicate that the sequence was created.

```
CREATE SEQUENCE customer_sequence START WITH 1000 INCREMENT BY 1;
```

Create the 'customers' table in the 'SQL Worksheet'. The 'Script Output' window should indicate that the table was created.

```
CREATE TABLE customers (
id NUMBER(4),
first_name VARCHAR2(20),
```

```
last_name VARCHAR2(20),
address VARCHAR2(30),
phone CHAR(10)
);
```

Populate the 'customers' table in the 'SQL Worksheet'. The 'Script Output' window should indicate that ten rows were inserted into the table.

```
INSERT INTO customers (id, first_name, last_name, address, phone)
VALUES (customer_sequence.NEXTVAL, 'Dan D.', 'Lion', '500 E 500 N # 8', '4357972222');
INSERT INTO customers (id, first_name, last_name, address, phone)
VALUES (customer_sequence.NEXTVAL, 'Hugh', 'Mungus', '321 Bear Lane', '8017778888');
INSERT INTO customers (id, first_name, last_name, address, phone)
VALUES (customer_sequence.NEXTVAL, 'Will E.', 'Makeit', '3515 Old Main Hill', '4357523322');
INSERT INTO customers (id, first_name, last_name, address, phone)
VALUES (customer_sequence.NEXTVAL, 'Betty', 'Whoant', '665 E 200 N # 4', '4357973344');
INSERT INTO customers(id, first_name, last_name, address, phone)
VALUES(customer_sequence.NEXTVAL, 'Hugh R.', 'Cool', '1800 E 1800 N', '4357877878');
INSERT INTO customers(id, first_name, last_name, address, phone)
VALUES (customer_sequence.NEXTVAL, 'Sally', 'Forth', '400 W 600 S # 15', '4357879000');
INSERT INTO customers(id, first_name, last_name, address, phone)
VALUES (customer_sequence.NEXTVAL, 'Rose E.', 'Vine', '1400 Preston Ave.', '8019843333');
INSERT INTO customers(id, first_name, last_name, address, phone)
VALUES (customer_sequence.NEXTVAL, 'Earl E.', 'Morning', '900 Jade Blvd. E', '8018774545');
INSERT INTO customers(id, first_name, last_name, address, phone)
VALUES (customer_sequence.NEXTVAL, 'Dewey', 'Doit', '100 N State Street', '8012222222');
INSERT INTO customers(id, first_name, last_name, address, phone)
VALUES (customer_sequence.NEXTVAL, 'Sam R.', 'Rye', '100 N Temple E', '8013453434');
```

Sequences use the 'NEXTVAL' method to increment automatically. Repeat the process by creating the 'order_sequence' sequence. The 'Script Output' window should indicate that the sequence was created.

```
CREATE SEQUENCE order_sequence START WITH 2000 INCREMENT BY 1;
```

Create the 'orders' table in the 'SQL Worksheet'. The 'Script Output' window should indicate that the table was created.

```
CREATE TABLE orders (
ord_no NUMBER(5),
ord_date DATE,
total_price NUMBER(5,2),
id NUMBER(4)
);
```

Populate the 'orders' table in the 'SQL Worksheet'. The 'Script Output' window should indicate that two rows were inserted into the table.

```
INSERT INTO orders (ord_no, ord_date, total_price, id)
VALUES (order_sequence.NEXTVAL, '11-NOV-02', 200, '1000');
INSERT INTO orders (ord_no, ord_date, total_price, id)
VALUES (order_sequence.NEXTVAL, '15-NOV-02', 315, '1001');
```

Create the 'product_sequence' sequence in the 'SQL Worksheet'. The 'Script Output' window should indicate that the sequence was created.

```
CREATE SEQUENCE product_sequence START WITH 3000 INCREMENT BY 1;
```

Create the 'products' table in the 'SQL Worksheet'. The 'Script Output' window should indicate that the table was created.

```
CREATE TABLE products (
pno NUMBER(5),
pdesc VARCHAR2(40),
price NUMBER(5,2),
onhand NUMBER(3),
weight NUMBER(3)
);
```

Populate the 'products' table in the 'SQL Worksheet'. The 'Script Output' window should indicate that four rows were inserted into the table.

```
INSERT INTO products(pno, pdesc, price, onhand, weight)
VALUES (product_sequence.NEXTVAL, 'Stanley Hammer HX200', 10, 100, 1);
INSERT INTO products(pno, pdesc, price, onhand, weight)
VALUES (product_sequence.NEXTVAL, 'Skil Drill Pack DR900', 20, 100, 2);
INSERT INTO products(pno, pdesc, price, onhand, weight)
VALUES (product_sequence.NEXTVAL, 'B and D Jigsaw JZ500', 50, 200, 2);
INSERT INTO products(pno, pdesc, price, onhand, weight)
VALUES (product_sequence.NEXTVAL, 'B and D Table Saw TS300', 100, 10, 5);
```

Create the 'ordprod_sequence' sequence in the 'SQL Worksheet'. The 'Script Output' window should indicate that the sequence was created.

```
CREATE SEQUENCE ordprod_sequence START WITH 4000 INCREMENT BY 1;
```

Create the 'ordprods' table in the 'SQL Worksheet'. The 'Script Output' window should indicate that the table was created.

```
CREATE TABLE ordprods (
bridgeid NUMBER(5),
quantity NUMBER(3),
subtotal NUMBER(5,2),
shipdate DATE,
```

```
status VARCHAR2(2),
ord_no NUMBER(5),
pno NUMBER(5)
);
```

Populate the 'ordprods' table in the 'SQL Worksheet'. The 'Script Output' window should indicate that five rows were inserted into the table.

```
INSERT INTO ordprods (bridgeid, quantity, subtotal, shipdate, status, ord_no, pno)
VALUES (ordprod_sequence.NEXTVAL, 2, 20, '25-OCT-02', 'SP', 2000, 3000);
INSERT INTO ordprods (bridgeid, quantity, subtotal, shipdate, status, ord_no, pno)
VALUES (ordprod_sequence.NEXTVAL, 1, 20, '25-OCT-02', 'SP', 2000, 3001);
INSERT INTO ordprods (bridgeid, quantity, subtotal, shipdate, status, ord_no, pno)
VALUES (ordprod_sequence.NEXTVAL, 3, 150, '28-OCT-02', 'SP', 2000, 3002);
INSERT INTO ordprods (bridgeid, quantity, subtotal, shipdate, status, ord_no, pno)
VALUES (ordprod_sequence.NEXTVAL, 2, 200, '28-OCT-02', 'SP', 2001, 3003);
INSERT INTO ordprods (bridgeid, quantity, subtotal, shipdate, status, ord_no, pno)
VALUES (ordprod_sequence.NEXTVAL, 2, 100, '28-OCT-02', 'SP', 2001, 3002);
```

Make all changes permanent by executing a 'COMMIT;'. The 'Script Output' window should indicate that all changes are 'committed'.

```
COMMIT;
```

Now that the data are in the database, three PHP files are used – 'dbGeneral.php', 'drop.php', and 'see_it.php' – to build a simple report generator to retrieve the full name of a customer.

PHP file 'dbGeneral.php' was introduced in Chapter 3, but I include it here for your convenience. Be sure to add your username (line 19), password (line 20), and server host (line 21) supplied by your tutor or IT expert in the 'setParms()' method (lines 17–22).

```php
1  <?php
2  // File dbGeneral.php
3  class dbGeneral
4  {
5  private $_schema;
6  private $_password;
7  private $_host;
8  private $_query;
9  private $_conn;
10 public $result;
11 function __construct($sql)
12 {
13 $this->_query = $sql;
14 $this->setParms();
15 $this->connDB();
16 }
```

```
17  function setParms()
18  {
19  $this->_schema = '';
20  $this->_password = '';
21  $this->_host = '';
22  }
23  function connDB()
24  {
25  if(!$this->_conn = oci_connect
26  ($this->_schema,$this->_password,$this->_host))
27  { echo 'error connecting'; }
28  }
29  function parse()
30  {
31  if(!$parse = oci_parse($this->_conn,$this->_query))
32  { echo 'error parsing'; }
33  else
34  { $this->result = $parse; }
35  }
36  function bind($bind,$choice,$length)
37  {
38  oci_bind_by_name($this->result,$bind,$choice,$length);
39  }
40  function exe()
41  {
42  oci_execute($this->result);
43  }
44  }
45  ?>
```

PHP file 'drop.php' creates a dynamic drop-down menu based on the data with a JavaScript event handler that submits the form once the user makes a selection.

```
1   <?php
2   // File drop.php
3   require_once 'dbGeneral.php';
4   $query = "SELECT * FROM customers";
5   $connect = new dbGeneral($query);
6   $connect->parse();
7   $stmt = $connect->result;
8   $connect->exe();
9   ?>
10  <html><body><div style="text-align:center;">
11  <form name="form_drop" method="post"
12  action="see_it.php">
13  <select name="choice"
14  onchange="document.form_drop.submit()">
```

```
15 <option value=999>CHOOSE BELOW</option>
16 <?php
17 while($row = oci_fetch_assoc($stmt))
18 {
19 $id = $row['ID'];
20 $val = $row['LAST_NAME'];
21 echo "<option value='$id'>$id";
22 echo "    $val</option>\n";
23 }
24 ?>
25 </select>
26 </form>
27 </div></body></html>
```

The logic begins by including 'dbGeneral' (line 3). A query is set (line 4). Next, a new instance of 'dbGeneral' is created (line 5). The query is parsed and executed (lines 6–8). The form (lines 11–26) uses method 'post' to send results to 'see_it.php'. A drop-down menu is created (lines 13–23). Drop-down selections (options) are dynamically generated in the 'while' loop based on the query (lines 17–23). A JavaScript event handler (line 14) submits the choice once it is selected from the drop-down menu.

```
 1 <?php
 2 // File see_it.php
 3 require_once 'dbGeneral.php';
 4 $choice = $_POST['choice'];
 5 $query = "SELECT * FROM customers ";
 6 $query .= "WHERE id=:choice";
 7 $connect = new dbGeneral($query);
 8 $connect->parse();
 9 $connect->bind(':choice', $choice, 4);
10 $stmt = $connect->result;
11 $connect->exe();
12 $row = oci_fetch_assoc($stmt);
13 $first = $row['FIRST_NAME'];
14 $last = $row['LAST_NAME'];
15 echo "<div style='text-align:center;'>";
16 echo "$first $last<br /></div>";
17 ?>
18 <html>
19 <p><div style="text-align:center;">
20 <form method="post" action="drop.php">
21 <input type="submit" value="back">
22 </form>
23 </div></html>
```

PHP file 'see_it.php' displays the drop-down box and the full name of the choice made by the user. The user's choice from the drop-down menu is posted (line 4). A query is set (lines 5 and 6). A new instance of 'dbGeneral' is created (line 7). The query is parsed and executed (lines 8–11). The bind variable is reconciled (line 9).

Be sure to set the appropriate length of the bind variable value, which in this case is 4 (line 9). The result set is placed in '$row' (line 12). Values of first and last name are retrieved (lines 13 and 14) and displayed (line 16). A button is created that, when pressed, returns processing to 'drop.php' (lines 20–22).

Load 'drop.php' into a browser. Figure 4.30 shows the drop-down box. Click the down arrow and choose '1002 Mungus'. Figure 4.31 shows the results. Click the 'back' button to return to the drop-down box web page.

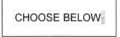

Figure 4.30 Display of Dynamically Derived Drop-Down Menu

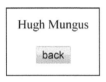

Figure 4.31 Display of Choice Made with 'back' Button

Sophisticated Report Generation Application

Let's build an even more sophisticated report generator. Three PHP files are used – 'dbGeneral.php', 'rpt. php', and 'getTbl.php' – to build a report generator for customer, order, product, and ordprod data. PHP file 'dbGeneral.php' is the same. PHP file 'rpt.php' consists of a fixed HTML drop-down menu with a JavaScript event handler that submits the form once a choice has been made.

```
 1  <?php
 2  // File rpt.php
 3  ?>
 4  <html><body bgcolor = BURLYWOOD>
 5  <body><div style="text-align:center;">
 6  <form method="POST" action="getTbl.php">
 7  <font color=BLUE size=+1>Select a Report:  </font>
 8  <select name="rpt" onchange="submit()"; >
 9  <option value=999 selected="SELECTED">CHOOSE BELOW</option>
10  <option value=1>Customer Report</option>
11  <option value=2>Order Report</option>
12  <option value=3>Product Report</option>
13  <option value=4>Ordprod Report</option>
14  </select>
15  </form>
16  <p></p></div></body></html>
```

The drop-down menu provides fixed options for reports (lines 9–13). The JavaScript event handler (line 8) submits the form to 'getTbl.php' (line 6) once a choice is made.

```php
1  <?php
2  // File getTbl.php
3  ?>
4  <html><head><style type="text/css">
5  table.center {
6  margin-left:auto;
7  margin-right:auto;
8  }
9  th.c1 { background-color: #FFB6C1; color: black; }
10 tr.d1 td { background-color: #DCDCDC; color: black; }
11 tr.d2 td { background-color: #FFFFFF; color: black; }
12 </style></head><body style="background-color:burlywood;">
13 <?php
14 require_once 'dbGeneral.php';
15 $rpt = $_POST["rpt"];
16 if ($rpt == 1)
17 { $query = "SELECT * FROM customers ORDER BY id"; }
18 else if ($rpt == 2)
19 { $query = "SELECT * FROM orders ORDER BY ord_no"; }
20 else if ($rpt == 3)
21 { $query = "SELECT * FROM products ORDER BY pno"; }
22 else if ($rpt == 4)
23 { $query = "SELECT * FROM ordprods ORDER BY bridgeid"; }
24 $connect = new dbGeneral($query);
25 $connect->parse();
26 $stmt = $connect->result;
27 $connect->exe();
28 $ncols = OCINumCols($stmt);
29 echo "<table class='center' border='1'><tr>";
30 for ($i = 1; $i <= $ncols; ++$i)
31 {
32 echo "<th class='c1'>";
33 echo OCIColumnName($stmt, $i);
34 echo "</th>";
35 }
36 echo "</tr>";
37 $j = 0;
38 while($row = oci_fetch_assoc($stmt))
39 {
40 if ($j % 2) {echo "<tr class='d1'>";}
41 else {echo "<tr class='d2'>";}
42 for ($i = 1; $i <= $ncols; ++$i)
43 {
44 echo "<td>";
45 $columnName = OCIColumnName($stmt, $i);
46 echo $row[$columnName];
47 echo "</td>";
48 }
```

```
49  ++$j;
50  echo "</tr>";
51  }
52  echo "</table><p><div style='text-align:center;'>";
53  echo "<form action='rpt.php'>";
54  echo "<input type='submit' value='back' /></form></div>";
55  ?>
56  </body></html>
```

PHP file 'getTbl.php' gets the appropriate data based on the choice made by the user and displays the report. If the choice is '1', the 'CUSTOMER' table is queried (lines 16 and 17). If the choice is '2', the 'ORDERS' table is queried (lines 18 and 19). If the choice is '3', the 'PRODUCTS' table is queried (lines 20 and 21). If the choice is '4', the 'ORDPRODS' table is queried (lines 22 and 23). Oracle API 'OCINumCols' (line 28) returns the number of columns from the chosen database table. Oracle API 'OCIColumnName' (line 33) returns the column name from the chosen database table. Lines 30–35 display the field names from the chosen table. Lines 38–51 display the data from the chosen table. The modulus '%' (line 40) is used to alternate colors in the table. CSS (lines 9–11) was created to adjust the colors. Finally, a form is created (lines 53 and 54), which includes a 'submit' button (line 54) to redirect to 'rpt.php' when pressed. Load 'rpt.php' in a browser. Figure 4.32 shows the drop-down box. Click the down arrow and choose 'Product Report'. Figure 4.33 shows the results. Use the 'back' button to return to the drop-down box web page.

Figure 4.32 Display of Report Drop-Down Menu

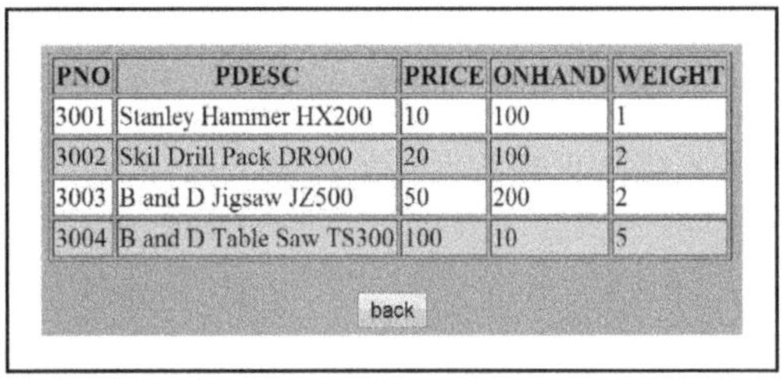

PNO	PDESC	PRICE	ONHAND	WEIGHT
3001	Stanley Hammer HX200	10	100	1
3002	Skil Drill Pack DR900	20	100	2
3003	B and D Jigsaw JZ500	50	200	2
3004	B and D Table Saw TS300	100	10	5

back

Figure 4.33 Display of Chosen Report with 'back' Button

Report Generation Application Using Ref Cursors

An alternative way to create a report generator is to use PL/SQL 'Ref Cursors'. A *'Ref Cursor'* is a special PL/SQL data type that creates a cursor variable at run time. One advantage is the ability of a 'Ref Cursor' to pass result sets. A second advantage is speed because PL/SQL is precompiled and is thereby faster than interpreting an SQL statement. A third advantage is security because 'Ref Cursors' are protected by the Oracle system.

The first step is to create a PL/SQL 'Ref Cursor'. Open an 'Oracle SQL Developer' connection. In an 'SQL Worksheet', create the 'Ref Cursor' procedure 'tbl_ref' with the following PL/SQL. Run the script. 'Script Output' should indicate that the procedure was compiled.

```
1  CREATE OR REPLACE PROCEDURE tbl_ref
2  (p_refcur OUT SYS_REFCURSOR)
3  IS
4  BEGIN
5  OPEN p_refcur FOR SELECT * FROM customers;
6  END;
```

The parameter 'p_refcur' is defined as 'OUT' (line 2), which means that its value is returned to the calling environment. The type definition is 'SYS_REFCURSOR' (line 2), which means that it will hold a cursor (data set). An 'OPEN' is issued (line 5), which places the results of the SELECT statement into 'p_refcur'.

The second step is to modify the 'dbGeneral' class by adding a 'bind_refcursor()' method. Don't forget to add your information in the 'setParms()' method.

```
1  <?php
2  // File dbGeneral.php
3  class dbGeneral
4  {
5  private $_schema;
6  private $_password;
7  private $_host;
8  private $_query;
9  private $_conn;
10 public $result;
11 function __construct($sql)
12 {
13 $this->_query = $sql;
14 $this->setParms();
15 $this->connDB();
16 }
17 function setParms()
18 {
19 $this->_schema = '';
20 $this->_password = '';
21 $this->_host = '';
22 }
23 function connDB()
24 {
25 if(!$this->_conn = oci_connect
26 ($this->_schema,$this->_password,$this->_host))
27 { echo 'error connecting'; }
28 }
29 function parse()
30 {
31 if(!$parse = oci_parse($this->_conn,$this->_query))
32 { echo 'error parsing'; }
33 else
34 { $this->result = $parse; }
```

```
35 }
36 function bind($bind,$choice,$length)
37 {
38 oci_bind_by_name($this->result,$bind,$choice,$length);
39 }
40 function exe()
41 {
42 oci_execute($this->result);
43 }
44 function bind_refcursor()
45 {
46 $curs = oci_new_cursor($this->_conn);
47 $this->parse();
48 oci_bind_by_name
49 ($this->result,':data',$curs,-1,OCI_B_CURSOR);
50 $this->exe();
51 oci_execute($curs);
52 $this->result = $curs;
53 }
54 }
55 ?>
```

The 'bind_refcursor()' method (lines 44–53) handles the ref cursor reconciliation process. This process is beyond the scope of this book, so I won't cover it here. Just use the method as it is presented.

The third step is to create PHP file 'drop_ref.php', which creates a drop-down box using data retrieved from the 'Ref Cursor'.

```
 1 <?php
 2 // File drop_ref.php
 3 require_once 'dbGeneral.php';
 4 $query = "BEGIN tbl_ref(:data); END;";
 5 $connect = new dbGeneral($query);
 6 $connect->bind_refcursor();
 7 $stmt = $connect->result;
 8 ?>
 9 <html><body><div style="text-align:center;">
10 <form name="form_drop" method="post"
11 action="see_it_ref.php">
12 <select name="choice"
13 onchange="document.form_drop.submit()">
14 <option value=999>CHOOSE BELOW</option>
15 <?php
16 while($row = oci_fetch_assoc($stmt))
17 { $id = $row['ID'];
18 $val = $row['LAST_NAME'];
19 echo "<option value='$id'>$id";
20 echo "    $val</option>\n"; }
```

```
21  ?>
22  </select>
23  </form>
24  </div></body></html>
```

The query (line 4) calls the PL/SQL procedure 'tbl_ref' with a 'BEGIN–END' block. The 'bind_refcursor()' method (line 6) binds the 'Ref Cursor' to the PHP program, which makes the result set available. The form 'posts' data to 'see_it_ref.php' (lines 10 and 11). The drop-down menu (lines 12–20) is dynamically created from the result set generated from the ref cursor.

The fourth step is to create PHP file 'see_it_ref.php', which displays the results.

```
1   <?php
2   // File see_it_ref.php
3   require_once 'dbGeneral.php';
4   $choice = $_POST['choice'];
5   $query = "SELECT * FROM customers WHERE id=:choice";
6   $connect = new dbGeneral($query);
7   $connect->parse();
8   $connect->bind(':choice', $choice, 4);
9   $stmt = $connect->result;
10  $connect->exe();
11  $row = oci_fetch_assoc($stmt);
12  $first = $row['FIRST_NAME'];
13  $last = $row['LAST_NAME'];
14  echo "<div style='text-align:center; '>";
15  echo "$first $last<br /></div>";
16  ?>
17  <html>
18  <p><div style="text-align:center;">
19  <form method="post" action="drop_ref.php">
20  <input type="submit" value="back">
21  </form>
22  </div></html>
```

The query (line 5) is created based on the choice from the drop-down menu (line 4). A new instance of 'dbGeneral' is created (line 6). The query is parsed and executed (lines 7–10). The result set is reconciled (line 11). Finally, the results are displayed (lines 12 and 13).

The final step is to load 'drop_ref.php' in a browser. Figure 4.34 shows the drop-down box. Click the down arrow and choose '1002 Mungus'. Figure 4.35 shows the results.

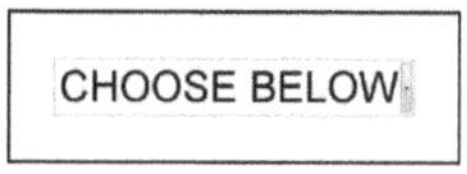

CHOOSE BELOW

Figure 4.34 Display of Dynamically Derived Drop-Down Menu Using REF CURSOR

Figure 4.35 Display of Choice Made with 'back' Button

The results are the same as the simple report generation application. The only difference is how the data is retrieved. In the original report generation application, an SQL query is used to build the result set. In this application, a PL/SQL 'Ref Cursor' is used to build the result set. The 'Ref Cursor' application is more complicated, but more efficient and secure because the PL/SQL procedure is protected inside the Oracle database. Go through each of the applications in this chapter line by line to ensure that you understand what the code is accomplishing.

Summary

The goal of this chapter was to help you gain a fundamental understanding of input validation to mitigate potentially harmful data from entering a website. Another goal was to learn how to create a safe report generation application. The process I use in this chapter to build applications is the one I use when I have to tackle a 'real-world' programming project. Of course, you don't have to follow my methodology, but I have tested it several times in the past and it has never failed me.

5   XML in Action

Overview

XML is structured in a simple and common format (in plain text) and provides a platform-neutral, efficient way of sharing and storing data. As such, an XML document can be shared by computers with completely different components, interfaces, configurations, and operating systems.

Two techniques for working with XML are presented. First, the 'SimpleXMLElement' class is introduced, explained, and implemented as a means to convert XML into an object that can be processed with normal property selectors and array iterators. Second, XPath is introduced, explained, and implemented as a means of finding information in an XML document.

Learning Objectives

After completing this chapter, you will gain a fundamental understanding of the topic by creating, modifying, traversing, and saving XML content. The following objectives summarize the skills the chapter will help you develop:

1   Learn the definition of XML and its characteristics.
2   Learn the five basic reasons why you should use XML.
3   Learn the structure of an XML document.
4   Learn the rules that ensure that an XML document is well-formed.
5   Learn about the 'SimpleXML' extension and 'SimpleXMLElement' class.
6   Learn two ways to create an instance of the 'SimpleXMLElement' class.
7   Learn about the 'foreach' construct.
8   Learn how to create and save an XML document.
9   Learn how to display the XML tree of an XML document.
10 Learn how to display and save XML document content.
11 Learn how to modify an XML document.
12 Learn how to remove nodes and values from an XML document.
13 Learn how to add attributes and elements to an XML document.
14 Learn how to use 'XPath' with XML.

XML

Extensible markup language (XML) is a standard for describing how information is structured. Specifically, *XML* is a text-based markup language that is the standard for data interchange on the web. It provides a foundation for creating documents that can be used on a wide variety of platforms and for storing data in a simple, common format in plain text.

The ubiquitous capacity and common format of XML allow computers to share information even if they have completely different system components, configurations, and operating systems. XML allows people to create their own customized markup applications for exchanging information.

XML Tags

XML uses tags in the same way as HTML. Unlike HTML, XML does not have a fixed range of tags and attributes. Within certain rules, you can name tags and attributes whatever you want unless you are working on a large collaborative project that needs to use a standardized vocabulary. The big difference is that an HTML tag tells you how a page is organized, while an XML document contains no information about the layout or structure of a page.

XML tags cannot include any whitespace or punctuation other than the hyphen '-', underscore '_' or period '.'. Tags cannot begin with 'xml' in any combination of uppercase or lowercase letters.

XML Data

XML stores data in a hierarchical (tree) structure according to meaning and without any reference to web page presentation. That is, XML provides an elegant way to separate data from format. An XML document may not even represent a page or even exist as a physical file on the server.

An XML document can be generated dynamically by a database in response to an incoming request. The server analyzes the request, queries the database to get the most current information, and sends the result to the recipient formatted as XML.

Five Basic Reasons to Use XML

XML is almost ubiquitous in terms of information sharing between computer systems. The five basic reasons for this ubiquity include simplicity, organization, accessibility, standardization, and reusability.

Simplicity is provided by XML because it is easy to create and understand. Such simplicity allows you freedom to develop based on your needs.

Organization is provided by XML because it allows you to build your website by segmenting the design process. Data is on one page, while formatting rules are on another. Once you have a general idea of what information you need to produce, you can write the data page first and then work on the design. XML thereby allows you to produce your website in stages and stay organized in the process.

Accessibility is provided by XML by enabling you to compartmentalize your work. Separating data (from format) makes it accessible when changes are needed without impacting format. If you write both segments (data and format) in HTML, you create sections that incorporate the formatting instructions with the information you need to display on the page. When changes are needed, you must wade through all the code to find a few lines because data and format are not separated. In addition, you risk causing unforeseen errors because any change can potentially impact the format since both segments are in the same place. Separating data from format thereby makes changes easy, less error prone, and less time consuming.

Standardization is provided by XML because it is an international standard. As such, anyone in the world has the ability to view and understand your document.

Reusability is provided by XML because you can make one data page and use it over and over again. That is, you can create as many display pages as you want for that data. XML allows you to generate different styles and formats based on one page of information.

XML Structure

Seeing the contents of an XML document is a good way to understand its basic structure. The following XML document 'cars.xml' contains three car elements.

```
 1  <?xml version="1.0" encoding="ISO-8859-1"?>
 2  <cars>
 3  <identity sno="fm12345">
 4  <make>Ford</make>
 5  <model>Mustang</model>
 6  </identity>
 7  <identity sno="ha98764">
 8  <make>Honda</make>
 9  <model>Accord</model>
10  </identity>
11  <identity sno="mm11111">
12  <make>Mazda</make>
13  <model>Miata</model>
14  </identity>
15  </cars>
```

Create text file 'cars.xml' on your file system (i.e., Linux) for use in an upcoming example. The XML declaration (sometimes referred to as the XML prolog) in line 1 tells browsers and processors that the document is XML. If used, the declaration must be the first entry in the document. There cannot be anything else before it, not even blank lines or comments. The *root element* '<cars>' (lines 2 and 15) contains everything else inside the document. An *element* describes the data that it contains, and can also contain other elements and attributes. An *attribute* provides additional information about elements, but cannot contain other elements.

At the next level are three '<identity>' elements (lines 3–6, 7–10, and 11–14), each of which has a 'sno' attribute (lines 3, 7, and 11). Within each '<identity>' element are two elements named '<make>' and '<model>', which each contain text. The text inside an element is referred to as a text element (or text node).

XML Nodes

XML can define seven nodes – root, element, attribute, text, comment, processing instructions, and namespace. The *root node* contains everything in the XML document, including the root element. An *element node* can contain other element nodes, a text node, or be empty. An *attribute node* is a name–value pair in an element's opening tag. A *text node* is the literal text between element opening and closing tags. A *comment node* contains comments. A *processing instruction node* passes instructions to the application processing an XML document. A *namespace node* provides a way to prevent clashes between elements from different sources.

XML Rules

An XML document must be well-formed to be considered viable. A *well-formed* XML document must conform to the seven rules of XML syntax. First, it can only have one root element. Second, every start tag must have a matching closing tag. Third, empty elements can omit the closing tag, but if they include one it must have a forward slash before the closing angle bracket '/>'. Fourth, elements must be properly nested. Fifth, attribute values must be in quotes. Sixth, in the content of an element or attribute value '<' and '&' must be replaced by HTML entities '<' and '&', respectively. Seventh, an XML declaration is allowed only at the start of the document.

SimpleXML

The 'SimpleXML' extension provides a very simple and easily usable toolset to convert XML to an object that can be processed with normal property selectors and array iterators. When using the 'SimpleXML' extension, all created objects are instances of the 'SimpleXMLElement' class.

The 'SimpleXML' extension converts an XML document into an object in the following manner. Elements are converted into single attributes of the 'SimpleXMLElement' object (or 'SimpleXML' object for short). When there is more than one element on one level, they are placed inside an array. Attributes are accessed using associative arrays, where an index corresponds to the attribute name. Text data from elements are converted into strings. If an element has more than one text node, they are arranged in the order they are found.

The 'SimpleXML' extension is fast and easy when performing basic tasks, such as reading XML files, extracting data from XML strings, and editing text nodes or attributes. However, when dealing with advanced XML, like namespaces, it is better to use XML DOM (a standard way of accessing and manipulating XML documents).

Create an Instance of the 'SimpleXMLElement' Class

The easiest way to create an instance of the 'SimpleXMLElement' class is to load the XML document from a file with 'simplexml_load_file()'. If you need to work with an advanced object, use 'simplexml_import_dom()' to return an instance of 'SimpleXML' from a DOM object.

```php
1  <?php
2  // File load_simplexml.php
3  $file= 'cars.xml';
4  $xml = simplexml_load_file($file);
5  foreach($xml->identity as $id)
6  {
7  echo $id['sno'] . ' ' .
8  $id->make . ' ' . $id->model;
9  echo '<br />';
10 }
11 ?>
```

The 'simplexml_load_file()' construct creates an instance of the 'SimpleXMLElement' class based on 'cars. xml' and places it in the '$xml' variable (line 4). The 'foreach()' construct (lines 5–10) iterates over the newly created object. As such, the 'sno' attribute (which uniquely identifies each car), make, and model are displayed for each '<identity>' element (lines 7–9).

Load PHP file 'load_simplexml.php' in a web browser. Figure 5.1 displays the results.

```
fm12345 Ford Mustang
ha98764 Honda Accord
mm11111 Mazda Miata
```

Figure 5.1 Display of XML from 'cars.xml' Using 'simplexml'

A second way to create an instance of 'SimpleXMLElement' is to create an instance of the 'DOMDocument' class and convert it to 'SimpleXML'.

```php
1  <?php
2  // File load_dom.php
```

```
 3  $xml = 'cars.xml';
 4  $dom = new DOMDocument;
 5  $dom->load($xml);
 6  $xml = simplexml_import_dom($dom);
 7  foreach($xml->identity as $id)
 8  {
 9  echo $id['sno'] . ' ' .
10  $id->make . ' ' . $id->model;
11  echo '<br />';
12  }
13  ?>
```

First, I create an instance of DOM and place it in '$dom' (line 4). Second, I load 'cars.xml' into the DOM object (line 5). Third, I create a 'SimpleXML' object from the DOM object (line 6). The 'foreach()' construct (lines 7–12) iterates through the XML document and displays the results.

　Load PHP file 'load_dom.php' in a browser. Figure 5.2 displays the results.

```
fm12345 Ford Mustang
ha98764 Honda Accord
mm11111 Mazda Miata
```

Figure 5.2　Display of XML from 'cars.xml' Using 'DOM'

Foreach

The 'foreach()' construct provides an easy way to iterate over arrays and objects. For objects, the syntax is 'foreach ('list' as 'object in list')'. When working with XML, the *list* holds the contents of the XML document, and the *object in list* is the current element in the XML document.

　When 'foreach()' commences, the internal object pointer automatically resets to the first object in the list. With each loop, the value of the current object from 'list' is assigned to 'object in list' and the internal object pointer is advanced by one. Be careful to use 'object in list' within the loop rather than 'list'. Using 'list' inside the loop causes a *fatal* error.

Create and Save an XML Document

If you use an earlier version of 'Google Chrome' web browser, you may have to download 'XML Tree' to enable XML data to be displayed in a user-friendly way. The software is free and easy to install.

　PHP file 'stereo_xml.php' creates an XML document and displays it. It does not save it. I always display results before saving to ensure that the code works and XML is created as expected.

```
1  <?php
2  // File stereo_xml.php
3  $newXML = new SimpleXMLElement('<root></root>');
4  $stereo1 = $newXML->addChild('stereo');
```

```
 5  $stereo1->addAttribute('id','ow191');
 6  $stereo1->addChild('name','Joyous Sound');
 7  $stereo1->addChild('preamp','Spectral');
 8  $stereo1->addChild('amp','Linn');
 9  $stereo1->addChild('cdp','Nagra');
10  $stereo1->addChild('speakers','Opera');
11  $stereo1->addChild('wire','Wireworld');
12  $stereo1->addChild('wire','JPS Labs');
13  $stereo1->addChild('wire','Shunyata');
14  $stereo1->addChild('price','$20,000.00');
15  $stereo2 = $newXML->addChild('stereo');
16  $stereo2->addAttribute('id','ms299');
17  $stereo2->addChild('name','Nirvana');
18  $stereo2->addChild('preamp','Belles');
19  $stereo2->addChild('amp','Belles');
20  $stereo2->addChild('cdp','Esoteric');
21  $stereo2->addChild('speakers','Focal');
22  $stereo2->addChild('wire','Shunyata');
23  $stereo2->addChild('price','$10,000.00');
24  $stereo3 = $newXML->addChild('stereo');
25  $stereo3->addAttribute('id','jj101');
26  $stereo3->addChild('name','Heaven');
27  $stereo3->addChild('preamp','MBL');
28  $stereo3->addChild('amp','MBL');
29  $stereo3->addChild('cdp','MBL');
30  $stereo3->addChild('speakers','MBL');
31  $stereo3->addChild('wire','MIT');
32  $stereo3->addChild('wire','Nordost');
33  $stereo3->addChild('price','$120,000.00');
34  $stereo4 = $newXML->addChild('stereo');
35  $stereo4->addAttribute('id','dp530');
36  $stereo4->addChild('name','Ear Candy');
37  $stereo4->addChild('preamp','AudioPax');
38  $stereo4->addChild('amp','Linn');
39  $stereo4->addChild('cdp','Linn');
40  $stereo4->addChild('cdp','Esoteric');
41  $stereo4->addChild('speakers','Energy');
42  $stereo4->addChild('wire','Crystal');
43  $stereo4->addChild('wire','JPS Labs');
44  $stereo4->addChild('wire','Wireworld');
45  $stereo4->addChild('wire','Shunyata');
46  $stereo4->addChild('price','$30,000.00');
47  header ('Content-Type: text/xml');
48  echo $newXML->asXML();
49  ?>
```

I start by creating an instance of the 'SimpleXMLElement' class and include the 'root' node (line 3). I continue by using the 'addChild()' method (line 4) to add a child element. Next, I use the 'addAttribute' method (line 5) to add an identifier to the '<stereo>' element. The remaining lines for '$stereo1' (lines 6–14) complete the first stereo system.

The same logic is used to create the remaining stereo systems. Notice that some systems have multiple 'wire' elements (e.g., 'stereo1' → lines 11–13) and one system (i.e., 'stereo4' → lines 39 and 40) has two 'cdp' entries.

The 'header' line (line 47) informs the browser that content is to be displayed. The final line (line 48) uses the 'asXML()' method to actually display the content. Load 'stereo_xml.php' to see the results.

Before saving the XML document, create a directory (e.g., 'xml_docs') to hold it and ensure that the permissions of the directory are set to allow 'writing'. I use '777' permissions (which gives full permissions on the folder) to save the XML document because I want to make sure that the save works. However, consult your IT expert, in case more restrictive permissions are deemed appropriate.

```
mkdir xml_docs
chmod 777 xml_docs
```

The next example modifies 'stereo_xml.php' to save the XML document. Modifications include removing the last two lines and adding six new ones. Open a new PHP file 'stereo_xml_save.php' and copy the contents of 'stereo_xml.php' into it.

```
 1  <?php
 2  // File stereo_xml_save.php
 3  $newXML = new SimpleXMLElement('<root></root>');
 4  $stereo1 = $newXML->addChild('stereo');
 5  $stereo1->addAttribute('id','ow191');
 6  $stereo1->addChild('name','Joyous Sound');
 7  $stereo1->addChild('preamp','Spectral');
 8  $stereo1->addChild('amp','Linn');
 9  $stereo1->addChild('cdp','Nagra');
10  $stereo1->addChild('speakers','Opera');
11  $stereo1->addChild('wire','Wireworld');
12  $stereo1->addChild('wire','JPS Labs');
13  $stereo1->addChild('wire','Shunyata');
14  $stereo1->addChild('price','$20,000.00');
15  $stereo2 = $newXML->addChild('stereo');
16  $stereo2->addAttribute('id','ms299');
17  $stereo2->addChild('name','Nirvana');
18  $stereo2->addChild('preamp','Belles');
19  $stereo2->addChild('amp','Belles');
20  $stereo2->addChild('cdp','Esoteric');
21  $stereo2->addChild('speakers','Focal');
22  $stereo2->addChild('wire','Shunyata');
23  $stereo2->addChild('price','$10,000.00');
24  $stereo3 = $newXML->addChild('stereo');
25  $stereo3->addAttribute('id','jj101');
26  $stereo3->addChild('name','Heaven');
27  $stereo3->addChild('preamp','MBL');
28  $stereo3->addChild('amp','MBL');
```

```
29  $stereo3->addChild('cdp','MBL');
30  $stereo3->addChild('speakers','MBL');
31  $stereo3->addChild('wire','MIT');
32  $stereo3->addChild('wire','Nordost');
33  $stereo3->addChild('price','$120,000.00');
34  $stereo4 = $newXML->addChild('stereo');
35  $stereo4->addAttribute('id','dp530');
36  $stereo4->addChild('name','Ear Candy');
37  $stereo4->addChild('preamp','AudioPax');
38  $stereo4->addChild('amp','Linn');
39  $stereo4->addChild('cdp','Linn');
40  $stereo4->addChild('cdp','Esoteric');
41  $stereo4->addChild('speakers','Energy');
42  $stereo4->addChild('wire','Crystal');
43  $stereo4->addChild('wire','JPS Labs');
44  $stereo4->addChild('wire','Wireworld');
45  $stereo4->addChild('wire','Shunyata');
46  $stereo4->addChild('price','$30,000.00');
47  $dom = new DomDocument();
48  $dom->preserveWhiteSpace = false;
49  $dom->formatOutput = true;
50  $dom->loadXML($newXML->asXML());
51  $dom->save('xml_docs/stereo.xml');
52  echo 'XML Document Saved';
53  ?>
```

Start by removing the 'header' (line 47) and 'echo' (line 48) statements. Add line 47 to create a new DOM object. Add line 48 to disallow any whitespace with the 'preserveWhiteSpace' method. Add line 49 to turn on formatting with the 'formatOutput' method. Add line 50 to load 'SimpleXML' output into the DOM object with the 'loadXML' method. The parameter '$newXML->asXML()' inside 'loadXML()' actually creates the XML output. Add line 51 to save the XML document with the 'save' method. Finally, add line 52 to display that the document was saved.

Load file 'stereo_xml_save.php' in a browser to save the XML document. Figure 5.3 indicates that the document was saved.

```
XML Document Saved
```

Figure 5.3 Display Showing that XML Was Saved

Just to be sure, check the contents of 'stereo.xml' in the 'xml_docs' directory. To accomplish this, change to the 'xml_docs' directory, issue list command 'ls', and edit the xml document as shown.

```
cd xml_docs
ls
vi stereo.xml
```

The contents of 'stereo.xml' should exactly match the following code.

```xml
<?xml version="1.0"?>
<root>
  <stereo id="ow191">
    <name>Joyous Sound</name>
    <preamp>Spectral</preamp>
    <amp>Linn</amp>
    <cdp>Nagra</cdp>
    <speakers>Opera</speakers>
    <wire>Wireworld</wire>
    <wire>JPS Labs</wire>
    <wire>Shunyata</wire>
    <price>$20,000.00</price>
  </stereo>
  <stereo id="ms299">
    <name>Nirvana</name>
    <preamp>Belles</preamp>
    <amp>Belles</amp>
    <cdp>Esoteric</cdp>
    <speakers>Focal</speakers>
    <wire>Shunyata</wire>
    <price>$10,000.00</price>
  </stereo>
  <stereo id="jj101">
    <name>Heaven</name>
    <preamp>MBL</preamp>
    <amp>MBL</amp>
    <cdp>MBL</cdp>
    <speakers>MBL</speakers>
    <wire>MIT</wire>
    <wire>Nordost</wire>
    <price>$120,000.00</price>
  </stereo>
  <stereo id="dp530">
    <name>Ear Candy</name>
    <preamp>AudioPax</preamp>
    <amp>Linn</amp>
    <cdp>Linn</cdp>
    <cdp>Esoteric</cdp>
    <speakers>Energy</speakers>
    <wire>Crystal</wire>
    <wire>JPS Labs</wire>
    <wire>Wireworld</wire>
    <wire>Shunyata</wire>
    <price>$30,000.00</price>
  </stereo>
</root>
```

Notice that the XML document is saved in a user-friendly format. Using DOM in PHP file 'stereo_xml_save. php' allows finer formatting control over the XML document. DOM was unnecessary in PHP file 'stereo_xml. php' because the browser takes care of formatting when displaying XML. XML document 'stereo.xml' is used in this chapter to illustrate the flexibility of 'SimpleXML'.

Display the Tree of an XML Document

Examining the XML tree of a document shows how the document is structured, which makes extraction of desired data very easy. The next example uses PHP file 'display_tree.php' to display the XML tree when loaded in a browser.

```
1  <?php
2  // File display_tree.php
3  $xml = simplexml_load_file('xml_docs/stereo.xml');
4  echo '<pre>';
5  print_r($xml);
6  echo '</pre>';
7  ?>
```

I start by converting 'stereo.xml' into a 'SimpleXML' object and placing the object into '$xml' (line 3). I continue by dynamically generating preformatted text with '<pre>' (line 4), printing the object in human-readable form with 'print_r()' (line 5), and ending preformatted text with '</pre>' (line 6).

Load 'display_tree.php'. Figure 5.4 shows the first node of the tree. Notice that data is stored in multidimensional arrays.

```
SimpleXMLElement Object
(
    [stereo] => Array
        (
            [0] => SimpleXMLElement Object
                (
                    [@attributes] => Array
                        (
                            [id] => ow191
                        )

                    [name] => Joyous Sound
                    [preamp] => Spectral
                    [amp] => Linn
                    [cdp] => Nagra
                    [speakers] => Opera
                    [wire] => Array
                        (
                            [0] => Wireworld
                            [1] => JPS Labs
                            [2] => Shunyata
                        )
```

Figure 5.4 Display of Tree Structure from 'stereo.xml'

Since the XML document has many stereo systems, 'stereo' is an array of 'SimpleXML' objects beginning with an index of zero. Each stereo contains the '@attributes' array with 'id' as the index. '@attributes' must be an array because each element can have more than one attribute. For the first stereo system, the 'id' is 'ow191'. Each stereo system also includes several elements, including 'name', 'preamp', 'amp', 'cdp', 'speakers', 'wire', and 'price'. Since the 'wire' element of the first stereo system has more than one value, it becomes an array with three elements – 'Wireworld', 'JPS Labs', and 'Shunyata'.

Knowing the tree structure of even the most complex XML document facilitates easy access to elements and attributes. It also helps debug problems because the XML tree shows how content is stored in the system.

Display the Content of an XML Document

The 'SimpleXML' extension enables easy access to XML content. The XML tree shows that each element node '<stereo>' is a 'SimpleXML' object. Since each '<stereo>' has child nodes, you can access them as properties.

PHP file 'stereo_names.php' displays 'name' elements of the first two stereo systems. Line 3 converts 'stereo.xml' into a 'SimpleXML' object and loads it into '$xml'. The 'name' of the first stereo system is displayed (line 4) with index '0' and a pointer to 'name'. The name of the second stereo system is then displayed (line 5) with an index of '1' and a pointer to 'name'. The XML tree (see Figure 5.4) shows that the first stereo system is element zero and the second is element one.

```
1  <?php
2  // File stereo_names.php
3  $xml = simplexml_load_file('xml_docs/stereo.xml');
4  echo $xml->stereo[0]->name . '<br />';
5  echo $xml->stereo[1]->name;
6  ?>
```

```
Joyous Sound
Nirvana
```

Figure 5.5 Display of First and Second Stereo 'names'

Load 'stereo_names.php' in a browser. Figure 5.5 shows the results.

PHP file 'all_names.php' displays 'name' elements of all four stereo systems when loaded in a browser. Figure 5.6 shows the results.

```
1  <?php
2  // File all_names.php
3  $xml = simplexml_load_file('xml_docs/stereo.xml');
4  foreach($xml->stereo as $stereo)
5  { echo $stereo->name . '<br />'; }
6  ?>
```

```
Joyous Sound
Nirvana
Heaven
Ear Candy
```

Figure 5.6 Display of All Stereo 'names'

The 'foreach' construct (lines 4 and 5) uses '$xml->stereo' to identify the stereo systems in the XML document, which enables easy traversal.

PHP file 'specific_nodes.php' displays the second and third 'wire' elements of the fourth stereo system when loaded in a browser. Figure 5.7 shows the results.

```php
1  <?php
2  // File specific_nodes.php
3  $xml = simplexml_load_file('xml_docs/stereo.xml');
4  echo $xml->stereo[3]->wire[1] . '<br />';
5  echo $xml->stereo[3]->wire[2] . '<br />';
6  ?>
```

```
JPS Labs
Wireworld
```

Figure 5.7 Display of Fourth Stereo System Second and Third 'wires'

Since the fourth stereo system (see Figure 5.4) has multiple 'wires', I use indexing to access the second and third wire elements (lines 4 and 5).

PHP file 'all_values.php' displays 'name', 'preamp', 'amp', 'cdp', 'speakers', 'wire', and 'price' elements of all stereo systems. Figure 5.8 displays the results.

```php
1  <?php
2  // File all_values.php
3  $xml = simplexml_load_file('xml_docs/stereo.xml');
4  foreach($xml->stereo as $stereo)
5  {
6  echo '<em>' . $stereo->name . '</em> ';
7  echo '<strong>' . $stereo['id'] . '</strong> ';
8  echo $stereo->preamp . ', ' . $stereo->amp;
9  $num = count($stereo->cdp);
10 $i = 1;
11 echo ', &lt;&lt;';
12 foreach($stereo->cdp as $cdp)
13 {
14 if($i < $num)
```

```
15 { echo $cdp . ', '; }
16 elseif($i == $num)
17 { echo $cdp; }
18 $i++;
19 }
20 echo '&gt;&gt;, ';
21 echo $stereo->speakers . ', ';
22 $num = count($stereo->wire);
23 $i = 1;
24 echo '(';
25 foreach($stereo->wire as $wire)
26 {
27 if($i < $num)
28 { echo $wire . ', '; }
29 elseif($i == $num)
30 { echo $wire; }
31 $i++;
32 }
33 echo '), and ' . $stereo->price . '<br />';
34 }
35 ?>
```

Joyous Sound **ow191** Spectral, Linn, <<Nagra>>, Opera, (Wireworld, JPS Labs, Shunyata), and $20,000.00
Nirvana **ms299** Belles, Belles, <<Esoteric>>, Focal, (Shunyata), and $10,000.00
Heaven **jj101** MBL, MBL, <<MBL>>, MBL, (MIT, Nordost), and $120,000.00
Ear Candy **dp530** AudioPax, Linn, <<Linn, Esoteric>>, Energy, (Crystal, JPS Labs, Wireworld, Shunyata), and $30,000.00

Figure 5.8 Display of Various Elements of All Stereo Systems

The 'outer' foreach()' loop (lines 4–34) traverses all 'stereo' systems within the 'SimpleXML' object. The code inside this loop is complex because the '<cdp>' and '<wire>' elements can have more than one entry per stereo system. To find the exact number of these elements, I use the 'count()' function and assign the result to '$num' (lines 9 and 22). To traverse the '<cdp>' and '<wire>' elements, I use a 'foreach()' for both.

The first 'inner' 'foreach()' (lines 12–19) traverses the 'cdp' array. The logic inside is a bit complex for aesthetics only. That is, I place a comma after each 'cdp', except for the final one. I accomplish this logic by creating a counter '$i' and initialize it to '1' (line 10). Inside the loop, I check to see if the counter is less than '$num' (line 14). If so, I display the CD player followed by a comma ',' (line 15). If not, I display the CD player without a comma ',' (lines 16 and 17). I end the loop by incrementing the counter (line 18).

The second 'inner' 'foreach()' (lines 25–32) traverses the 'wire' array. Like the first 'inner' loop, I create a counter '$i' and initialize it to '1' (line 23). Inside the loop, I check to see if the counter is less than '$num' (line 27). If so, I display the CD player followed by a comma ',' (line 28). If not, I display the CD player without a comma ',' (lines 29 and 30). I end the loop by incrementing the counter (line 31).

PHP file 'names_wires.php' displays 'name' and 'wire' for each system. The code is pretty simple because I just display everything on its own line.

```
 1  <?php
 2  // File names_wires.php
 3  $xml = simplexml_load_file('xml_docs/stereo.xml');
 4  foreach($xml->stereo as $stereo)
 5  {
 6  echo '<strong>' . $stereo->name . '</strong><br />';
 7  foreach($stereo->wire as $wire)
 8  { echo $wire . '<br />'; }
 9  echo '<br />';
10  }
11  ?>
```

The 'outer' 'foreach()' (lines 4–10) traverses all stereo systems. The 'inner' 'foreach()' (lines 7 and 8) displays all 'wires' within a stereo system. Load the file in a browser. Figure 5.9 shows the results.

Joyous Sound
Wireworld
JPS Labs
Shunyata

Nirvana
Shunyata

Heaven
MIT
Nordost

Ear Candy
Crystal
JPS Labs
Wireworld
Shunyata

Figure 5.9 Display of All 'names' with Corresponding 'wires'

PHP file 'elements_attributes.php' displays 'name', 'id' attribute, and 'wire' for each system when loaded in a browser. Figure 5.10 shows the results.

```
 1  <?php
 2  // File elements_attributes.php
 3  $xml = simplexml_load_file('xml_docs/stereo.xml');
 4  foreach($xml->stereo as $stereo)
 5  {
 6  echo '<strong>' . $stereo->name . '</strong>';
 7  echo '<strong style="color:green;">';
```

```
 8 echo '  ' . $stereo['id'];
 9 echo '</strong></br />';
10 foreach($stereo->wire as $wire)
11 { echo $wire . '<br />'; }
12 echo '<br />';
13 }
14 ?>
```

Joyous Sound ow191
Wireworld
JPS Labs
Shunyata

Nirvana ms299
Shunyata

Heaven jj101
MIT
Nordost

Ear Candy dp530
Crystal
JPS Labs
Wireworld
Shunyata

Figure 5.10 Display of All 'names', 'wires', and 'id' Attributes

The 'outer' 'foreach()' (lines 4–13) traverses all stereo systems. I start by displaying the name of the system (line 6). The opening tag of each '<stereo>' element contains an attribute called 'id'. So, I use '$stereo['id']' to display the value of this attribute (line 8). The 'inner' 'foreach()' (lines 10 and 11) displays all 'wires' within a stereo system.

PHP file 'attributes.php' displays the name of the third stereo system and its corresponding 'id' attribute. Figure 5.11 shows the results. Since the index of the first node is zero, an index of '2' is used to access the third element and attribute (lines 5 and 6).

```
1 <?php
2 // File attributes.php
3 $xml = simplexml_load_file('xml_docs/stereo.xml');
4 echo 'Stereo System: ';
5 echo $xml->stereo[2]->name;
6 echo ' (' . $xml->stereo[2]['id'] . ')';
7 ?>
```

Stereo System: Heaven (jj101)

Figure 5.11 Display of Third 'name' and 'id' Attributes

PHP file 'names_attributes.php' displays all stereo system names and corresponding 'id' values with a 'foreach()' loop (lines 4–8). Figure 5.12 shows the results.

```php
1  <?php
2  // File names_attributes.php
3  $xml = simplexml_load_file('xml_docs/stereo.xml');
4  foreach($xml->stereo as $stereo)
5  {
6  echo $stereo->name . ' (' . $stereo['id'] . ')';
7  echo '<br />';
8  }
9  ?>
```

Joyous Sound (ow191)
Nirvana (ms299)
Heaven (jj101)
Ear Candy (dp530)

Figure 5.12 Display of All 'names' and 'id' Attributes

PHP file 'specific_wire.php' displays all names, corresponding 'id' attribute values, and the first 'wire' of each stereo system with a 'foreach()' loop (lines 4–8). Figure 5.13 shows the results.

```php
1  <?php
2  // File specific_wire.php
3  $xml = simplexml_load_file('xml_docs/stereo.xml');
4  foreach($xml->stereo as $stereo)
5  {
6  echo $stereo->name . ' (' . $stereo['id'] . ')';
7  echo ' ' . $stereo->wire[0] . '<br />';
8  }
9  ?>
```

Joyous Sound (ow191) Wireworld
Nirvana (ms299) Shunyata
Heaven (jj101) MIT
Ear Candy (dp530) Crystal

Figure 5.13 Display of All 'names' and 'id' Attributes with First 'wire'

PHP file 'see_xml.php' displays node information for the second stereo system. The 'header' statement (line 4) informs the browser to display content as XML and the 'asXML()' method (line 5) returns a well-formed XML string based on the SimpleXML element. Figure 5.14 shows the results.

```php
1  <?php
2  // File see_xml.php
3  $xml = simplexml_load_file('xml_docs/stereo.xml');
4  header('Content-Type: text/xml');
5  echo $xml->stereo[1]->asXML();
6  ?>
```

```xml
<stereo id="ms299">
   <name>Nirvana</name>
   <preamp>Belles</preamp>
   <amp>Belles</amp>
   <cdp>Esoteric</cdp>
   <speakers>Focal</speakers>
   <wire>Shunyata</wire>
   <price>$10,000.00</price>
</stereo>
```

Figure 5.14 Display of Second Stereo System as XML

PHP file 'see_all_xml.php displays the entire contents of the XML document. As in the previous example, the 'header' statement (line 4) informs the browser to display content as XML and the 'asXML()' method (line 5) returns a well-formed XML string based on the SimpleXML element.

```php
1  <?php
2  // File see_all_xml.php
3  $xml = simplexml_load_file('xml_docs/stereo.xml');
4  header('Content-Type: text/xml');
5  echo $xml->asXML();
6  ?>
```

Save the Content of an XML Document

If you encounter a problem when trying to save a file, the reason may be related to inadequate file permissions. We already changed file permissions earlier in the chapter to ensure that files can be saved. It doesn't hurt, however, to check file permissions again. If the file permissions will not allow you to save, use the 'chmod' Linux command as follows:

```
chmod 777 xml_docs
```

PHP file 'save_xml.php' saves a copy of the XML document into file 'stereo_copy.xml'. Figure 5.15 shows the results. Just to be sure, check the contents of 'stereo_copy.xml' in the 'xml_docs' directory.

```
1  <?php
2  // File save_xml.php
3  $xml = simplexml_load_file('xml_docs/stereo.xml');
4  if(@$xml->asXML('xml_docs/stereo_copy.xml'))
5  { echo 'XML saved'; }
6  else
7  { echo 'Could not save XML'; }
8  ?>
```

XML saved

Figure 5.15 Display Showing that Copy of Stereo Was Saved

The 'asXML()' method returns an XML document, from a 'SimpleXML' object, as a string. When used without an argument, the method returns a string containing XML of the current object. When used with a file as an argument, the XML is saved to the file (line 4). I precede the condition inside the 'if' statement with the '@' symbol in line 4 to suppress any error messages that might be generated.

To save a portion of an XML document, load the document, and use 'file_put_contents()'. PHP file 'save_stereo2.php' saves the second stereo system XML in 'stereo2.xml'. Figure 5.16 shows that the document was saved.

```
1  <?php
2  // File save_stereo2.php
3  $xml = simplexml_load_file('xml_docs/stereo.xml');
4  $output = "<?xml version='1.0' encoding='utf-8'?>\n";
5  $output .= $xml->stereo[1]->asXML();
6  if(file_put_contents('xml_docs/stereo2.xml',$output))
7  { echo 'XML saved'; }
8  else
9  { echo 'Could not save XML'; }
10 ?>
```

XML saved

Figure 5.16 Display Showing that Second Stereo System Was Saved

Line 4 assigns a string that identifies a file as XML (prolog) to '$output'. Line 5 appends the contents of the second stereo system to '$output'. That is, the first line of '$output' is the prolog, and the lines that follow are the contents of the second stereo system.

Verify that the contents of 'stereo2.xml' reflect the appropriate data from the second stereo system with the following commands.

cd xml_docs
vi stereo2.xml

First, change to the 'xml_docs' directory. Then edit the file 'stereo2.xml'. Figure 5.17 shows the results.

```
<?xml version='1.0' encoding='utf-8'?>
<stereo id="ms299">
    <name>Nirvana</name>
    <preamp>Belles</preamp>
    <amp>Belles</amp>
    <cdp>Esoteric</cdp>
    <speakers>Focal</speakers>
    <wire>Shunyata</wire>
    <price>$10,000.00</price>
</stereo>
```

Figure 5.17 Display of XML in File Structure

When saving small XML output, the code in PHP file 'save_stereo2.php' works fine. However, when saving a large amount of XML data, spacing issues can make it less readable. One solution is to use DOM.

PHP file 'save_stereo_dom.php' uses the 'DOMDocument' object to format the output. Methods 'preserve-WhiteSpace()' and 'formatOutput()' clean the XML document. Method 'loadXML()' loads the data into DOMDocument object and method 'save()' saves the file. Figure 5.18 shows the results.

```php
1  <?php
2  // File save_stereo_dom.php
3  $xml = simplexml_load_file('xml_docs/stereo.xml');
4  $output = "<?xml version='1.0' encoding='utf-8'?>\n";
5  $output .= $xml->stereo[1]->asXML();
6  $xml = simplexml_load_string($output);
7  $file = "xml_docs/stereo_dom.xml";
8  if(is_writable(dirname($file)))
9  {
10 $dom = new DomDocument();
11 $dom->preserveWhiteSpace = false;
12 $dom->formatOutput = true;
13 $dom->loadXML($xml->asXML());
14 $dom->save($file);
15 echo "XML saved";
16 }
17 else
18 { echo "Cannot save XML"; }
19 ?>
```

```
XML saved
```

Figure 5.18 Display Showing that Refined XML Was Saved

Specifically, I begin by converting 'stereo.xml' into a 'SimpleXML' object (line 3). Next, I create string output of the prolog followed by the contents of the second stereo system and assign to '$output' (lines 4 and 5). I continue by loading string '$output' into '$xml' as a 'SimpleXML' object (line 6). I assign the name of the file I will create to '$file' (line 7). I then check if the directory is 'writable' (line 8). If so, I create a new 'DOMDocument' object (line 10), format it (lines 11 and 12), load the object that holds the second stereo system (line 13), and save it (line 14). Figure 5.19 shows the contents of file 'stereo_dom.xml'.

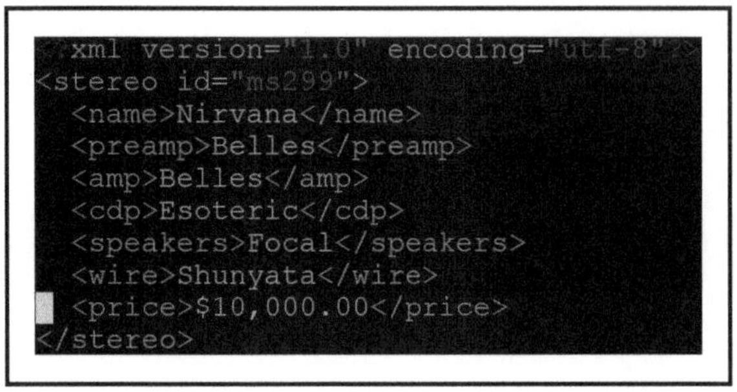

Figure 5.19 Display of Refined XML in File Structure

Comparing Figure 5.19 with Figure 5.17, notice that spacing in the XML document 'stereo_dom.xml' (Figure 5.19) removes whitespace before ending tag '</stereo>'. Even though spacing issues in this case are minor, as more data is added, readability becomes more problematic. Although 'stereo_dom.xml' is readable, it is not well-formed because it does not have a root element that contains the XML data (review the 'XML Rules' section earlier in the chapter for details).

Well-Formed XML

PHP file 'well_formed.php' creates a new XML document with a root element container populated with stereo systems two and four from 'stereo.xml'. Since I added a root element container, the document is now well-formed! Load 'well_formed.php' in a browser. Figure 5.20 shows the results.

```php
1  <?php
2  // File well_formed.php
3  $xml = simplexml_load_file('xml_docs/stereo.xml');
4  $output = "<?xml version='1.0' encoding='utf-8'?>\n";
5  $output .= "<root>\n";
6  $output .= $xml->stereo[1]->asXML();
7  $output .= $xml->stereo[3]->asXML();
8  $output .= "\n</root>";
9  if(file_put_contents('xml_docs/stereo_data.xml',$output))
10 { echo 'XML saved'; }
11 else
12 { echo 'Could not save XML'; }
13 ?>
```

```
XML saved
```

Figure 5.20 Display Showing that Well-Formed Second and Fourth XML Elements Were Saved

I begin by creating a prolog string (line 4) and assigning it to '$output'. I continue building '$output' by adding an opening 'root' tag (line 5). Next, I add the second and fourth stereo systems to '$output' (lines 6 and 7). I finish '$output' by adding a closing 'root' tag (line 8). I save the contents of '$output' to the 'stereo_data.xml' file (line 9).

It is always a good idea to verify that a file was saved properly. The following Linux commands will help you do this.

```
cd xml_docs
vi stereo_data.xml
```

Tags '<root>' and '</root>' should contain (surround) the 'stereo' nodes that contain the data. Now that 'stereo_data.xml' is well-formed, it can be converted to a 'SimpleXML' object and easily traversed.

PHP file 'traverse.php' loads 'stereo_data.xml', converts it to a 'SimpleXML' object, traverses the object, and displays some data. Load 'traverse.php' into a browser. Figure 5.21 shows the results.

```
1  <?php
2  // File traverse.php
3  $xml = simplexml_load_file('xml_docs/stereo_data.xml');
4  foreach($xml->stereo as $stereo)
5  {
6  echo $stereo->name . ' ' . $stereo->price;
7  echo '<br />';
8  }
9  ?>
```

```
Nirvana $10,000.00
Ear Candy $30,000.00
```

Figure 5.21 Display Showing Traversal of Well-Formed Elements

I load 'stereo_data.xml' and convert it into a 'SimpleXML' object (line 3). I then use a 'foreach()' loop (lines 4–8) to traverse the stereo systems in the XML document. Lines 6 and 7 display the 'name' and 'price' of the two systems.

PHP file 'well_formed.php' created a well-formed document (stereo_data.xml), but the spacing is still not quite right. Specifically, the spacing for element '<stereo>' is not consistent. DOM can be used to fix the problem.

PHP file 'cleanse.php' recreates 'stereo_data.xml' from the original 'stereo.xml' and uses DOM to format the data properly. Figure 5.22 shows the results. Edit 'stereo_data.xml' in the 'xml_docs' directory to verify contents.

```
 1  <?php
 2  // File cleanse.php
 3  $xml = simplexml_load_file('xml_docs/stereo.xml');
 4  $output = "<?xml version='1.0' encoding='utf-8'?>\n";
 5  $output .= "<root>\n";
 6  $output .= $xml->stereo[1]->asXML();
 7  $output .= $xml->stereo[3]->asXML();
 8  $output .= "\n</root>";
 9  $xml = simplexml_load_string($output);
10  $file = "xml_docs/stereo_data.xml";
11  if(is_writable(dirname($file)))
12  {
13  $dom = new DomDocument();
14  $dom->preserveWhiteSpace = false;
15  $dom->formatOutput = true;
16  $dom->loadXML($xml->asXML());
17  $dom->save($file);
18  echo "XML saved";
19  }
20  else
21  { echo "Cannot save XML"; }
22  ?>
```

XML saved

Figure 5.22 Display Showing that Refined Well-Formed Elements Were Saved

I begin by loading 'stereo.xml' into '$xml' as a 'SimpleXML' object (line 3). I continue by building '$output' (lines 4–8). Next, I load string '$output' into '$xml' as a 'SimpleXML' object (line 9). I can overwrite '$xml' with data from the new object because all necessary data from 'stereo.xml' was already extracted into '$output'. I create '$file' (line 9) to hold file information for saving the data. If the directory is 'writable', I use 'DOMDocument' methods to format data properly before saving (lines 13–17).

Modify an XML Document

'SimpleXML' objects can be modified in three ways. First, values of text and attributes can be changed. Second, attribute or element nodes can be removed. Third, new nodes and attributes can be added.

PHP file 'change.php' reduces the price of each stereo system by 10 percent and displays results to the browser. Nothing is saved.

```
 1  <?php
 2  // File change.php
 3  $xml = simplexml_load_file('xml_docs/stereo.xml');
 4  foreach ($xml->stereo as $stereo)
```

```
 5  {
 6  $reduced = substr($stereo->price, 1);
 7  $reduced = str_replace(",","",$reduced);
 8  $reduced = $reduced * .9;
 9  $stereo->price = '$' . number_format($reduced,2);
10  }
11  header ('Content-Type: text/xml');
12  echo $xml->asXML();
13  ?>
```

Since 'price' is a string, it must first be converted to a number. So, I remove the dollar sign from each 'price' element value with 'substr()' (line 6). Next, I remove the comma with 'str_replace()' (line 7). I then reduce 'price' by '10%' (line 8). I convert 'price' back into a string (line 9) by concatenating a dollar sign to the properly formatted number (decimals and a comma between grouped thousands) via the 'number_format()' function. Finally, I display results to a browser (lines 11 and 12).

The XML document is not actually changed because it is not saved. Figure 5.23 shows a partial display of the results (price of 'Joyous Sound' is reduced to $18,000).

```
<stereo id="ow191">
   <name>Joyous Sound</name>
   <preamp>Spectral</preamp>
   <amp>Linn</amp>
   <cdp>Nagra</cdp>
   <speakers>Opera</speakers>
   <wire>Wireworld</wire>
   <wire>JPS Labs</wire>
   <wire>Shunyata</wire>
   <price>$18,000.00</price>
</stereo>
```

Figure 5.23 Display Showing Partial Results from Modified XML

The following code modifies only the first stereo system. The 'price' of the system is reduced by '15%', the 'id' is changed, and the name of the speakers is changed. Load the file in a browser. Figure 5.24 shows the changes made to the first stereo system.

```
1  <?php
2  // File change_specific.php
3  $xml = simplexml_load_file('xml_docs/stereo.xml');
4  $reduced = substr($xml->stereo[0]->price, 1);
5  $reduced = str_replace(",","",$reduced);
6  $reduced = $reduced * .85;
```

```
 7  $xml->stereo[0]->price = '$' . number_format($reduced,2);
 8  $xml->stereo[0]['id'] = 'fw191';
 9  $xml->stereo[0]->speakers = 'Focal';
10  header ('Content-Type: text/xml');
11  echo $xml->asXML();
12  ?>
```

```
<stereo id="fw191">
   <name>Joyous Sound</name>
   <preamp>Spectral</preamp>
   <amp>Linn</amp>
   <cdp>Nagra</cdp>
   <speakers>Focal</speakers>
   <wire>Wireworld</wire>
   <wire>JPS Labs</wire>
   <wire>Shunyata</wire>
   <price>$17,000.00</price>
</stereo>
```

Figure 5.24 Display Showing Partial Results from Again Modified XML

I begin by removing '$' from the 'price' of the first stereo system (line 4). I continue by removing the comma (line 5) and reducing 'price' by '15%' (line 6). Next, I concatenate a dollar sign to the properly formatted number (line 7). I change the 'id' (line 8) and 'speakers' (line 9) of the first stereo system. I finish by displaying contents to a browser (lines 10 and 11).

PHP file 'adjust.php' modifies only the first stereo system and saves the results in 'stereo_adj.xml'. Load the file in a browser. Figure 5.25 shows the results. Just to be sure, check the contents of 'stereo_adj.xml' in the 'xml_docs' directory.

```
 1  <?php
 2  // adjust.php
 3  $xml = simplexml_load_file('xml_docs/stereo.xml');
 4  $reduced = substr($xml->stereo[0]->price, 1);
 5  $reduced = str_replace(",","",$reduced);
 6  $reduced = $reduced * .85;
 7  $xml->stereo[0]->price = '$' . number_format($reduced,2);
 8  $xml->stereo[0]['id'] = 'fw191';
 9  $xml->stereo[0]->speakers = 'Focal';
10  if($xml->asXML('xml_docs/stereo_adj.xml'))
11  { echo 'XML saved'; }
```

```
12 else
13 { echo 'Could not save XML'; }
14 ?>
```

```
XML saved
```

Figure 5.25 Display Showing that Modified XML Was Saved

The logic in 'adjust.php' is the same as in 'change_specific.php', except that the results are saved to 'stereo_adj.php' (line 10) and there is no 'header()' to display results.

PHP file 'remove.php' removes some nodes from all stereo systems. Changes are not permanent since the XML is not saved. Figure 5.26 shows partial results, verifying that the first stereo system no longer has an 'id' attribute or nodes 'cdp', 'wire', or 'price'.

```php
1  <?php
2  // File remove.php
3  $xml = simplexml_load_file('xml_docs/stereo.xml');
4  foreach ($xml->stereo as $stereo)
5  {
6  unset($stereo['id']);
7  unset($stereo->cdp);
8  unset($stereo->wire);
9  unset($stereo->price);
10 }
11 header ('Content-Type: text/xml');
12 echo $xml->asXML();
13 ?>
```

```
<stereo>
   <name>Joyous Sound</name>
   <preamp>Spectral</preamp>
   <amp>Linn</amp>
   <speakers>Opera</speakers>
</stereo>
```

Figure 5.26 Display Showing Partial Results after Deleted Pieces

The 'unset()' function is used to remove 'id' (line 6), 'cdp' (line 7), 'wire' (line 8), and 'price' (line 9) from all stereo systems. Nothing is actually changed because results are only displayed (line 11 and 12).

PHP file 'remove_specific.php' removes some nodes from the first stereo system. Changes are not permanent since XML is not saved. Figure 5.27 shows the results.

```php
1  <?php
2  // File remove_specific.php
3  $xml = simplexml_load_file('xml_docs/stereo.xml');
4  unset($xml->stereo[0]['id']);
5  unset($xml->stereo[0]->cdp);
6  unset($xml->stereo[0]->wire);
7  unset($xml->stereo[0]->price);
8  header ('Content-Type: text/xml');
9  echo $xml->asXML();
10 ?>
```

```xml
<stereo>
   <name>Joyous Sound</name>
   <preamp>Spectral</preamp>
   <amp>Linn</amp>
   <speakers>Opera</speakers>
</stereo>
```

Figure 5.27 Display Showing Deleted Pieces from First Element

Lines 4–7 remove 'id', 'cdp', 'wire', and 'price' from the first stereo system. No changes are actually made because XML is not saved. Lines 8 and 9 display results.

PHP file 'remove_save.php' removes some nodes from all stereo systems and saves the results in 'stereo_less.xml'. I begin by removing 'id', 'cdp', 'wire', and 'price' from all stereo systems (lines 4–10). To preserve proper formatting, I use DOM. First, I create a new 'DOMDocument' (line 11). Second, I do not preserve whitespace in the document (line 12). Third, I format output correctly by setting 'formatOutput' to 'true' (line 13). Fourth, I load the 'asXML()' output into the object (line 14) and save to 'stereo_less.xml' (line 15). By saving the results to a new file name, I preserve the original data in 'stereo.xml'.

```php
1  <?php
2  // File remove_save.php
3  $xml = simplexml_load_file('xml_docs/stereo.xml');
4  foreach ($xml->stereo as $stereo)
5  {
6  unset($stereo['id']);
7  unset($stereo->cdp);
8  unset($stereo->wire);
9  unset($stereo->price);
10 }
11 $dom = new DomDocument();
12 $dom->preserveWhiteSpace = false;
```

```
13 $dom->formatOutput = true;
14 $dom->loadXML($xml->asXML());
15 $dom->save('xml_docs/stereo_less.xml');
16 ?>
```

The contents of 'stereo_less.xml' should look like the following code.

```
<?xml version="1.0"?>
<root>
  <stereo>
    <name>Joyous Sound</name>
    <preamp>Spectral</preamp>
    <amp>Linn</amp>
    <speakers>Opera</speakers>
  </stereo>
  <stereo>
    <name>Nirvana</name>
    <preamp>Belles</preamp>
    <amp>Belles</amp>
    <speakers>Focal</speakers>
  </stereo>
  <stereo>
    <name>Heaven</name>
    <preamp>MBL</preamp>
    <amp>MBL</amp>
    <speakers>MBL</speakers>
  </stereo>
  <stereo>
    <name>Ear Candy</name>
    <preamp>AudioPax</preamp>
    <amp>Linn</amp>
    <speakers>Energy</speakers>
  </stereo>
</root>
```

Add Attributes and Elements to an XML Document

With 'SimpleXML', it is relatively easy to add attributes and elements to an XML document. PHP file 'add_attribute.php' adds an attribute to an existing element tag and displays the results.

```
1  <?php
2  // File add_attribute.php
3  $xml = simplexml_load_file('xml_docs/stereo.xml');
4  foreach ($xml->stereo as $stereo)
5  {
```

```
 6  if(strpos($stereo->speakers,'Opera') !== false)
 7  { $stereo->speakers->addAttribute('type','monitor'); }
 8  else
 9  { $stereo->speakers->addAttribute('type','floor'); }
10  }
11  header ('Content-Type: text/xml');
12  echo $xml->asXML();
13  ?>
```

Function 'strpos()' finds the position of the first occurrence of 'Opera' in the element value of each 'speaker' (line 6). If the string contains the word 'Opera', attribute 'type' is assigned 'monitor' (line 7). Otherwise, attribute 'type' is assigned 'floor' (line 9). Results are then displayed (lines 11 and 12). Figure 5.28 shows that attribute 'monitor' was added to 'Opera' speakers for the first stereo system.

```
<stereo id="ow191">
   <name>Joyous Sound</name>
   <preamp>Spectral</preamp>
   <amp>Linn</amp>
   <cdp>Nagra</cdp>
   <speakers type="monitor">Opera</speakers>
   <wire>Wireworld</wire>
   <wire>JPS Labs</wire>
   <wire>Shunyata</wire>
   <price>$20,000.00</price>
</stereo>
```

Figure 5.28 Display Showing Added Attribute to XML

PHP file 'save_attribute.php' contains the same basic logic, but saves changes to 'stereo_add.xml'. In this case, we need not worry about XML formatting because modifications are inside element tags. That is, no structural changes are made to the XML document. Figure 5.29 shows the results.

```
 1  <?php
 2  // File save_attribute.php
 3  $xml = simplexml_load_file('xml_docs/stereo.xml');
 4  foreach ($xml->stereo as $stereo)
 5  {
 6  if(strpos($stereo->speakers,'Opera') !== false)
 7  { $stereo->speakers->addAttribute('type','monitor'); }
 8  else
 9  { $stereo->speakers->addAttribute('type','floor'); }
10  }
```

```
11  ob_start();
12  if($xml->asXML('xml_docs/stereo_add.xml'))
13  { echo 'XML saved'; }
14  else
15  { echo 'XML not saved'; }
16  ob_flush();
17  ob_end_clean();
18  ?>
```

```
XML saved
```

Figure 5.29 Display Showing that Added Attribute to XML Was Saved

Function 'ob_start()' (line 11) turns on output buffering. While output buffering is active, no output is sent from the script. Instead, output is stored in an internal buffer. Line 12 saves the changes to 'stereo_add.xml'. Function 'ob_flush()' (line 16) outputs what is stored in the internal buffer. Function 'ob_clean()' (line 17) erases the output buffer. Programming flexibility is increased by being able to control the output buffering process. The contents of 'stereo_add.xml' should look like the following code.

```xml
<?xml version="1.0"?>
<root>
  <stereo id="ow191">
    <name>Joyous Sound</name>
    <preamp>Spectral</preamp>
    <amp>Linn</amp>
    <cdp>Nagra</cdp>
    <speakers type="monitor">Opera</speakers>
    <wire>Wireworld</wire>
    <wire>JPS Labs</wire>
    <wire>Shunyata</wire>
    <price>$20,000.00</price>
  </stereo>
  <stereo id="ms299">
    <name>Nirvana</name>
    <preamp>Belles</preamp>
    <amp>Belles</amp>
    <cdp>Esoteric</cdp>
    <speakers type="floor">Focal</speakers>
    <wire>Shunyata</wire>
    <price>$10,000.00</price>
  </stereo>
  <stereo id="jj101">
    <name>Heaven</name>
    <preamp>MBL</preamp>
```

```
    <amp>MBL</amp>
    <cdp>MBL</cdp>
    <speakers type="floor">MBL</speakers>
    <wire>MIT</wire>
    <wire>Nordost</wire>
    <price>$120,000.00</price>
  </stereo>
  <stereo id="dp530">
    <name>Ear Candy</name>
    <preamp>AudioPax</preamp>
    <amp>Linn</amp>
    <cdp>Linn</cdp>
    <cdp>Esoteric</cdp>
    <speakers type="floor">Energy</speakers>
    <wire>Crystal</wire>
    <wire>JPS Labs</wire>
    <wire>Wireworld</wire>
    <wire>Shunyata</wire>
    <price>$30,000.00</price>
  </stereo>
</root>
```

PHP file 'add_elements.php' adds new child elements to the first stereo system by matching the 'id' attribute' and displays results (without saving). Figure 5.30 shows the added elements to the first stereo system.

```
1  <?php
2  // File add_elements.php
3  $xml = simplexml_load_file('xml_docs/stereo.xml');
4  foreach ($xml->stereo as $stereo)
5  {
6  if($stereo['id'] == "ow191")
7  {
8  $distributor = $stereo->addChild('distributor');
9  $distributor->addChild('company','Sound Hounds');
10 $distributor->addChild('location','LA, CA');
11 $distributor->addChild('country','USA');
12 }
13 }
14 header ('Content-Type: text/xml');
15 echo $xml->asXML();
16 ?>
```

```
<stereo id="ow191">
  <name>Joyous Sound</name>
  <preamp>Spectral</preamp>
  <amp>Linn</amp>
  <cdp>Nagra</cdp>
  <speakers>Opera</speakers>
  <wire>Wireworld</wire>
  <wire>JPS Labs</wire>
  <wire>Shunyata</wire>
  <price>$20,000.00</price>
 − <distributor>
     <company>Sound Hounds</company>
     <location>LA, CA</location>
     <country>USA</country>
   </distributor>
</stereo>
```

Figure 5.30 Display Showing Added Elements to XML

Line 6 checks if 'id' is 'ow191'. If so, 'child' node 'distributor' is added to this element (line 8). Under 'distributor', elements 'company', 'location', and 'country' are added, with their respective values (lines 9–11). Results are then displayed to a browser (lines 14 and 15).

PHP file 'add_save_elements.php' adds a new 'child' node to the element with 'id' of 'ow191' and saves changes to 'stereo_add_save.xml'. Figure 5.31 shows the modified first stereo system in 'stereo_add_save.xml'.

```php
1  <?php
2  // File add_save_elements.php
3  $xml = simplexml_load_file('xml_docs/stereo.xml');
4  foreach ($xml->stereo as $stereo)
5  {
6  if($stereo['id'] == "ow191")
7  {
8  $distributor = $stereo->addChild('distributor');
9  $distributor->addChild('company','Sound Hounds');
10 $distributor->addChild('location','LA, CA');
11 $distributor->addChild('country','USA');
12 }
13 }
14 ob_start();
15 $dom = new DomDocument();
16 $dom->preserveWhiteSpace = false;
17 $dom->formatOutput = true;
18 $dom->loadXML($xml->asXML());
```

```
19  $dom->save('xml_docs/stereo_add_save.xml');
20  ob_end_clean();
21  ?>
```

```
<stereo id="ow191">
  <name>Joyous Sound</name>
  <preamp>Spectral</preamp>
  <amp>Linn</amp>
  <cdp>Nagra</cdp>
  <speakers>Opera</speakers>
  <wire>Wireworld</wire>
  <wire>JPS Labs</wire>
  <wire>Shunyata</wire>
  <price>$20,000.00</price>
  <distributor>
    <company>Sound Hounds</company>
    <location>LA, CA</location>
    <country>USA</country>
  </distributor>
</stereo>
```

Figure 5.31 Display Showing that Added Elements to XML Were Saved

I start by loading 'stereo.xml' into '$xml' as a 'SimpleXML' object. I continue by traversing each 'stereo' element (lines 4–13). If 'id' is 'ow191', I add a 'child' node 'distributor' with its own children (lines 8–11). I continue by starting a new output buffer (line 14), cleaning the output and saving it to 'stereo_add_save.xml' with 'DOMDocument' (lines 15–19), and clearing the output buffer (line 20).

XPath

XML path language (XPath) is a W3C standard for identifying elements and attributes in an XML document. XPath uses relative paths dependent on the current context, so if the path is already inside a node you can refer to its child node without starting from the root element. XPath can be implemented in PHP on 'SimpleXML' objects to run XPath queries on XML data.

XPath Basic Symbols

A leading forward slash '/' indicates the root element and subsequent forward slashes indicate the path from parent to child. A single period '.' represents the current node. Two periods '..' represent the parent node. An asterisk '*' represents any element. Two forward slashes '//' selects all descendants of the current node as well as the current node itself. To identify an attribute, prefix its name with '@'.

PHP file 'xpath_names.php' extracts and displays all stereo system names from 'stereo.xml'. This is accomplished by using '//name' to select all descendants. Figure 5.32 shows the name of each stereo system.

```
1  <?php
2  // File xpath_names.php
3  $xml = simplexml_load_file('xml_docs/stereo.xml');
4  $names = $xml->xpath('//name');
5  echo '<ul>';
6  foreach($names as $name)
7  { echo "<li>$name</li>"; }
8  echo '</ul>';
9  ?>
```

- Joyous Sound
- Nirvana
- Heaven
- Ear Candy

Figure 5.32 Display Showing All 'name' Elements from XML with XPath

Line 4 extracts 'name' elements. The 'foreach' loop (lines 6 and 7) traverses the names and displays each 'name' value (line 7).

PHP file 'xpath_attributes.php' extracts and displays all 'id' attributes from 'stereo.xml'. This is accomplished by using '//@id' to select all descendant attributes. Figure 5.33 shows the results.

```
1  <?php
2  // File xpath_attributes.php
3  $xml = simplexml_load_file('xml_docs/stereo.xml');
4  $ids = $xml->xpath('//@id');
5  echo '<ul>';
6  foreach($ids as $id)
7  { echo "<li>$id</li>"; }
8  echo '</ul>';
9  ?>
```

- ow191
- ms299
- jj101
- dp530

Figure 5.33 Display Showing All 'id' Attributes from XML with XPath

Line 4 extracts 'id' attributes. The 'foreach' loop (lines 6 and 7) traverses the 'id' attributes and displays each value (line 7).

PHP file 'xpath_finer.php' demonstrates how to move through the hierarchy path of the XML document.

```
 1  <?php
 2  // File xpath_finer.php
 3  $xml = simplexml_load_file('xml_docs/stereo.xml');
 4  $linns = $xml->xpath('//amp[.="Linn"]');
 5  echo '<ul>';
 6  foreach($linns as $linn)
 7  {
 8  $name = $linn->xpath('../name');
 9  $preamp = $linn->xpath('../preamp');
10  $amp = $linn->xpath('../amp');
11  $cdp = $linn->xpath('../cdp');
12  $speakers = $linn->xpath('../speakers');
13  $wire = $linn->xpath('../wire');
14  $price = $linn->xpath('../price');
15  echo "System: " . $name[0] . '<br />';
16  echo "Preamp: " . $preamp[0] . '<br />';
17  echo "Amp: " . $amp[0] . '<br />';
18  echo "CD Player: ";
19  foreach($cdp as $cd)
20  { echo $cd . ' '; }
21  echo "<br />Speakers: " . $speakers[0] . '<br />';
22  echo "Wire: ";
23  foreach($wire as $w)
24  { echo $w . ' '; }
25  echo "<br />Price: " . $price[0] . '<br />';
26  echo '<p>';
27  }
28  ?>
```

Before I explain the code, let's review. A single period '.' indicates the current node. To access elements within the selected nodes, use '../*elementname*'. A double period '..' indicates the parent node.

So, I use '//amp[.="Linn"]' (line 4) to select 'amp' nodes with the value of 'Linn'. I use the 'outer' 'foreach' loop (lines 6–27) to traverses all nodes with 'Linn' amps. I use '../name' to access the 'name' element for each of these amps (line 8). Lines 9–14 use the same logic to access 'preamp', 'amp', 'cdp', 'speakers', 'wire', and 'price' elements. I display 'name', 'preamp', and 'amp' (lines 15–17). A double period must be used to access these elements because the outer loop is at the '<amp>' node level. Since a stereo system can have more than one 'cdp' and 'wire', I use 'foreach' loops (lines 19 and 20 for 'cdp' and lines 23 and 24 for 'wire') to display them. Figure 5.34 shows the results.

```
System: Joyous Sound
Preamp: Spectral
Amp: Linn
CD Player: Nagra
Speakers: Opera
Wire: Wireworld JPS Labs Shunyata
Price: $20,000.00

System: Ear Candy
Preamp: AudioPax
Amp: Linn
CD Player: Linn Esoteric
Speakers: Energy
Wire: Crystal JPS Labs Wireworld Shunyata
Price: $30,000.00
```

Figure 5.34 Display Showing Data Using XPath

PHP file 'xpath_implode.php' extracts and displays all stereo elements and attributes. Since '<stereo>' nodes can have more than one 'cdp' and 'wire' element, a way must be found to deal with this circumstance. In the previous example, 'foreach' loops were used. The 'implode()' function is used as a viable alternative to nested loops because it returns a string from the elements of an array. Remember that the XML document is converted to a 'SimpleXML' object that stores XML data in arrays. The function accepts a 'separator' parameter that specifies what to put between the array elements. A comma is used as the 'separator' parameter. Figure 5.35 shows the results.

```php
1  <?php
2  // File xpath_implode.php
3  $font = '<b style=color:red>';
4  $end = '</b>';
5  $xml = simplexml_load_file('xml_docs/stereo.xml');
6  $stereos = $xml->xpath('stereo');
7  echo "<ul>";
8  foreach ($stereos as $stereo)
9  {
10 $id = $stereo->xpath('./@id');
11 $name = $stereo->xpath('./name');
12 $preamp = $stereo->xpath('./preamp');
13 $amp = $stereo->xpath('./amp');
14 $cdp = $stereo->xpath('./cdp');
15 $speakers = $stereo->xpath('./speakers');
16 $wire = $stereo->xpath('./wire');
17 $price = $stereo->xpath('./price');
18 echo '<li>' . $name [0] . ' ';
19 echo '<b style=color:red>'. $id[0] . '</b></li>';
20 echo implode (', ', $cdp) . "<br />";
21 echo implode (', ', $wire) . "<br /><br />";
22 }
23 echo "</ul>";
24 ?>
```

- Joyous Sound ow191
  Nagra
  Wireworld, JPS Labs, Shunyata

- Nirvana ms299
  Esoteric
  Shunyata

- Heaven jj101
  MBL
  MIT, Nordost

- Ear Candy dp530
  Linn, Esoteric
  Crystal, JPS Labs, Wireworld, Shunyata

Figure 5.35 Display Showing Data with XPath and Implode

I use a CSS style attribute (line 3) to color code the 'id' attributes displayed. I use 'XPath' to load all stereo system nodes into '$stereos' (line 6). The 'foreach' loop (lines 8–22) traverses the 'stereo' nodes. Line 10 loads the 'id' attribute into '$id'. Lines 11–17 load the 'name', 'preamp', 'amp', 'cdp', 'speakers', 'wire', and 'price' element values into their respective variables. Lines 20 and 21 use 'implode()' to extract and display 'cdp' and 'wire' elements easily and elegantly.

Summary

The goal of this chapter was to gain skills in efficiently creating, modifying, saving, and working with XML documents. I used explanations and examples to help you gain the commensurate skills.

6 Standard PHP Library and the Iterator Interface

Overview

Two topics are covered in this chapter – the Standard PHP Library and the Iterator interface. The Standard PHP Library (SPL) is a collection of interfaces and classes that provides efficient data access through sophisticated types of looping for aggregate structures such as arrays, database result sets, XML trees, and directory listings. SPL is based on the Iterator interface, which is an effective mechanism for traversing the elements of an aggregate structure.

Learning Objectives

After completing this chapter, you will gain skills in two areas. First, I will show you how to use selected SPL classes to efficiently iterate over an aggregate structure. Second, I will show you how to use the Iterator interface to better understand the looping process and gain more control over aggregate structure iteration. Skills are enhanced through explanation and code examples. The following objectives summarize the skills the chapter will help you develop:

1 Learn the definition and characteristics of SPL.
2 Learn the definition and characteristics of the Iterator interface.
3 Learn the five methods that the Iterator interface is based upon.
4 Learn how to use selected SPL classes to iterate aggregate structures.
5 Learn how to use the Iterator interface with an array.
6 Learn how to use the Iterator interface with XML.
7 Learn how to use the Iterator interface with a database.
8 Learn the definition and characteristics of the 'IteratorAggregate' interface.
9 Learn how to use the 'IteratorAggregate' interface.

Definition and Characteristics of SPL

The ***Standard PHP Library*** (SPL) is a collection of interfaces and classes that provides efficient data access through sophisticated types of looping for aggregate structures. An ***aggregate structure*** is anything you want to loop over. Arrays, database result sets, XML trees, and directory listings are examples of aggregate structures because they hold elements that can be iterated over.

SPL implements the iterator design pattern. The ***iterator design pattern*** is an OOP design technique used to iterate over an aggregate structure and access its elements sequentially without exposing its underlying presentation.

The idea is to take the responsibility for access and traversal out of the aggregate structure and place it into an iterator object that defines a standard traversal protocol. A ***traversal protocol*** is a set of rules that explains the procedures for iterating an aggregate structure. So, I can place an aggregate structure into an iterator object, and let the iterator object take care of access and traversal of elements in a standard manner. This way, the internal structure is invisible to the outside world. For instance, if I place a database result set into an iterator object, I can manipulate the elements easily without even knowing the internal structure of the database result set! All of the traversal logic is handled by the iterator object.

Definition and Characteristics of the Iterator Interface

The Iterator interface is logically and functionally based on the iterator design pattern. The ***Iterator interface*** is a built-in interface that provides the necessary methods to efficiently interact with an iterator. An ***iterator*** is an object that provides a means to traverse an aggregate structure. All iterators (including SPL) implement the Iterator interface.

PHP provides two interfaces that allow a programmer to define how objects behave in a 'foreach' loop – 'Iterator' and 'IteratorAggregate'. The Iterator interface is discussed in this section. The IteratorAggregate interface is discussed at the end of the chapter.

PHP natively allows a programmer to iterate over objects with a 'foreach' loop. However, this process only works with public properties of an object. As such, public properties of the object are the only values that can normally be accessed through 'foreach' loop iteration.

Since encapsulation theory advocates using private or protected properties with getters and setters, the properties of the object cannot normally be accessed. The Iterator interface (and 'IteratorAggregate') provide a solution because they allow the programmer to define the logic that governs the values to return when an object is iterated over.

Before SPL interfaces and classes can be used with a 'foreach' loop, the aggregate structure must be placed into an iterator object. Once it is placed into an iterator object, not only can it be easily traversed with a 'foreach' loop; it also has the flexibility of any OOP object, such as inheritance, aggregation, encapsulation, polymorphism, and reflection. This type of flexibility is what OOP is all about!

Five Iterator Interface Methods

The Iterator interface requires the programmer to implement five methods – current, key, next, rewind, and valid. The 'current()' method returns the current value in the iteration. The 'key()' method returns the key value for the current value. The 'next()' method advances the iterator forward one step. The 'rewind()' method resets the pointer that is being used for the iteration. The 'valid()' method returns a Boolean value that indicates if the value exists in the current position of the iteration.

Selected SPL Classes

Although SPL functionality is based on the Iterator interface, the complexities involved are transparent to the programmer. This is because Iterator interface logic is internal to SPL classes and interfaces. As such, SPL is easy to program because the five Iterator interface methods do not have to be programmatically implemented.

The first SPL class I demonstrate is 'LimitIterator', which determines where to start iteration and how many times the loop should run. The first parameter of 'LimitIterator' is an object. The second parameter is the starting position (the first element starts at position zero). The third parameter indicates how many elements to include.

PHP file 'limit.php' implements 'LimitIterator'. The program begins by placing an array into an 'ArrayIterator' object that is itself wrapped in a 'LimitIterator' object limited to two values. The values of the limited object are then displayed.

```
1  <?php
2  // File limit.php
3  $numbers = array(5,10,8,35,50);
4  $iterator = new ArrayIterator($numbers);
5  $limiter = new LimitIterator($iterator,0,2);
6  foreach($limiter as $number)
7  { echo $number . '<br />'; }
8  ?>
```

Specifically, I assign the array to '$numbers', which consists of five numeric elements (line 3). I then place the array into an iterator object with 'ArrayIterator' and assign it to '$iterator' (line 4). I then wrap '$iterator' in a 'LimitIterator' object and assign it to '$limiter' (line 5), which holds the first two elements of the original array. I use 'foreach' (lines 6 and 7) to iterate the object in '$limiter' and display the elements in a browser, as shown in Figure 6.1.

```
5
10
```

Figure 6.1 Output Using 'ArrayIterator' and 'LimitIterator' SPL Classes

I can use the 'SimpleXMLElement' class to place an XML document into an iterator object, but it must be wrapped in an SPL iterator. This is because the 'SimpleXMLElement' class does not natively implement the Iterator interface.

An elegant way of creating a 'SimpleXMLIterator' object is to use it as the second parameter in the 'simple_load_file()' method. The next couple of examples use the following XML document, 'fish.xml' (all XML documents are available on the companion website):

```xml
<?xml version="1.0"?>
<aquarium>
<fish id='9'>
<name>angel fish</name>
<water>fresh</water>
<price>25</price>
</fish>
<fish id='16'>
<name>discus</name>
<water>fresh</water>
<price>18</price>
</fish>
<fish id='76'>
<name>neon tetra</name>
<water>fresh</water>
<price>12</price>
</fish>
<fish id='101'>
<name>tessalata eel</name>
```

```
<water>salt</water>
<price>75</price>
</fish>
<fish id='113'>
<name>clown fish</name>
<water>salt</water>
<price>25</price>
</fish>
<fish id='191'>
<name>antennata lion fish</name>
<water>salt</water>
<price>87</price>
</fish>
<fish id='39'>
<name>dinosaur bichir</name>
<water>fresh</water>
<price>110</price>
</fish>
</aquarium>
```

PHP file 'fish.php' uses the 'SimpleXMLIterator' class to place 'fish.xml' into an iterator object, wraps the object in a 'LimitIterator' object, and displays the names.

```
1  <?php
2  // File fish.php
3  $xml = simplexml_load_file('xml_docs/fish.xml',
4  'SimpleXMLIterator');
5  $limiter = new LimitIterator($xml,2,3);
6  foreach ($limiter as $fish)
7  { echo $fish->name . '<br />'; }
8  ?>
```

Assuming that 'fish.xml' is in the 'xml_docs' directory, I place the XML document into an iterator object by adding 'SimpleXMLIterator' as the second parameter in the 'simplexml_load_file()' method and assigning the object to '$xml' (lines 3 and 4). I then wrap '$xml' in a 'LimitIterator' object and assign it to '$limiter' (line 5). The 'foreach' loop (lines 6 and 7) iterates '$limiter' and displays the names of fish starting at the third element and continuing for three elements. So, the third, fourth, and fifth fish are displayed. Figure 6.2 shows the results.

```
neon tetra
tessalata eel
clown fish
```

Figure 6.2 Output Using 'SimpleXMLIterator' Wrapper and 'LimitIterator' Class

PHP file 'pcre.php' applies PCRE to an iterator to refine results with regular expressions. The SPL 'RegexIterator' class allows the programmer to use PCRE.

```
 1  <?php
 2  // File pcre.php
 3  $xml = simplexml_load_file('xml_docs/fish.xml',
 4  'SimpleXMLIterator');
 5  foreach($xml as $fish)
 6  {
 7  $match = new RegexIterator($fish->water,'#fresh#');
 8  foreach($match as $fresh)
 9  {
10  echo $fish->name . ' ' . $fresh;
11  echo ' $' . $fish->price . '.00<br />';
12  }
13  }
14  ?>
```

I start by placing 'fish.xml' into an iterator object (lines 3 and 4). I then traverse the object with a 'foreach' loop (lines 5–13). Inside the loop, I wrap all '<fish>' elements that live in fresh water into a 'RegexIterator' object and assign to '$match' (line 7). Specifically, the 'RegexIterator' object checks if there is a match for string 'fresh' in the '<water>' element of each '<fish>' node. The inner 'foreach' loop (lines 8–12) traverses '$match' elements and displays results. Figure 6.3 shows the results.

```
angel fish fresh $25.00
discus fresh $18.00
neon tetra fresh $12.00
dinosaur bichir fresh $110.00
```

Figure 6.3 Output Using 'SimpleXMLIterator' and 'RegexIterator' SPL Class

The next example uses the SPL 'AppendIterator' class to append two iterator objects together and loop through them sequentially in one operation. To illustrate, I use another XML document, 'more_fish.xml'.

```
<?xml version="1.0"?>
<aquarium>
<fish id='177'>
<name>cardinal fish</name>
<water>salt</water>
<price>27</price>
</fish>
<fish id='143'>
<name>orbiculate batfish</name>
<water>salt</water>
<price>32</price>
</fish>
<fish id='33'>
<name>bicolor goatfish</name>
<water>fresh</water>
```

```
<price>19</price>
</fish>
<fish id='172'>
<name>blue tang</name>
<water>salt</water>
<price>29</price>
</fish>
</aquarium>
```

PHP file 'append.php' appends two XML documents.

```
 1  <?php
 2  // File append.php
 3  $fish = simplexml_load_file('xml_docs/fish.xml',
 4  'SimpleXMLIterator');
 5  $moreFish = simplexml_load_file('xml_docs/more_fish.xml',
 6  'SimpleXMLIterator');
 7  $combined = new AppendIterator();
 8  $combined->append($fish);
 9  $combined->append($moreFish);
10  echo '<ol>';
11  foreach($combined as $fish)
12  {
13  echo '<li>' . $fish->name . ' ($' . $fish->price . ')';
14  echo ' &lt;' . $fish->water . '&gt;</li>'; }
15  echo '</ol>';
16  ?>
```

Assuming that 'fish.xml' and 'more_fish.xml' are in the 'xml_docs' directory, I place 'fish.xml' into an iterator object as '$fish' (lines 3 and 4) and 'more_fish.xml' into an iterator object as '$moreFish' (lines 5 and 6). I then create a new instance of 'AppendIterator' as '$combined' (line 7). I continue by appending '$fish' and '$moreFish' into '$combined' with method 'append()' (line 8 and 9). I finish by iterating '$combined' with a 'foreach' loop (lines 11–14) and displaying name, price, and water of each element (lines 13 and 14). Figure 6.4 shows the results.

```
 1.  angel fish ($25) <fresh>
 2.  discus ($18) <fresh>
 3.  neon tetra ($12) <fresh>
 4.  tessalata eel ($75) <salt>
 5.  clown fish ($25) <salt>
 6.  antennata lion fish ($87) <salt>
 7.  dinosaur bichir ($110) <fresh>
 8.  cardinal fish ($27) <salt>
 9.  orbiculate batfish ($32) <salt>
10.  bicolor goatfish ($19) <fresh>
11.  blue tang ($29) <salt>
```

Figure 6.4 Output Using 'SimpleXMLIterator' and 'AppendIterator' SPL Class

For large documents, 'LimitIterator' and 'AppendIterator' classes can be used to splice portions of data from multiple documents effectively, limiting what is displayed. PHP file 'splice.php' splices limited data from two XML documents and displays results.

```php
1  <?php
2  // File splice.php
3  $fish = simplexml_load_file('xml_docs/fish.xml',
4  'SimpleXMLIterator');
5  $moreFish = simplexml_load_file('xml_docs/more_fish.xml',
6  'SimpleXMLIterator');
7  $limit1 = new LimitIterator($fish,0,3);
8  $limit2 = new LimitIterator($moreFish,0,3);
9  $combined = new AppendIterator();
10 $combined->append($limit1);
11 $combined->append($limit2);
12 echo '<ol>';
13 foreach($combined as $fish)
14 {
15 echo '<li>' . $fish->name . ' ($' . $fish->price . ')';
16 echo ' &lt;' . $fish->water . '&gt;</li>'; }
17 echo '</ol>';
18 ?>
```

I place 'fish.xml' into an iterator object as '$fish' (lines 3 and 4) and 'more_fish.xml' into an iterator object as '$moreFish' (lines 5 and 6). I then create new instances of 'LimitIterator' as '$limit1' and '$limit2' to limit '$fish' and '$moreFish' to three elements each (lines 7 and 8). I continue by appending '$limit1' and '$limit2' with 'AppendIterator' and its 'append()' method as '$combined' (lines 9–11). I finish by iterating '$combined' with a 'foreach' loop (line 13–16) and displaying name, price, and water of each element (lines 15 and 16). Figure 6.5 shows the results.

```
1. angel fish ($25) <fresh>
2. discus ($18) <fresh>
3. neon tetra ($12) <fresh>
4. cardinal fish ($27) <salt>
5. orbiculate batfish ($32) <salt>
6. bicolor goatfish ($19) <fresh>
```

Figure 6.5 Output Using 'SimpleXMLIterator' and Various SPL Classes

The 'CachingIterator' class allows caching of multiple child elements from a parent element. A ***cache*** holds copies of recently accessed data and is designed to speed up processing by prioritizing for quick access. The next example uses this class and XML document 'composer.xml'.

```xml
<?xml version="1.0" encoding="ISO-8859-1"?>
<catalog>
```

```
<category>
Small chamber ensembles - 2-4 Players by New York Women Composers
</category>
<composer id="c1">
<name>Julie Mandel</name>
<composition>
<title>Trio for Flute, Viola and Harp</title>
<date><year>1994</year></date>
</composition>
<composition>
<title>Invention for Flute and Piano</title>
<date><year>1994</year></date>
</composition>
</composer>
<composer id="c2">
<name>Margaret De Wys</name>
<composition>
<title>Charmonium</title>
<date><year>1991</year></date>
</composition>
</composer>
<composer id="c3">
<name>Beth Anderson</name>
<composition>
<title>Little Trio</title>
<date><year>1984</year></date>
</composition>
<composition>
<title>Dr. Blood's Mermaid Lullaby</title>
<date><year>1980</year></date>
</composition>
<composition>
<title>Trio: Dream in D</title>
<date><year>1980</year></date>
</composition>
</composer>
<composer id="c4">
<name>Linda Bouchard</name>
<composition>
<title>Propos II</title>
<date><year>1985</year></date>
</composition>
<composition>
<title>Rictus En Miroir</title>
<date><year>1985</year></date>
</composition>
</composer>
</catalog>
```

PHP file 'composer.php' uses the 'CachingIterator' class to cache compositions for each composer.

```php
1  <?php
2  // File composer.php
3  $xml = simplexml_load_file('xml_docs/composer.xml',
4  'SimpleXMLIterator');
5  echo '<strong>' . $xml->category . '</strong><br />';
6  echo '<ol>';
7  foreach($xml->composer as $composer)
8  {
9  echo '<li>' . $composer->name . ' => ';
10 $compositions =
11 new CachingIterator($composer->composition);
12 echo '<ul>';
13 foreach($compositions as $comp)
14 {
15 echo '<li>';
16 echo $comp->title . '(' . $comp->date->year . ')';
17 echo '</li>';
18 }
19 echo '</ul></li>';
20 }
21 echo '</ol>';
22 ?>
```

Assuming 'composer.xml' is saved in 'xml_docs', I place 'composer.xml' into an iterator object as '$xml' (lines 3 and 4). With the first (outer) 'foreach' loop, I traverse each composer and display composer info (lines 7–20). I use the 'CachingIterator' class to create object '$compositions' that holds compositions for each composer (lines 10 and 11). I use the inner 'foreach' loop to traverse each composition by composer and display title and date (lines 13–18). Figure 6.6 shows the results.

Figure 6.6 Output Using 'SimpleXMLIterator' and 'CachingIterator' Class

The Iterator Interface with Arrays

To this point in the chapter, I have demonstrated *implicit* implementation of the Iterator interface (with SPL). ***Implicit*** implementation means that the details of the Iterator interface are transparent to the programmer. That is, the programmer does not have to know anything about how the Iterator interface is implemented.

Now, I will demonstrate *explicit* implementation of the Iterator interface. **Explicit** implementation means that the programmer has to know the details of the Iterator interface. That is, the programmer must explicitly use the methods of the Iterator interface to process the aggregate structure. PHP file 'explicit_array.php' creates an array and uses explicit iteration.

```php
1  <?php
2  // File explicit_array.php
3  $dude = array('name' => 'David', 'city' => 'London',
4  'country' => 'United Kingdom');
5  $iterator = new ArrayIterator($dude);
6  $iterator->rewind();
7  while($iterator->valid())
8  {
9  echo $iterator->key() . ': ' . $iterator->current() .
10 '<br />';
11 $iterator->next();
12 }
13 $iterator->rewind();
14 echo '<br />' . $iterator->key() . ': ' .
15 $iterator->current();
16 ?>
```

I begin by placing array '$dude' (lines 3 and 4) into an 'ArrayIterator' object as '$iterator' (line 5). I continue by explicitly setting the object to its first element with the 'rewind()' method (line 6). I then iterate the object as long as there are elements with the 'valid()' method (line 7). Next, I display key and current values with 'key()' and 'current()' methods respectively (line 9). I use the 'next()' method to move to the next element (line 11). After iteration, I reset the object to its first element again (line 13) and display the key and current values (lines 14 and 15). Figure 6.7 shows the results.

```
name: David
city: London
country: United Kingdom

name: David
```

Figure 6.7 Output Using Explicit Array Iteration Methods

Even more control over iteration can be gained by creating a custom Iterator interface class. PHP file 'array_interface.php' contains a custom array Iterator interface class. It is purposefully created to work with any array.

```php
1  <?php
2  // File array_interface.php
3  class array_interface implements Iterator
4  {
```

```
 5  private $var = array();
 6  public function __construct($array)
 7  {
 8  if (is_array($array))
 9  { $this->var = $array; }
10  }
11  public function rewind()
12  {
13  echo "rewinding data ... <p />";
14  reset($this->var);
15  }
16  public function current()
17  {
18  $var = current($this->var);
19  return $var;
20  }
21  public function key()
22  {
23  $var = key($this->var);
24  return $var;
25  }
26  public function next()
27  {
28  $var = next($this->var);
29  if($var) { echo " (next: $var)<br />"; }
30  return $var;
31  }
32  public function valid()
33  {
34  $var = $this->current() !== false;
35  return $var;
36  }
37  }
38  ?>
```

The 'array_interface' class (lines 3–37) implements the Iterator interface and includes all five methods – rewind, current, key, next, and valid. The constructor accepts an array (line 6), checks to see if it is actually an array (line 8), and, if so, assigns it to the '$var' property as '$this->var' (line 9). Since the class implements the Iterator interface, the array is automatically placed into an iterator object.

The 'rewind()' method (lines 11–15) displays 'rewinding ...' when invoked (line 13) and resets the array (line 14). The 'current()' method (lines 16–20) returns the current element when invoked (lines 18 and 19). The 'key()' method (lines 21–25) returns the key when invoked (lines 23 and 24). The 'next()' method (lines 26–31) moves the pointer of the iterator object to its next element (line 28), displays the value if available (line 29), and returns the value (line 30) when invoked. The 'valid()' method (lines 32–36) checks to see if the current element exists (line 34) and returns it (line 35).

With explicit implementation, the programmer can control what happens in each method of the Iterator interface. PHP file 'invoke_array_interface.php' instantiates a new instance of the 'array_interface' class.

```php
1  <?php
2  // File invoke_array_interface.php
3  require_once 'array_interface.php';
4  $values = array("horse","dog","cat");
5  $it = new array_interface($values);
6  $it->rewind();
7  while($it->valid())
8  {
9  echo $it->key() . '=> ' . $it->current();
10 $it->next() . '<br />';
11 }
12 echo '<p>';
13 foreach ($it as $a => $b)
14 {
15 echo $a . ' => ' . $b;
16 }
17 ?>
```

I begin by assigning an array to '$values' (line 4). I continue by creating a new instance of 'array_interface' as '$it' (line 5). Next, I rewind object '$it' (line 6). With a 'while' loop (lines 7–11), I traverse '$it'. I first check if there are any elements left to traverse (line 7) and continue by displaying the key, current, and next values with the object's methods (lines 9 and 10). Finally, I traverse '$it' with a 'foreach' loop (lines 13–16). The 'foreach' loop is very convenient because it automatically (implicitly) rewinds and then iterates the object. Figure 6.8 shows the results.

```
rewinding data ...

0=> horse (next: dog)
1=> dog (next: cat)
2=> cat

rewinding data ...

0 => horse (next: dog)
1 => dog (next: cat)
2 => cat
```

Figure 6.8 Output Using a Custom Iterator Interface Class for Arrays

Let's review. Whether implementing '$it' explicitly ('while' loop) or implicitly ('foreach' loop), the text 'rewinding data …' is displayed first because 'rewind()' is the first method invoked (lines 6 and 13). The 'valid()' method is then invoked to check if the current element exists (lines 7 and 13). Since the current element exists, the key and element are then displayed by the 'echo' statements in the 'while' (lines 9 and 10) and 'foreach' loops (line 15), respectively. The 'next()' method is then invoked to move to the next element (dog) (lines 10 and 13). The 'valid()' method is again invoked to check if the current element exists (lines 7 and 13). Since it does, the key and element are again displayed (lines 9 and 10 and line 15). The 'next()' method is then invoked to move to the next element (cat) (lines 10 and 13). The 'valid()' method is again invoked to check if the current element exists (lines 7 and 13). Since it does, the key and element are again displayed (lines 9 and 10 and line 15). The 'next()' method is then invoked to move to the next element (lines 10 and 13). Since it does not exist, 'next' is FALSE. When the 'valid()' method is invoked (lines 7 and 13), the current element does not exist and the loops terminate.

Line 13 is referenced over and over because 'foreach' loops implicitly invoke all of the Iterator interface methods. So, explicit implementation offers added flexibility, but is much more complex. In contrast, implicit implementation is very simple but allows no flexibility to the programmer. Most of the time, implicit implementation is fine but it doesn't hurt to know how to explicitly use the Iterator interface.

The Iterator Interface with XML

Explicit iteration can also be used to traverse an XML document. The next example uses 'projects.xml'.

```
<?xml version = "1.0" encoding="UTF-8" standalone="yes"?>
<document>
<employee badge='1'>
<name>Grace Kelly</name>
<hiredate>October 15, 2005</hiredate>
<projects>
<project>
<product id='111'>Printer</product>
<price>$111.00</price>
</project>
<project>
<product id='222'>Laptop</product>
<price>$989.00</price>
</project>
</projects>
</employee>
<employee badge='2'>
<name>Grant Cary</name>
<hiredate>October 20, 2005</hiredate>
<projects>
<project>
<product id='333'>Desktop</product>
<price>$2995.00</price>
</project>
<project>
<product id='444'>Scanner</product>
<price>$200.00</price>
</project>
</projects>
</employee>
<employee badge='3'>
<name>Clark Gable</name>
<hiredate>October 25, 2005</hiredate>
<projects>
<project>
<product id='555'>Keyboard</product>
<price>$129.00</price>
```

```
</project>
<project>
<product id='666'>Mouse</product>
<price>$25.00</price>
</project>
</projects>
</employee>
</document>
```

PHP file 'explicit_xml.php' demonstrates explicit traversal of XML.

```php
1  <?php
2  // File explicit_xml.php
3  $xml = simplexml_load_file('xml_docs/projects.xml',
4  'SimpleXMLIterator');
5  $xml->rewind();
6  while($xml->valid())
7  {
8  echo $xml->current()['badge'] . ' ';
9  echo $xml->current()->name;
10 foreach($xml->current()->projects->project
11 as $project)
12 { echo ' ' . $project->product['id'] . ' ' .
13 $project->product; }
14 echo '<br />';
15 $xml->next();
16 }
17 ?>
```

Assuming 'projects.xml' is in 'xml_docs', I place the XML document in an iterator object as '$xml' (lines 3 and 4). I rewind the object (line 5). Next, I use a 'while' loop (lines 6–16) to traverse the object. Line 6 checks if there are any elements left to traverse. Lines 8 and 9 display the 'badge' and 'name' respectively. Since 'projects' can have multiple elements, I use a 'foreach' loop (lines 10–13) to display the 'id' (line 12) and 'product' (line 13) values. I move to the next element with 'next()' (line 15). Load 'explicit_xml.php' in a browser. Figure 6.9 shows the results.

```
1 Grace Kelly 111 Printer 222 Laptop
2 Grant Cary 333 Desktop 444 Scanner
3 Clark Gable 555 Keyboard 666 Mouse
```

Figure 6.9 Output Using 'SimpleXMLIterator' and XML Iteration Methods

Even more control over iteration can be gained by creating a custom Iterator interface class. PHP file 'xml_interface.php' contains a custom XML Iterator interface class. It is purposefully created to work with any XML document.

```php
1  <?php
2  // File xml_interface.php
3  class xml_interface implements Iterator
4  {
5  private $_xml;
6  private $_position;
7  public function __construct($xml)
8  {
9  $this->_xml = $xml;
10  $this->_position = 0;
11  }
12  public function rewind()
13  { $this->_position = 0; }
14  public function current()
15  {
16  $var = $this->_xml->children()[$this->_position];
17  return $var;
18  }
19  public function key()
20  { $var = $this->_position;
21  return $var; }
22  public function next()
23  { $var = ++$this->_position;
24  return $var; }
25  public function valid()
26  {
27  $count = $this->_xml->count();
28  if($this->_position < $count)
29  { $var = TRUE; }
30  else
31  { $var = FALSE; }
32  return $var;
33  }
34  }
35  ?>
```

The 'xml_interface' class implements the Iterator interface. It includes all five methods – rewind, current, key, next, and valid.

The constructor (lines 7–11) accepts a 'SimpleXML' object (line 7). It then sets '$this->_xml' to the iterator object (line 9). It finishes by setting property '$this->_position' to zero (line 10), which is the 'key' value because it points to the current element in the iterator object.

The 'rewind()' method (lines 12 and 13) accepts no parameters. It sets the 'key' value (pointer) to zero (line 13).

The 'current()' method (lines 14–18) accepts no parameters. It uses 'SimpleXML' method 'children()' (line 16) to grab the child element at a given 'key' value and returns this value when invoked (line 17).

The 'key()' method (lines 19–21) accepts no parameters. It assigns the 'key' value to '$var' (line 20) and returns it when invoked (line 21).

202 SPL and the Iterator Interface

The 'next()' method (lines 22–24) increments the 'key' value of the iterator object to its next element (line 23) and returns it when invoked (line 24).

The 'valid()' method (lines 25–33) checks if the current element exists. Specifically, 'SimpleXML' method 'count()' (line 27) returns the number of elements and is compared against the 'key' value (line 28) to determine if the iterator object exists (valid) or does not exist (invalid). The iterator object exists if the 'key' is pointing to an element. When the 'key' points to nothing, it means that iteration of the object is finished (no elements left to traverse). It sets '$var' to 'TRUE' if valid (line 29) or 'FALSE' if invalid (line 31).

Although creating a custom Iterator interface is not trivial, it gives the programmer complete control over what happens when iterating an object. You may not use this often, but it is a very powerful tool to have in your programming arsenal.

PHP file 'invoke_xml_interface.php' instantiates a new instance of the 'xml_interface' class.

```php
1  <?php
2  // File invoke_xml_interface.php
3  require_once 'xml_interface.php';
4  $xml = simplexml_load_file('xml_docs/projects.xml');
5  $obj = new xml_interface($xml);
6  foreach($obj as $value)
7  {
8  echo '<strong>' . $value->name . ' ::: </strong>';
9  foreach($value->projects->project as $datum)
10 {
11 echo '*' . $datum->product['id'] . '* ';
12 echo $datum->product . ' ';
13 echo $datum->price . ' ';
14 }
15 echo '<br />';
16 }
17 ?>
```

I begin by placing 'projects.xml' into a 'SimpleXML' object (line 4). I continue by creating a new instance of the 'xml_interface' class with the 'SimpleXML' object as parameter (line 5). I use an outer 'foreach' loop (lines 6–16) to display info of each employee. I use the inner 'foreach' loop (lines 9–14) to display information about each project associated with an employee. The inner 'foreach' loop is needed because each employee can be associated with more than one project. Load 'invoke_xml_interface.php' in a browser. Figure 6.10 shows the results.

Grace Kelly ::: *111* Printer $111.00 *222* Laptop $989.00
Grant Cary ::: *333* Desktop $2995.00 *444* Scanner $200.00
Clark Gable ::: *555* Keyboard $129.00 *666* Mouse $25.00

Figure 6.10 Output Using a Custom Iterator Interface Class for XML

An alternative to the 'xml_interface' class is to use the document object model (DOM). DOM is even more flexible, but is more complex to implement. PHP file 'xml_interface_dom.php' contains the custom XML Iterator interface class using DOM. It is purposefully created to work with any XML document.

```php
1  <?php
2  // File xml_interface_dom.php
3  class xml_interface_dom implements Iterator
4  {
5  private $_xml;
6  private $_nodeVals;
7  private $_position;
8  public function __construct($xml)
9  {
10  $this->_xml = $xml;
11  $this->_position = 0;
12  $doc = new DOMDocument();
13  $doc->load($xml);
14  $items = $doc->getElementsByTagName('*');
15  $this->_nodeVals =
16  $doc->getElementsByTagName($items->item(1)->nodeName);
17  }
18  public function rewind()
19  { $this->_position = 0; }
20  public function current()
21  {
22  $var = $this->_nodeVals->item($this->_position);
23  return $var;
24  }
25  public function key()
26  {
27  $var = $this->_position;
28  return $var;
29  }
30  public function next()
31  {
32  $var = ++$this->_position;
33  return $var;
34  }
35  public function valid()
36  {
37  $count = $this->_nodeVals->length;
38  if($this->_position < $count)
39  { $var = TRUE; }
40  else
41  { $var = FALSE; }
42  return $var;
43  }
44  }
45  ?>
```

The 'xml_interface_dom' class implements the Iterator interface. It includes all five methods – rewind, current, key, next, and valid.

The constructor (lines 8–17) accepts an XML document (line 8), sets the document to '$this->_xml' (line 10), sets the 'key' to '$this->_position' (line 11), creates a new 'DOMDocument' object in '$doc' (line12), loads the XML document into DOM (line 13), sets '$items' to hold all XML elements (line 14), and sets '$this->_nodeVals' to hold a value from a given XML element (lines 15 and 16).

The 'rewind()' method (lines 18 and 19) accepts no parameters. It sets the 'key' to zero (line 19).

The 'current()' method (lines 20–24) returns the current element when invoked. The 'item()' method (line 22) grabs the element value at a given 'key' value. Then, the method returns this 'key' value (line 23).

The 'key()' method (lines 25–29) returns the key when invoked. The 'key' value is assigned to '$var' (line 27) and then returned (line 28).

The 'next()' method (lines 30–33) moves the 'key' value to the next element when invoked. It increments the 'key' (line 32) and returns it (line 33).

The 'valid()' method (lines 35–43) checks if the current element exists. The 'length()' method (line 37) retrieves the number of elements in the iterator object into '$count'. The current 'key' is compared to '$count' (line 38). If valid, 'TRUE' is assigned to '$var' (line 39). If not, 'FALSE' is assigned (line 41). The result is returned (line 42).

PHP file 'invoke_xml_interface_dom.php' instantiates a new instance of the 'xml_interface_dom' class.

```php
1  <?php
2  // File invoke_xml_interface_dom.php
3  require_once 'xml_interface_dom.php';
4  $xml = 'xml_docs/projects.xml';
5  $obj = new xml_interface_dom($xml);
6  foreach($obj as $value)
7  {
8  $name = $value->getElementsByTagName("name");
9  $nameVal = $name->item(0)->nodeValue;
10  echo '<strong>' . $nameVal . ' ::: </strong>';
11  $searchNode =
12  $value->getElementsByTagName("product");
13  $i = 0;
14  foreach($searchNode as $node)
15  {
16  $id[$i] = $node->getAttribute('id');
17  $i++;
18  }
19  $product = $value->getElementsByTagName("product");
20  $productVal1 = $product->item(0)->nodeValue;
21  $productVal2 = $product->item(1)->nodeValue;
22  $price = $value->getElementsByTagName("price");
23  $priceVal1 = $price->item(0)->nodeValue;
24  $priceVal2 = $price->item(1)->nodeValue;
25  echo '*' . $id[0] . '*' . ' ' .
26  $productVal1 . ' ';
27  echo $priceVal1 . ' ';
28  echo '*' . $id[1] . '*' . ' ' .
29  $productVal2 . ' ';
30  echo $priceVal2;
31  echo '<br />';
32  }
33  ?>
```

I begin by creating a new DOM instance in '$obj' (line 5). I then use the outer 'foreach' loop (lines 6–32) to process iterator object elements.

I retrieve the 'name' of each employee is in two stages. First, I use method 'getElementsByTagName()' to locate the 'name' element and place it in '$name' (line 8). Second, I use method 'item()' with 'nodeValue' to retrieve the value based on '$name' and place it in '$nameVal' (line 9).

I retrieve product 'id' attributes in two stages. First, I use method 'getElementsByTagName()' to locate 'product' elements and place them in '$searchNode' (lines 11 and 12). Second, I traverse the object in '$searchNode' with an inner 'foreach()' loop (lines 14–18). In this loop, I place 'id' attributes in array '$id' (lines 16 and 17).

I retrieve the 'product' elements in two stages. First, I use method 'getElementsByTagName()' to locate 'product' elements and place them in '$product' (line 19). Second, I retrieve the name of the first product with '$product->item(0)->nodeValue' (line 20) and the name of the second product with '$product->item(1)->nodeValue' (line 21).

I retrieve the 'price' elements in two stages. First, I use method 'getElementsByTagName()' to locate 'price' elements and place them in '$price' (line 22). Second, I retrieve the name of the first price with '$price->item(0)->nodeValue' (line 23) and the name of the second price with '$price->item(1)->nodeValue' (line 24). Finally, I display the retrieved data (lines 25–31).

Whew! This one is really complex! This is why I recommend that you use the 'SimpleXMLElement' class whenever possible. Load 'invoke_xml_interface_dom.php' in a browser. Figure 6.11 shows the results.

Grace Kelly ::: *111* Printer $111.00 ***222*** Laptop $989.00
Grant Cary ::: *333* Desktop $2995.00 ***444*** Scanner $200.00
Clark Gable ::: *555* Keyboard $129.00 ***666*** Mouse $25.00

Figure 6.11 Output Using a Custom DOM Iterator Interface Class for XML

The Iterator Interface with a Database

Using the Iterator interface with a database is more complicated because a database connection (to Oracle in our case) has to be established before there can be any processing. Once a connection is established, SQL and connection information can be sent to the Iterator interface.

I use two classes to demonstrate the Iterator interface with Oracle – 'dbAggregation' and 'dbIterator'. I use the 'dbAggregation' class to connect to the Oracle database and send connection information and the SQL statement to the 'dbIterator' class. I use the 'dbIterator' class to implement the Iterator interface. This class parses and executes the SQL statement, and includes the Iterator interface methods (customized to work with Oracle) that enable iteration with a 'foreach' loop.

PHP file 'dbAggregation.php' holds the 'dbAggregation' class. Be sure to include your username, password, and host server information in the 'setParms()' method.

```php
1  <?php
2  // File dbAggregation.php
3  class dbAggregation
4  {
5  private $_schema;
6  private $_password;
7  private $_host;
8  protected $_connection;
9  public function __construct()
10  {
```

```
11 $this->setParms();
12 $this->connDB();
13 }
14 public function setParms()
15 {
16 $this->_schema = '';
17 $this->_password = '';
18 $this->_host = '';
19 }
20 public function connDB()
21 {
22 $this->_connection = oci_connect($this->_schema,
23 $this->_password, $this->_host);
24 }
25 public function getResultSet($sql)
26 {
27 $results = new dbIterator($sql,$this->_connection);
28 return $results;
29 }
30 }
31 ?>
```

The 'dbAggregation' class has three private properties and one protected property (lines 5–8). It also contains a constructor and three public methods.

The constructor calls 'setParms()' (line 11) and 'connDB()' (line 12) methods. It has no parameters.

The 'setParms()' method (lines 14–19) sets the Oracle username, password, and host server to their respective private properties. It also has no parameters.

The 'connDB()' method (lines 20–24) connects to the database with API 'oci_connect()' (lines 22 and 23). It has no parameters.

The 'getResultSet()' method (lines 25–29) creates a new instance of the 'dbIterator' class with the SQL statement and connection information as parameters (line 27). It then returns the result set to the calling environment (line 28).

Since the 'dbAggregation' class creates a new instance of the 'dbIterator' class, aggregation is taking place. PHP file 'dbIteration.php' holds the 'dbIteration' class.

```
1 <?php
2 // File dbIterator.php
3 class dbIterator implements Iterator
4 {
5 public $sql;
6 public $connection;
7 protected $_result = array();
8 protected $_valid;
9 private $_stmt;
10 public function __construct($sql,$connection)
11 {
12 $this->sql = $sql;
```

```
13  $this->connection = $connection;
14  if(!$this->_stmt = oci_parse($connection,$sql))
15  { echo "failed to parse"; };
16  if(!oci_execute($this->_stmt))
17  {echo "failed to execute"; }
18  }
19  public function next()
20  {
21  $this->_result = oci_fetch_assoc($this->_stmt);
22  if(!$this->_result)
23  { $this->_valid = false; }
24  else
25  { $this->_valid = true; }
26  }
27  public function current()
28  {
29  return $this->_result;
30  }
31  public function key()
32  { }
33  public function valid()
34  {
35  return $this->_valid;
36  }
37  public function rewind()
38  {
39  if(!($this->_result))
40  {
41  oci_free_statement($this->_stmt);
42  if(!$this->_stmt = oci_parse($this->connection,
43  $this->sql))
44  { echo "failed to parse"; };
45  if(!oci_execute($this->_stmt))
46  {echo "failed to execute"; }
47  }
48  $this->_result = oci_fetch_assoc($this->_stmt);
49  if(!$this->_result)
50  { $this->_valid = false; }
51  else
52  { $this->_valid = true; }
53  }
54  }
55  ?>
```

I use the 'dbIterator' class to implement the Iterator interface, which converts an SQL result set into an iterator object that can then be traversed with a 'foreach' loop.

The class begins by implementing 'Iterator' (line 3). The class contains two public properties, two protected properties, and one private property (lines 5–9).

The constructor (lines 10–18) accepts the SQL statement and connection information as parameters (line 10). It then sets the '$this->sql' property to the SQL statement (line 12), sets the '$this->connection' property to the connection information (line 13), parses the SQL (line 14), and executes the SQL (line 16).

The remainder of the class includes five Iterator interface methods. The methods included are next, current, key, rewind, and valid – with appropriate logic for iterating an Oracle object.

The 'next()' method uses API 'oci_fetch_assoc' to get the next element in the iterator object (lines 19–26). It begins by setting the result to '$this->_result' (line 21). If the next element exists, the '$this->_valid' property is set to 'true' (line 25). If not, the '$this->_valid' property is set to 'false' (line 23).

The 'current()' method (lines 27–30) returns the value of the current element in the object. It accepts no parameters. The 'key()' method is not used in Oracle so no logic is included.

The 'valid()' method (lines 33–26) returns the '$this->_valid' property. It accepts no parameters.

The 'rewind()' method (lines 37–53) checks if there is a result set (line 39). If not, it uses API 'oci_free_statement' (line 41) to reset the pointer to the first element in the object (if no result set has been created). It then uses the connection information and the SQL statement as parameters to API 'oci_parse' to parse the query (lines 42 and 43). Finally, it uses API 'oci_execute' to run the parsed query (line 45). The 'rewind()' method continues by using API 'oci_fetch_assoc' to fetch the value of the current element (line 48). If data exists, '$this->_valid' is set to 'true' (line 52). If not, it is set to 'false' (line 50).

In general terms, the 'dbIterator' class connects to an Oracle database, uses Oracle APIs to parse, execute, and fetch an Oracle database table result set based on an SQL statement, and uses the Iterator interface methods to traverse an Oracle iterator object.

PHP file 'implement.php' uses the 'dbAggregation' and 'dbIterator' classes to iterate an Oracle database table 'customers'. This table was created in Chapter 4.

```php
1  <?php
2  // File implement.php
3  require_once 'dbAggregation.php';
4  require_once 'dbIterator.php';
5  $tbl = "customers";
6  $query = "SELECT * FROM $tbl";
7  $conn = new dbAggregation();
8  $result = $conn->getResultSet($query);
9  echo '<p><h2>Iterator Test</h2></p>';
10 foreach($result as $row)
11 {
12 foreach($row as $field => $value)
13 { echo "$field: $value<br />"; }
14 echo '<br />';
15 }
16 ?>
```

I start by including 'dbAggregation' and 'dbIterator' classes. I continue by selecting all records from the 'customers' table (line 6). I create a new instance of 'dbAggregation' as '$conn' (line 7). I use method 'getResult()' from '$conn' with '$query' as parameter to get the result set (line 8).

The method creates a new instance of 'dbIterator' using aggregation with the SQL statement and connection information as parameters. The new instance of 'dbIterator' parses the query, executes the query, and converts the SQL result set into an iterator object. The 'dbIterator' iterator object is then assigned to '$results' in the 'dbAggregation' object, which is returned to '$result' in the calling environment. Look inside 'dbIterator.php' for details.

I traverse each element of the iterator object '$result' with a 'foreach' loop (lines 10–15). I use an inner 'foreach' loop (lines 12 and 13) because each element of '$result' contains multiple sub-element values. This makes sense because database tables are typically two-dimensional structures consisting of rows and columns.

Load PHP file 'implement.php' in a web browser. Figure 6.12 shows a partial view of the results (a total of ten records should be displayed).

Iterator Test

ID: 1001
FIRST_NAME: Dan D.
LAST_NAME: Lion
ADDRESS: 500 E 500 N # 8
PHONE: 4357972222

Figure 6.12 Output Using 'dbAggregation' Class and a Database Iterator Interface

Definition and Characteristics of the 'IteratorAggregate' Interface

The Iterator interface implements an internal iterator. ***Internal iterators*** hide the implementation details of the aggregate structure upon which they work. That is, the Iterator interface automatically handles iteration of the aggregate structure through its internal methods – 'rewind()', 'valid()', 'current()', 'key()', and 'next()'. Details of iterator implementation are hidden.

The 'IteratorAggregate' interface creates an external iterator. ***External iterators*** are local to the calling environment. That is, all manipulations of external iterators are controlled manually. For instance, 'next' won't be called until you call it! With an internal iterator, 'next' (as well as the other methods) is called automatically.

The interface employs the 'getIterator()' method to retrieve an external iterator. Method 'getIterator()' must have public visibility so the calling environment has access. Upon instantiation of a new object that implements 'IteratorAggregate', the 'getIterator' method is automatically invoked. As such, an external iterator is automatically returned to the calling environment.

The 'IteratorAggregate' Interface

A simple example demonstrates how the 'IteratorAggregate' interface works. PHP file 'array_aggregate.php' contains the class that implements the interface and PHP file 'invoke_array_aggregate.php' contains the code that invokes the class. Notice that the class implements an 'IteratorAggregate' rather than an 'Iterator' (Iterator interface).

```php
1  <?php
2  // File array_aggregate.php
3  class array_aggregate implements IteratorAggregate
4  {
5  private $_wiz;
6  public function __construct($arr)
7  {
8  $this->_wiz = $arr;
9  }
10  public function getIterator()
```

```
11 {
12 return new ArrayIterator($this->_wiz);
13 }
14 }
15 ?>
```

I use class 'array_aggregate' (lines 3–14) to implement the 'IteratorAggregate' interface. The constructor accepts an array (line 6) and assigns the array to '$this->_wiz' (line 8). The 'getIterator()' method (lines 10–13) places the array into an 'ArrayIterator' object that is subsequently wrapped in an 'IteratorAggregate' interface object and automatically returned to the calling environment as an external iterator (line 12). The method uses aggregation because it creates a new object inside the method (that is inside the class).

```
1 <?php
2 // File invoke_array_aggregate.php
3 require_once 'array_aggregate.php';
4 $list = array('lions','tigers','bears','Oh My!');
5 $obj = new array_aggregate($list);
6 foreach($obj as $value)
7 {
8 echo $value . '<br />';
9 echo "\n";
10 }
11 ?>
```

I use PHP file 'invoke_array_aggregate.php' to assign an array to '$list' (line 4). I then create a new instance of 'array_aggregate' with '$list' as parameter (line 5). The new object automatically invokes method 'getIterator()', which returns an external iterator (based on array '$list') to the calling environment. The external iterator is placed in '$obj'. I use a 'foreach()' loop to traverse the '$obj' and display results (lines 6–10). Load 'invoke_array_aggregate.php' in a browser. Figure 6.13 shows the results.

```
lions
tigers
bears
Oh My!
```

Figure 6.13 Output Using the 'IteratorAggregate' Interface for an Array

The 'IteratorAggregate' interface can also be used with XML. In the next example, I demonstrate how to place an XML document 'fish.xml' (introduced earlier in the chapter) into an external iterator. PHP file 'xml_aggregate.php' contains the class and 'invoke_xml_aggregate.php' invokes it.

```
1 <?php
2 // File xml_aggregate.php
3 class xml_aggregate implements IteratorAggregate
```

```
 4 {
 5 private $_obj;
 6 public function __construct($obj)
 7 {
 8 $this->_obj = $obj;
 9 }
10 public function getIterator()
11 {
12 return $this->_obj;
13 }
14 }
```

Class 'xml_aggregate' accepts a 'SimpleXML' object (line 6), automatically wraps it in an 'IteratorAggregate' object, and sets the result to the '$this->_obj' property (line 8). Method 'getIterator()' automatically returns an external iterator to the calling environment (lines 10–13).

PHP file 'invoke_xml_aggregate.php' places 'fish.xml' into a 'SimpleXML' object. A new instance of 'xml_aggregate' is then created.

```
 1 <?php
 2 // File invoke_xml_aggregate.php
 3 require_once 'xml_aggregate.php';
 4 $xml = simplexml_load_file('xml_docs/fish.xml');
 5 $obj = new xml_aggregate($xml);
 6 foreach($obj as $value)
 7 {
 8 if($value->water == 'salt')
 9 {
10 echo $value['id'] . ':: ' . $value->name . ' =>';
11 echo ' $' . $value->price . '<br />' . "\n";
12 }
13 }
14 ?>
```

I place 'fish.xml' into a 'SimpleXML' object as '$xml' (line 4). I then create a new instance of 'xml_aggregate' with '$xml' as parameter (line 5). When I create the new instance, 'getIterator()' is automatically invoked. This method returns an external iterator (based on the XML document) to the calling environment and places it in '$obj'. I use a 'foreach()' loop (lines 6–13) to traverse '$obj' and display results. Load 'invoke_xml_aggregate.php' in a browser. Figure 6.14 shows the results.

```
101:: tessalata eel => $75
113:: clown fish => $25
191:: antennata lion fish => $87
```

Figure 6.14 Output Using the 'IteratorAggregate' Interface for XML

Summary

The goal of this chapter was to promote skill development in two areas. First, code examples of selected SPL classes were presented (with feedback) to promote skills in efficiently iterating a container. Second, Iterator interface examples were presented (with feedback) to promote understanding of the looping process and promote skills in gaining more control over container iteration.

Admittedly, creating custom Iterator interfaces is difficult. However, I truly believe that developing skills in this area is very beneficial for students who want to pursue technical careers in industry.

7 XML Database Transformation and AJAX

Overview

Both XML and relational databases store data, and both have established techniques for extracting the data they contain. Relational databases have mature management systems that can efficiently and reliably maintain large quantities of structured data, so they are better for handling large volumes of data within a multiuser system. XML databases have no equivalent XML management system, but they contain both the data and the informative relationship structuring of that data that both machines and people can read. Relational database systems should therefore be considered for managing large data stores in a multiuser environment, while XML should be considered for data delivered to client programs and between components of a distributed system. Creating XML documents from relational database queries and vice versa is a natural way to combine the benefits of both technologies.

Learning Objectives

After completing this chapter, you will gain skills in creating XML from a database and vice versa, and creating AJAX-driven applications that generate reports from XML documents. The following objectives summarize the skills the chapter will help you develop:

1   Learn how to create XML from a database table
2   Learn how to create a database table from XML.
3   Learn how to create a sophisticated XML generation application.
4   Learn about AJAX and how it works.
5   Learn how to create an AJAX 'DOM' application for XML reports.
6   Learn how to create an AJAX 'SimpleXML' application for XML reports.
7   Learn how to create an application to display XML trees.
8   Learn how to incorporate 'iframes' into the XML tree application.

Extracting XML from a Database Table

It is relatively easy to extract XML from a database table because each row becomes a top-level node and individual fields in each row populate child elements. In this section, I use the 'dbGeneral' class first introduced in Chapter 3 for database interaction. I include the class in this section for your convenience. If you need to review the class, consult Chapter 3 for a detailed explanation.

   PHP file 'dbGeneral.php' holds the 'dbGeneral' class. Be sure to add your username, password, and host server to the 'setParms()' method.

```php
1  <?php
2  // File dbGeneral.php
3  class dbGeneral
4  {
5  private $_schema;
6  private $_password;
7  private $_host;
8  private $_query;
9  private $_conn;
10 public $result;
11 function __construct($sql)
12 {
13 $this->_query = $sql;
14 $this->setParms();
15 $this->connDB();
16 }
17 function setParms()
18 {
19 $this->_schema = '';
20 $this->_password = '';
21 $this->_host = '';
22 }
23 function connDB()
24 {
25 if(!$this->_conn = oci_connect($this->_schema,
26 $this->_password, $this->_host))
27 { echo 'error connecting'; }
28 }
29 function parse()
30 {
31 if(!$parse = oci_parse($this->_conn, $this->_query))
32 { echo 'error parsing'; }
33 else
34 { $this->result = $parse; }
35 }
36 function bind($bind, $choice, $length)
37 {
38 oci_bind_by_name($this->result, $bind,
39 $choice, $length);
40 }
41 function exe()
42 {
43 oci_execute($this->result);
44 }
45 }
46 ?>
```

Briefly, 'dbGeneral' contains five 'private' properties (lines 5–9), one 'public' property (line 10), a constructor (lines 11–16), and five methods. The constructor sets an incoming SQL statement to '$this->_query' (line 13) and invokes the 'setParms()' and 'connDB()' methods (lines 14 and 15). Method 'setParms()' (lines 17–22) sets the username, password, and server needed to interact with Oracle. Method 'connDB()' (lines 23–28) connects to Oracle. Method 'parse()' (lines 29–35) prepares (parses) the SQL statement for processing. Method 'bind()' (lines 36–40) binds a value to a bind variable. Finally, method 'exe()' (lines 41–44) runs the SQL statement.

PHP file 'db_to_xml.php' creates and displays an XML document from the 'web_site' table created in Chapter 3. If you have not created the 'web_site' table, review Chapter 3 for details and instructions. The 'web_site' table contains four fields: 'vid', 'vuser', 'pwd', and 'lvl'.

```php
1  <?php
2  // File db_to_xml.php
3  require_once 'dbGeneral.php';
4  $newXML = new SimpleXMLElement('<root></root>');
5  $query = "SELECT * FROM web_site";
6  $connect = new dbGeneral($query);
7  $connect->parse();
8  $stmt = $connect->result;
9  $connect->exe();
10 while($row = oci_fetch_assoc($stmt))
11 {
12 $login = $newXML->addChild('schema');
13 $login->addChild('vid',$row['VID']);
14 $login->addChild('vuser',$row['VUSER']);
15 $login->addChild('pwd',$row['PSWD']);
16 $login->addChild('lvl',$row['LVL']);
17 }
18 header ('Content-Type: text/xml');
19 echo $newXML->asXML();
20 ?>
```

I begin by creating an instance of 'SimpleXML' as '$newXML' (line 4) with '<root></root>' as parameter (to create a container for the XML document). Next, I create a new instance of 'dbGeneral' (line 6) with an SQL statement (line 5) as parameter. I use methods 'parse()' and 'exe()' (lines 7–9) from 'dbGeneral' to retrieve data into '$stmt' from the 'web_site' table.

From each row of data returned from the table, I contain each node with '<schema>' (line 12). I use method 'addChild()' (lines 13–16) to place field values into their respective XML elements. Finally, I display results (lines 18 and 19).

Load 'db_to_xml.php' in a browser. Figure 7.1 shows the first 'schema' node. Five 'schema' nodes are actually displayed in the browser.

```
<root>
   <schema>
      <vid>001</vid>
      <vuser>ben</vuser>
      <pwd>1649869de3d29daab675ad252
      b9bd02248fd9ea7</pwd>
      <lvl>1</lvl>
   </schema>
</root>
```

Figure 7.1 Display Showing Partial XML Document Created from a Database Table

To save the newly created XML document, check permissions. To ensure that the document is saved, use the most unrestrictive permissions (consult your IT expert with questions regarding permissions). Run the following command (I assume that the current location is 'public_html').

```
chmod 777 xml_docs
```

PHP file 'db_to_xml_save.php' creates XML from the table and saves results.

```
 1  <?php
 2  // File db_to_xml_save.php
 3  require_once 'dbGeneral.php';
 4  $newXML = new SimpleXMLElement('<root></root>');
 5  $query = "SELECT * FROM web_site";
 6  $connect = new dbGeneral($query);
 7  $connect->parse();
 8  $stmt = $connect->result;
 9  $connect->exe();
10  while($row = oci_fetch_assoc($stmt))
11  {
12  $login = $newXML->addChild('schema');
13  $login->addChild('vid',$row['VID']);
14  $login->addChild('vuser',$row['VUSER']);
15  $login->addChild('pwd',$row['PSWD']);
16  $login->addChild('lvl',$row['LVL']);
17  }
18  ob_start();
19  $dom = new DomDocument();
20  $dom->preserveWhiteSpace = false;
21  $dom->formatOutput = true;
22  $dom->loadXML($newXML->asXML());
23  $dom->save('xml_docs/new_db.xml');
24  ob_end_clean();
25  ?>
```

The logic is exactly the same as 'db_to_xml.php' prior to line 18. In line 18, I start an output buffer session. By doing this, anything that I wish to display is sent to a buffer. When I close the buffer, its contents are displayed in a browser. Using a buffer is a good idea in web programming, because the programmer controls when output is displayed. In line 19, I create a new 'DOMDocument' object as '$dom'. I continue by turning off whitespace, turning on formatting, loading the newly created XML into '$dom', and saving the XML to a file (lines 20–23). I end by closing the buffer (line 24). Check the contents of 'new_db.xml' to verify that the XML was saved properly.

Creating a Database Table from XML

The first step is to create a new database table to hold data from XML. So, open 'Oracle SQL Developer' and run the following code (without line numbers):

```
1  CREATE TABLE menu
2  (
```

```
3  NAMES VARCHAR2(30 BYTE),
4  PRICES VARCHAR2(10 BYTE),
5  DESCRIPTIONS VARCHAR2(100 BYTE),
6  CALORIES NUMBER(4,0)
7  );
```

Start by issuing 'CREATE TABLE menu' (line 1) with its corresponding fields (lines 3–6). Table 'menu' should now be created. Data type 'VARCHAR2' is a variable-length string (see lines 3–5). So, 'NAMES' (line 3) can be anywhere from 0 to 30 characters long. Data type 'NUMBER' is a number (line 6). So, 'CALORIES' (line 6) can be up to four digits with no decimal places.

Create XML document 'menu.xml' in the 'xml_docs' directory (the XML document is available on the companion website).

```xml
<?xml version="1.0"?>
<breakfast_menu>
<food>
<name>Belgian Waffles</name>
<price>$5.95</price>
<description>two of our famous Belgian Waffles with plenty of real maple syrup</description>
<calories>650</calories>
</food>
<food>
<name>Strawberry Belgian Waffles</name>
<price>$7.95</price>
<description>light Belgian waffles covered with strawberries and whipped cream</description>
<calories>900</calories>
</food>
<food>
<name>Berry-Berry Belgian Waffles</name>
<price>$8.95</price>
<description>light Belgian waffles covered with an assortment of fresh berries and whipped
      cream</description>
<calories>900</calories>
</food>
<food>
<name>French Toast</name>
<price>$4.50</price>
<description>thick slices made from our homemade sourdough bread</description>
<calories>600</calories>
</food>
<food>
<name>Homestyle Breakfast</name>
<price>$6.95</price>
<description>two eggs, bacon or sausage, toast, and our ever-popular hash browns</description>
<calories>950</calories>
</food>
</breakfast_menu>
```

PHP file 'xml_to_db.php' adds the XML data to the 'menu' table with the SQL 'INSERT' statement. Be sure that 'menu.xml' is available in the directory.

```
1  <?php
2  // File xml_to_db.php
3  require_once 'dbGeneral.php';
4  $xml = simplexml_load_file('xml_docs/menu.xml');
5  foreach($xml->food as $food)
6  {
7  $name = $food->name;
8  $price = $food->price;
9  $description = $food->description;
10 $calories = $food->calories;
11 $query = "INSERT INTO menu VALUES
12 ('$name', '$price', '$description', '$calories')";
13 $connect = new dbGeneral($query);
14 $connect->parse();
15 $connect->result;
16 $connect->exe();
17 }
18 ?>
```

I begin by placing 'menu.xml' in a 'SimpleXML' object as '$xml' (line 4). I use a 'foreach' loop (lines 5–17) to add each XML element to the 'menu' table in the database. With lines 7–10, I grab element values from each XML node. With lines 11 and 12, I place the SQL 'INSERT' statement into '$query'. I then create a new instance of 'dbGeneral' with '$query' as parameter (line 13). I continue by processing the query (lines 14–16).

Load 'xml_to_db.php' into a web browser. Use 'Oracle SQL Developer' to verify that the data was added properly. There should be five records in the 'menu' table.

XML Generation Application

To create an XML generation application, I use three classes – 'dbAggregation', 'dbIterator', and 'xmlOutput'. Classes 'dbAggregation' and 'dbIterator' were introduced and fully explained in Chapter 6, so refer back to this chapter if you need a detailed explanation of the logic.

The 'dbAggregation' class sets the username, password, and host server (lines 16–18) in the 'setParms()' method. It also connects to the Oracle database (lines 22 and 23) in the 'connDB()' method, instantiates a new 'dbIterator' instance and returns (gets) the result back to the calling environment (lines 27 and 28) in the 'getResultSet()' method.

```
1  <?php
2  // File dbAggregation.php
3  class dbAggregation
4  {
5  private $_schema;
6  private $_password;
7  private $_host;
8  protected $_connection;
9  public function __construct()
```

```
10 {
11 $this->setParms();
12 $this->connDB();
13 }
14 public function setParms()
15 {
16 $this->_schema = '';
17 $this->_password = '';
18 $this->_host = '';
19 }
20 public function connDB()
21 {
22 $this->_connection = oci_connect($this->_schema,
23 $this->_password, $this->_host);
24 }
25 public function getResultSet($sql)
26 {
27 $results = new dbIterator($sql, $this->_connection);
28 return $results;
29 }
30 }
31 ?>
```

The 'dbIterator' class implements an Iterator interface (line 3). Its constructor accepts the connection to Oracle from 'dbAggregation' (line 10) and processes the SQL (lines 12–17). The class also contains the Iterator interface logic (lines 19–53), including methods 'next()' (lines 19–26), 'current()' (lines 27–30), 'valid()' (lines 33–36), and 'rewind()' (lines 37–53). The 'key()' method is included with no logic because Oracle doesn't use it. However, the 'key()' method *must* be present because it is required in an Iterator interface.

```
1 <?php
2 // File dbIterator.php
3 class dbIterator implements Iterator
4 {
5 public $sql;
6 public $connection;
7 protected $_result = array();
8 protected $_valid;
9 private $_stmt;
10 public function __construct($sql,$connection)
11 {
12 $this->sql = $sql;
13 $this->connection = $connection;
14 if(!$this->_stmt = oci_parse($connection,$sql))
15 { echo "failed to parse"; };
16 if(!oci_execute($this->_stmt))
17 {echo "failed to execute"; }
18 }
19 public function next()
```

```
20 {
21 $this->_result = oci_fetch_assoc($this->_stmt);
22 if(!$this->_result)
23 { $this->_valid = false; }
24 else
25 { $this->_valid = true; }
26 }
27 public function current()
28 {
29 return $this->_result;
30 }
31 public function key()
32 {}
33 public function valid()
34 {
35 return $this->_valid;
36 }
37 public function rewind()
38 {
39 if(!($this->_result))
40 {
41 oci_free_statement($this->_stmt);
42 if(!$this->_stmt =
43 oci_parse($this->connection, $this->sql))
44 { echo "failed to parse"; };
45 if(!oci_execute($this->_stmt))
46 {echo "failed to execute"; }
47 }
48 $this->_result = oci_fetch_assoc($this->_stmt);
49 if(!$this->_result)
50 { $this->_valid = false; }
51 else
52 { $this->_valid = true; }
53 }
54 }
55 ?>
```

The 'xmlOutput' class (lines 3–42) accepts the result set created by classes 'dbAggregation' and 'dbIterator', and creates the XML document. The class uses four 'private' properties (lines 5–8). The constructor sets the result set, choice, and XML file name (lines 11–13) and invokes the 'write()' method (line 14). Specifically, the constructor sets the result set to '$this->_result' (line 11), sets choice (display or save) to '$this->_choice' (line 12), sets the XML document to '$this->_xmlfile' (line 13), and invokes method 'write()' (line 14). The 'write()' method (lines 16–39) creates the XML.

The 'write()' method is pretty complex. It begins by creating a new instance of 'XMLWriter' (line 18), which is an extension that generates streams or files containing XML data. The 'XMLWriter' extension includes several methods to generate XML. If the choice is to display ('see') the XML, the 'openMemory()' method is invoked (line 20). If the choice is to save the XML, the 'openUri()' and 'setIndent()' methods are invoked (lines 23 and 24). The 'write()' method continues by building the XML document from the result set.

The 'startDocument()' method (line 26) begins the XML document. The startElement()' method (line 27) creates the element tags. The 'writeElement()' method (line 33) adds element values from the database table. The 'endElement()' (lines 35 and 37) and 'endDocument()' (line 38) methods close the XML document.

The 'flush()' method (lines 40 and 41) is the final method in the 'xmlOutput' class. It displays the XML in a browser or saves the XML, depending on choice.

```php
1  <?php
2  // File xmlOutput.php
3  class xmlOutput
4  {
5  private $_result;
6  private $_xml;
7  private $_choice;
8  private $_xmlfile;
9  public function __construct($result, $choice, $xmlfile)
10 {
11 $this->_result = $result;
12 $this->_choice = $choice;
13 $this->_xmlfile = $xmlfile;
14 $this->write();
15 }
16 public function write()
17 {
18 $this->_xml = new XMLWriter();
19 if($this->_choice == 'see')
20 { $this->_xml->openMemory(); }
21 else
22 {
23 $this->_xml->openUri($this->_xmlfile);
24 $this->_xml->setIndent(true);
25 }
26 $this->_xml->startDocument();
27 $this->_xml->startElement('root');
28 foreach($this->_result as $row)
29 {
30 $this->_xml->startElement('row');
31 foreach($row as $field => $value)
32 {
33 $this->_xml->writeElement($field, $value);
34 }
35 $this->_xml->endElement();
36 }
37 $this->_xml->endElement();
38 $this->_xml->endDocument();
39 }
40 public function flush()
41 { return $this->_xml->flush(); }
42 }
43 ?>
```

PHP file 'xml_flush.php' displays tXML based on the 'menu' table. It includes 'dbAggregation', 'dbIterator', and 'xmlOutput' classes to do its magic.

```php
1  <?php
2  // File xml_flush.php
3  require_once 'dbAggregation.php';
4  require_once 'dbIterator.php';
5  require_once 'xmlOutput.php';
6  $tbl = "menu";
7  $query = "SELECT * FROM $tbl";
8  $conn = new dbAggregation();
9  $result = $conn->getResultSet($query);
10 $xml = new xmlOutput($result,'see','');
11 header('Content-Type: text/xml');
12 $see = $xml->flush();
13 echo $see;
14 ?>
```

I begin by creating a query (lines 6 and 7). I continue by creating a new instance of 'dbAggregation' as '$conn' (line 8). I use 'getResultSet()' to get the database result set into '$result' (line 9). I continue by creating a new instance of 'xmlOutput' as '$xml' (line 10). Since the choice is 'see', I want to display the XML. So, I inform the browser (line 11), use 'flush()' (line 12), and display (line 13). Load 'xml_flush.php' in a browser. Figure 7.2 displays the first 'row' node. Five 'row' nodes are actually displayed in the browser.

```
<row>
   <NAMES>Belgian Waffles</NAMES>
   <PRICES>$5.95</PRICES>
   <DESCRIPTIONS>two of our famou
   s Belgian Waffles with plenty
   of real maple syrup</DESCRIPTI
   ONS>
   <CALORIES>650</CALORIES>
</row>
```

Figure 7.2 Generate XML with 'dbAggregation', 'dbIterator', and 'xmlOutput'

Before attempting to save the XML document, be sure that the directory has 'write' permissions with the following commands (if necessary).

chmod 777 xml_docs

Since 'menu.xml' was created earlier in the chapter, delete it. The reason is that we want to create it and save it with the PHP program that follows.

rm-rf xml_docs/menu.xml

PHP file 'xml_save.php' saves the XML based on the 'menu' table.

```
 1  <?php
 2  // File xml_save.php
 3  require_once 'dbAggregation.php';
 4  require_once 'dbIterator.php';
 5  require_once 'xmlOutput.php';
 6  $tbl = "menu";
 7  $query = "SELECT * FROM $tbl";
 8  $conn = new dbAggregation();
 9  $result = $conn->getResultSet($query);
10  $xml = new xmlOutput
11  ($result,'save','xml_docs/menu.xml');
12  $xml->flush();
13  ?>
```

The logic is the same as 'xml_flush.php' except that we don't need the 'header' statement because our choice is 'save' (line 11). That is, we don't need to tell the browser to do anything because we are saving rather than displaying. Verify that 'menu.xml' was created and saved in the 'xml_docs' directory.

AJAX

Asynchronous JavaScript and XML (AJAX) is a method of sending and receiving data asynchronously from a server-side application using JavaScript. With asynchronous data transmission, the web browser (and server) can continue doing other things while the AJAX data request is being fulfilled by the server.

AJAX is possible because web browsers offer objects that can make independent HTTP requests with the help of JavaScript. An AJAX application includes an HTML page that contains user interface elements that interact with JavaScript functions. JavaScript functions enable HTTP requests by communicating with the web browser. The web browser sends the HTTP request to the server and waits for a response. The server processes the request and can respond in XML markup, plain text, images or data from a database. Figure 7.3 depicts how AJAX works.

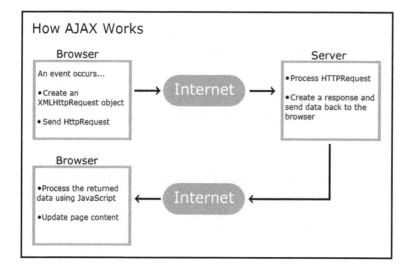

Figure 7.3 Graphical Representation of the AJAX Process (http://www.w3schools.com/ajax/ajax_intro.asp)

The AJAX process has six steps. First, the HTTP object is created. Second, the web browser sends the HTTP request to the server. Third, the server processes the HTTP request. Fourth, the server creates a response and sends it back to the web browser. Fifth, the web browser processes the response. Sixth, the web browser updates web page content.

JavaScript file 'demo.js' demonstrates AJAX. You don't need to save this file because I use it for explanation purposes only.

```
 1 // File demo.js
 2 var xhr;
 3 xhr = new XMLHttpRequest();
 4 function showRpt(str)
 5 {
 6 var url="demo.php";
 7 xhr.open("POST",url,true);
 8 xhr.setRequestHeader("Content-Type",
 9 "application/x-www-form-urlencoded");
10 xhr.onreadystatechange=function()
11 {
12 if (xhr.readyState==4 ||
13 xhr.readyState=="complete")
14 {document.getElementById("txtHint").innerHTML =
15 xhr.responseText;}
16 }
17 xhr.send("response="+str+"&sid="+Math.random());
18 }
```

First, I create a new instance of the HTTP request object and place it in variable 'xhr' (lines 2 and 3).

```
var xhr;
xhr = new XMLHttpRequest();
```

The 'XMLHttpRequest' object defines the API used to send HTTP or HTTPS requests directly to a web server and loads the server response data directly back to the PHP script (line 6).

```
var url="demo.php";
```

Next, I use the 'open()' method (line 7) to tell the web browser to send the HTTP request to the server.

```
xhr.open("POST",url,true);
```

The first argument tells the server whether to 'get' or 'post'. In this case, I use method 'post'. The second argument is the URL of the PHP file used by the server to generate the content of the request. The third argument tells the server how to process the request – 'true' for asynchronous and 'false' for synchronous.

Since I chose 'post', I must use method 'setRequestHeader()' to tell the server to include header information (lines 8 and 9).

```
xhr.setRequestHeader("Content-Type","application/x-www-form-urlencoded");
```

I use method 'send()' (line 17) to tell the server to process the request.

```
xhr.send("response="+str+"&sid="+Math.random());
```

I continue by checking the state of the request (line 10).

```
xhr.onreadystatechange=function()
```

JavaScript event 'onreadystatechange' is triggered every time property 'readyState' changes status.
   I check if the request was processed (lines 12 and 13).

```
if (xhr.readyState==4 || xhr.readyState=="complete")
```

The 'readyState' property holds the status of the 'XMLHttpRequest' object. If 'readyState' is '4', the request is finished and the response is ready.
   I tell the web browser to finish the AJAX process by updating the contents of the web page (lines 14 and 15).

```
{document.getElementById("txtHint").innerHTML = xhr.responseText;}
```

The response created by the server is saved in property 'responseText'. 'document.getElementByID("txtHint"). innerHTML' updates web page content by using the DOM to place the response after the HTML tag with 'id' of 'txtHint'.

AJAX DOM Application for XML Reports

To apply what we have learned so far, I build an application with a drop-down menu for choosing reports from two XML documents. I use the 'DOMDocument' class to extract data from XML.
   The '*DOMDocument*' class represents an entire HTML or XML document and serves as the root of the document tree. The XML documents used for this application are 'customer.xml' and 'catalog.xml'. Both documents are available on the companion website. Owing to their large size, they are not provided in text.

Application Scripts for AJAX DOM

I use eight scripts in this application – 'xml.php', 'select_xml.js', 'get_xml.php', 'all.php', 'cat.php', 'usa.php', 'uk.php', and 'eu.php'. PHP file 'xml.php' contains the drop-down logic and JavaScript event handler.

```
 1  <?php
 2  // File xml.php
 3  ?>
 4  <html><body style="background-color:BURLYWOOD;">
 5  <head><script src="select_xml.js"></script></head>
 6  <body><div style="text-align:center;">
 7  <form>
 8  <h3 style="color:crimson;">Select XML:  </h3>
 9  <select name="rpt" onchange="showRpt(this.value)">
10  <option value=999 selected="SELECTED">CHOOSE ONE</option>
11  <option value="All">All Customers</option>
12  <option value="Catalog">Entire Catalog</option>
```

```
13  <option value="USA">USA Catalog</option>
14  <option value="UK">UK Catalog</option>
15  <option value="EU">EU Catalog</option>
16  </select>
17  </form>
18  <p><div style="color:blue;" id="txtHint">
19  <b>XML info will be listed here.</b></div>
20</p></body></html>
```

Line 5 tells PHP where to find the AJAX script. Line 9 contains the JavaScript event handler, which invokes function 'showRpt()' when a selection is made from the drop-down menu. Lines 9–16 create the drop-down menu. The response from the HTTP request is placed after line 18 because it contains the '<div>' tag with 'id' of 'txtHint'.

The JavaScript event handler 'onchange' (line 9) is key. It is triggered when the state changes. In our case, the state changes when a menu selection is made. A choice from the menu tells PHP to run 'showRpt()' from 'select_xml.js', which creates an AJAX request. So, the state changes from processing 'xml.php' to 'select_xml.js'. The parameter for 'showRpt()' is 'this.value', which indicates the current choice. The 'this' keyword in JavaScript serves the same purpose as the 'this' keyword in PHP.

```
<select name="rpt" onchange="showRpt(this.value)">
```

I use JavaScript file 'select_xml.js' to create and process the HTTP request. The 'AJAX' section (earlier in the chapter) explains how the code works in detail.

```
 1  // File select_xml.js
 2  var xhr;
 3  xhr = new XMLHttpRequest();
 4  function showRpt(str)
 5  {
 6  var url="get_xml.php";
 7  xhr.open("POST",url,true);
 8  xhr.setRequestHeader("Content-Type",
 9  "application/x-www-form-urlencoded");
10  xhr.onreadystatechange=function()
11  {
12  if (xhr.readyState==4 ||
13  xhr.readyState=="complete")
14  {document.getElementById("txtHint").innerHTML =
15  xhr.responseText;}
16  }
17  xhr.send("response="+str+"&sid="+Math.random());
18  }
```

I begin by creating a new instance of 'XMLHttpRequest' as 'xhr' (line 3). I continue with function 'showRpt()' (lines 4–18). The function identifies the PHP file to use for the request (line 6), how to open the request (lines 7–9), how to check when the request is completed (lines 10–16), where to place the response (lines 14 and 15), and how to send the response (line 17).

The server calls PHP file 'get_xml.php' to process the response.

```php
1  <?php
2  // File get_xml.php
3  $response = $_POST["response"];
4  if ($response == 999)
5  {
6  echo "<h3 style='color:RED;'>";
7  echo "Choose one of the reports Silly!</h3>";
8  }
9  else
10 {
11 if ($response == "All") { header('Location: all.php'); }
12 else if ($response == "Catalog") { header('Location: cat.php'); }
13 else if ($response == "USA") { header('Location: usa.php'); }
14 else if ($response == "UK") { header('Location: uk.php'); }
15 else if ($response == "EU") { header('Location: eu.php'); }
16 }
17 ?>
```

I begin by posting the response from the drop-down form (line 3). If an incorrect response was chosen from the menu, I display a message (lines 4–8). With lines 9–16, I redirect (based on the choice from the drop-down menu) to a PHP file that generates the appropriate response content.

PHP file 'all.php' creates a 'DOMDocument' object, parses the 'customer.xml' document, and displays data from 'customer.xml'.

```php
1  <?php
2  // File all.php
3  $xmlDoc = new DOMDocument();
4  $xmlDoc->load('xml_docs/customer.xml');
5  $x = $xmlDoc->getElementsByTagName('row');
6  for ($i=0; $i<($x->length); $i++)
7  {
8  $first = $x->item($i)->getElementsByTagName('FIRST_NAME')->
9  item(0)->childNodes->item(0)->nodeValue;
10 $last = $x->item($i)->getElementsByTagName('LAST_NAME')->
11 item(0)->childNodes->item(0)->nodeValue;
12 $addr = $x->item($i)->getElementsByTagName('ADDRESS')->
13 item(0)->childNodes->item(0)->nodeValue;
14 $phone = $x->item($i)->getElementsByTagName('PHONE')->
15 item(0)->childNodes->item(0)->nodeValue;
16 echo "<div style='text-align:center;'>";
17 echo "<p>" . $last . "," . $first . "<br>" . $addr .
18 "<br>" . $phone . "</p></div>";
19 }
20 ?>
```

I begin by creating a 'DOMDocument' object as '$xmlDoc' (line 3). I load 'customer.xml' into the object (line 4). I continue by placing all 'row' elements from the XML into '$x' (line 5). I use a 'for' loop to process the XML document (lines 6–19).

To grab the value of 'FIRST_NAME' from each node, I use the 'item', 'getElementsByTagName', 'childNodes', and 'nodeValue' methods (lines 8 and 9). I use 'item' initially to grab the *i*th element. Within the *i*th element, I use method 'getElementsByTagName' to identify the element name and 'item(0)' to identify the element level. In our case, 'FIRST_NAME' is at the top level. Next, I use 'childNodes->item(0)->nodeValue' to grab the value of 'FIRST_NAME'. Whew! The DOM is very tough! I use the same logic to get the other element values.

PHP file 'cat.php' creates a 'DOMDocument' object, parses the 'catalog.xml' document, and displays data from 'catalog.xml'.

```php
1  <?php
2  // File cat.php
3  $xmlDoc = new DOMDocument();
4  $xmlDoc->load('xml_docs/catalog.xml');
5  $x = $xmlDoc->getElementsByTagName('CD');
6  for ($i=0; $i<($x->length); $i++)
7  {
8  $title = $x->item($i)->getElementsByTagName('TITLE')->
9  item(0)->childNodes->item(0)->nodeValue;
10 $artist = $x->item($i)->getElementsByTagName('ARTIST')->
11 item(0)->childNodes->item(0)->nodeValue;
12 $country = $x->item($i)->getElementsByTagName('COUNTRY')->
13 item(0)->childNodes->item(0)->nodeValue;
14 $company = $x->item($i)->getElementsByTagName('COMPANY')->
15 item(0)->childNodes->item(0)->nodeValue;
16 $price = $x->item($i)->getElementsByTagName('PRICE')->
17 item(0)->childNodes->item(0)->nodeValue;
18 $year = $x->item($i)->getElementsByTagName('YEAR')->
19 item(0)->childNodes->item(0)->nodeValue;
20 echo "<div style='text-align:center;'>";
21 echo "<p>" . $title . "<br>" . $artist . "<br>" . $country .
22 "<br>" . $company . "<br>" . $price . "<br>". $year . "</p></div>";
23 }
24 ?>
```

I begin by creating a 'DOMDocument' object (line 3) and use method 'load()' from the object to load 'catalog. xml' (line 4). I continue by placing all 'CD' elements from the XML into '$x' (line 5). Next, I extract all 'catalog' XML data (lines 8–19), and display it (lines 20–22). To grab the values from each element, I use the same logic presented in 'all.php' except the element names are different.

PHP file 'usa.php' creates a 'DOMDocument' object, parses the 'catalog.xml' document, and displays 'catalog' data for 'USA' only.

```php
1  <?php
2  // File usa.php
3  $xmlDoc = new DOMDocument();
4  $xmlDoc->load('xml_docs/catalog.xml');
```

```
 5  $x = $xmlDoc->getElementsByTagName('CD');
 6  for ($i=0; $i<($x->length); $i++)
 7  {
 8  if($x->item($i)->getElementsByTagName('COUNTRY')->
 9  item(0)->childNodes->item(0)->nodeValue == "USA")
10  {
11  $title = $x->item($i)->getElementsByTagName('TITLE')->
12  item(0)->childNodes->item(0)->nodeValue;
13  $artist = $x->item($i)->getElementsByTagName('ARTIST')->
14  item(0)->childNodes->item(0)->nodeValue;
15  $country = $x->item($i)->getElementsByTagName('COUNTRY')->
16  item(0)->childNodes->item(0)->nodeValue;
17  $company = $x->item($i)->getElementsByTagName('COMPANY')->
18  item(0)->childNodes->item(0)->nodeValue;
19  $price = $x->item($i)->getElementsByTagName('PRICE')->
20  item(0)->childNodes->item(0)->nodeValue;
21  $year = $x->item($i)->getElementsByTagName('YEAR')->
22  item(0)->childNodes->item(0)->nodeValue;
23  echo "<div style='text-align:center;'>";
24  echo "<p>" . $title . "<br>" . $artist . "<br>" . $country .
25  "<br>" . $company . "<br>" . $price . "<br>". $year . "</p></div>";
26  }
27  }
28  ?>
```

The code follows the same logic as 'cat.php', but only displays data from 'COUNTRY' 'USA' using an 'if' statement (lines 8 and 9). I first create a 'DOMDocument' object (line 3) and use method 'load()' from the object to load 'catalog.xml' (line 4). I continue by placing all 'CD' elements from the XML into '$x' (line 5). Next, I extract all 'catalog' XML data (lines 11–22), and display it (lines 23–25). To grab the values from each element, I use the same logic presented in 'cat.php'.

PHP file 'uk.php' creates a 'DOMDocument' object, parses the 'catalog.xml' document, and displays 'catalog' data for 'UK' only.

```
 1  <?php
 2  // File uk.php
 3  $xmlDoc = new DOMDocument();
 4  $xmlDoc->load('xml_docs/catalog.xml');
 5  $x = $xmlDoc->getElementsByTagName('CD');
 6  for ($i=0; $i<($x->length); $i++)
 7  {
 8  if($x->item($i)->getElementsByTagName('COUNTRY')->
 9  item(0)->childNodes->item(0)->nodeValue == "UK")
10  {
11  $title = $x->item($i)->getElementsByTagName('TITLE')->
12  item(0)->childNodes->item(0)->nodeValue;
13  $artist = $x->item($i)->getElementsByTagName('ARTIST')->
14  item(0)->childNodes->item(0)->nodeValue;
15  $country = $x->item($i)->getElementsByTagName('COUNTRY')->
```

```
16 item(0)->childNodes->item(0)->nodeValue;
17 $company = $x->item($i)->getElementsByTagName('COMPANY')->
18 item(0)->childNodes->item(0)->nodeValue;
19 $price = $x->item($i)->getElementsByTagName('PRICE')->
20 item(0)->childNodes->item(0)->nodeValue;
21 $year = $x->item($i)->getElementsByTagName('YEAR')->
22 item(0)->childNodes->item(0)->nodeValue;
23 echo "<div style='text-align:center;'>";
24 echo "<p>" . $title . "<br>" . $artist . "<br>" . $country .
25 "<br>" . $company . "<br>" . $price . "<br>". $year . "</p></div>";
26 }
27 }
28 ?>
```

The code follows the same logic as 'usa.php', but only displays data from 'COUNTRY' 'UK' using an 'if' statement (lines 8 and 9). I first create a 'DOMDocument' object (line 3) and use method 'load()' from the object to load 'catalog.xml' (line 4). I continue by placing all 'CD' elements from the XML into '$x' (line 5). Next, I extract all 'catalog' XML data (lines 11–22), and display it (lines 23–25). To grab the values from each element, I use the same logic presented in 'cat.php'.

PHP file 'eu.php' creates a 'DOMDocument' object, parses the 'catalog.xml' document, and displays 'catalog' data for 'EU' only.

```
1  <?php
2  // File eu.php
3  $xmlDoc = new DOMDocument();
4  $xmlDoc->load('xml_docs/catalog.xml');
5  $x = $xmlDoc->getElementsByTagName('CD');
6  for ($i=0; $i<($x->length); $i++)
7  {
8  if($x->item($i)->getElementsByTagName('COUNTRY')->
9  item(0)->childNodes->item(0)->nodeValue == "EU")
10 {
11 $title = $x->item($i)->getElementsByTagName('TITLE')->
12 item(0)->childNodes->item(0)->nodeValue;
13 $artist = $x->item($i)->getElementsByTagName('ARTIST')->
14 item(0)->childNodes->item(0)->nodeValue;
15 $country = $x->item($i)->getElementsByTagName('COUNTRY')->
16 item(0)->childNodes->item(0)->nodeValue;
17 $company = $x->item($i)->getElementsByTagName('COMPANY')->
18 item(0)->childNodes->item(0)->nodeValue;
19 $price = $x->item($i)->getElementsByTagName('PRICE')->
20 item(0)->childNodes->item(0)->nodeValue;
21 $year = $x->item($i)->getElementsByTagName('YEAR')->
22 item(0)->childNodes->item(0)->nodeValue;
23 echo "<div style='text-align:center;'>";
24 echo "<p>" . $title . "<br>" . $artist . "<br>" . $country .
25 "<br>" . $company . "<br>" . $price . "<br>". $year . "</p></div>";
```

```
26 }
27 }
28 ?>
```

The code follows the same logic as 'usa.php', but only displays data from 'COUNTRY' 'EU' using an 'if' statement (lines 8 and 9). I first create a 'DOMDocument' object (line 3) and use method 'load()' from the object to load 'catalog.xml' (line 4). I continue by placing all 'CD' elements from the XML into '$x' (line 5). Next, I extract all 'catalog' XML data (lines 11–22), and display it (lines 23–25). To grab the values from each element, I use the same logic presented in 'cat.php'.

I know that this seems like a lot of code. But did you notice that I reused code in many places? When I build an application, I try to reuse code wherever possible.

Before testing the application, be sure to save the files with the names provided – 'xml.php', 'select_xml. js', 'get_xml.php', 'all.php', 'cat.php', 'usa.php', 'uk.php', and 'eu.php'. In addition, be sure that 'customer. xml' and 'catalog.xml' are saved in the 'xml_docs' directory. Load 'xml.php' in a browser. Figure 7.4 shows the initial screen display with the drop-down menu.

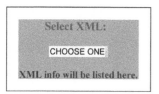

Figure 7.4 Display AJAX-Enabled Form with Drop-Down Menu of XML Data Options

Click the drop-down menu arrow and choose 'All Customers'. Figure 7.5 shows partial results (there should be ten customers displayed). To view the entire catalog, USA entries, UK entries, or EU entries, click on the appropriate menu item.

Figure 7.5 Output 'All Customer' Partial Data Using 'DOMDocument' Class

AJAX 'SimpleXML' Application for XML Reports

If you haven't already noticed, using the 'DOM' is a *royal* pain! So, I am going to show you how to build the same application with much less code. The application provides a drop-down menu for choosing reports from two XML documents, but uses 'SimpleXML' instead of 'DOM'. 'SimpleXML' makes XML extraction *much* easier.

Like the 'DOM' application, the XML documents I use are 'customer.xml' and 'catalog.xml'. Both documents are available on the companion website.

Application Scripts for AJAX 'SimpleXML'

I use eight scripts in this application – 'xml_simple.php', 'select_simple.js', 'get_simple.php', 'all_simple.php', 'cat_simple.php', 'usa_simple.php', 'uk_simple.php', and 'eu_simple.php'.

PHP file 'xml_simple.php' contains the drop-down logic and JavaScript event handler.

```
1  <?php
2  // File xml_simple.php
3  ?>
4  <html><body style="background-color:BURLYWOOD;">
5  <head><script src="select_simple.js"></script></head>
6  <body><div style="text-align:center;">
7  <form>
8  <h3 style="color:crimson;">Select XML:  </h3>
9  <select name="rpt" onchange="showRpt(this.value)">
10 <option value=999 selected="SELECTED">CHOOSE ONE</option>
11 <option value="All">All Customers</option>
12 <option value="Catalog">Entire Catalog</option>
13 <option value="USA">USA Catalog</option>
14 <option value="UK">UK Catalog</option>
15 <option value="EU">EU Catalog</option>
16 </select>
17 </form>
18 <p><div style="color:blue;"
19 id="txtHint"><b>XML info will be listed here.</b></div>
20 </p></body></html>
```

The logic in 'xml_simple.php' is almost the same as 'xml.php'. The only difference is the name of the JavaScript file, which is 'select_simple.js' (line 5).

JavaScript file 'select_simple.js' instantiates the 'XMLHttpRequest' object and processes the HTTP request. The logic is the same as 'select_xml.js' except I use 'get_simple.php' to process the AJAX request (line 6).

```
1  // File select_simple.js
2  var xhr;
3  xhr = new XMLHttpRequest();
4  function showRpt(str)
5  {
6  var url="get_simple.php";
```

```
 7  xhr.open("POST",url,true);
 8  xhr.setRequestHeader("Content-Type",
 9  "application/x-www-form-urlencoded");
10  xhr.onreadystatechange=function()
11  {
12  if (xhr.readyState==4 || xhr.readyState=="complete")
13  {document.getElementById("txtHint").innerHTML =
14  xhr.responseText;}
15  }
16  xhr.send("response="+str+"&sid="+Math.random());
17  }
```

PHP file 'get_simple.php' processes the request.

```
 1  <?php
 2  // File get_simple.php
 3  $response = $_POST["response"];
 4  if ($response == 999)
 5  {
 6  echo "<h3 style='color:RED;'>";
 7  echo "Choose one of the reports Silly!</h3>";
 8  }
 9  else
10  {
11  if ($response == "All")
12  { header('Location: all_simple.php'); }
13  else if ($response == "Catalog")
14  { header('Location: cat_simple.php'); }
15  else if ($response == "USA")
16  { header('Location: usa_simple.php'); }
17  else if ($response == "UK")
18  { header('Location: uk_simple.php'); }
19  else if ($response == "EU")
20  { header('Location: eu_simple.php'); }
21  }
22  ?>
```

I begin by posting the response (line 3). I then check to see which menu item was selected from the drop-down menu (lines 11–20) and redirect to the appropriate PHP file for final processing.

PHP file 'all_simple.php' converts the XML into a 'SimpleXML' object, parses the 'customer.xml' document, and displays the data.

```
 1  <?php
 2  // File all_simple.php
 3  $xml = simplexml_load_file('xml_docs/customer.xml');
 4  echo "<html><head><style type='text/css'>";
```

```
 5 echo "table.center{ margin-left:auto; margin-right:auto; }";
 6 echo "<div style='text-align:center;'>";
 7 echo "</style></head><table class='center'>";
 8 foreach($xml->row as $row)
 9 {
10 echo "<tr><td>";
11 echo $row->ID . ' ' . $row->FIRST_NAME . ' ' .
12 $row->LAST_NAME;
13 echo ' ' . $row->ADDRESS. ' ' . $row->PHONE . "<br />";
14 echo "</tr></td>";
15 };
16 echo "</table></div></html>";
17 ?>
```

I begin by creating a 'SimpleXML' object from 'customer.xml' as '$xml' (line 3). I then use a 'foreach' loop (lines 8–15) to iterate through the object. Wow! Look how simple the code is compared with the 'DOMDocument' version! The only reason I would ever use the 'DOMDocument' version is if I needed its advanced features.

PHP file 'cat_simple.php' converts the XML into a 'SimpleXML' object, parses the 'catalog.xml' document, and displays the data.

```
 1 <?php
 2 // File cat_simple.php
 3 $xml = simplexml_load_file('xml_docs/catalog.xml');
 4 echo "<html><head><style type='text/css'>";
 5 echo "table.center{ margin-left:auto; margin-right:auto; }";
 6 echo "<div style='text-align:center;'>";
 7 echo "</style></head><table class='center'>";
 8 foreach($xml->CD as $cd)
 9 {
10 echo "<tr><td>";
11 echo $cd->TITLE . ' ' . $cd->ARTIST . ' ' . $cd->COUNTRY;
12 echo ' ' . $cd->COMPANY . ' ' . $cd->PRICE . ' ' .
13 $cd->YEAR . "<br />";
14 echo "</tr></td>";
15 };
16 echo "</table></div></html>";
17 ?>
```

I begin by creating a 'SimpleXML' object from 'catalog.xml' as '$xml' (line 3). I then use a 'foreach' loop (lines 8–15) to iterate through the object.

PHP file 'usa_simple.php' converts the XML into a 'SimpleXML' object, parses the 'catalog.xml' document, and displays the data for 'USA' only.

```
 1 <?php
 2 // File usa_simple.php
 3 $xml = simplexml_load_file('xml_docs/catalog.xml');
```

```
 4 echo "<html><head><style type='text/css'>";
 5 echo "table.center{ margin-left:auto; margin-right:auto; }";
 6 echo "<div style='text-align:center;'>";
 7 echo "</style></head><table class='center'>";
 8 foreach($xml->CD as $cd)
 9 {
10 if($cd->COUNTRY == "USA")
11 {
12 $country = $cd->COUNTRY;
13 echo "<tr><td>";
14 echo $cd->TITLE . ' ' . $cd->ARTIST . ' ' . $cd->COUNTRY;
15 echo ' ' . $cd->COMPANY . ' ' . $cd->PRICE . ' ' .
16 $cd->YEAR . "<br />";
17 echo "</tr></td>";
18 }
19 }
20 echo "</table></div></html>";
21 ?>
```

I use the same logic as 'cat_simple.php' but only display data from 'COUNTRY' 'USA' by using an 'if' statement (line 10).

PHP file 'uk_simple.php' converts the XML into a 'SimpleXML' object, parses the 'catalog.xml' document, and displays the data for 'UK' only.

```
 1 <?php
 2 // File uk_simple.php
 3 $xml = simplexml_load_file('xml_docs/catalog.xml');
 4 echo "<html><head><style type='text/css'>";
 5 echo "table.center{ margin-left:auto; margin-right:auto; }";
 6 echo "<div style='text-align:center;'>";
 7 echo "</style></head><table class='center'>";
 8 foreach($xml->CD as $cd)
 9 {
10 if($cd->COUNTRY == "UK")
11 {
12 $country = $cd->COUNTRY;
13 echo "<tr><td>";
14 echo $cd->TITLE . ' ' . $cd->ARTIST . ' ' . $cd->COUNTRY;
15 echo ' ' . $cd->COMPANY . ' ' . $cd->PRICE . ' ' .
16 $cd->YEAR . "<br />";
17 echo "</tr></td>";
18 }
19 }
20 echo "</table></div></html>";
21 ?>
```

I use the same logic as 'cat_simple.php' but only display data from 'COUNTRY' 'UK' by using an 'if' statement (line 10).

PHP file 'eu_simple.php' converts the XML into a 'SimpleXML' object, parses the 'catalog.xml' document, and displays the data for 'EU' only.

```php
1  <?php
2  // File eu_simple.php
3  $xml = simplexml_load_file('xml_docs/catalog.xml');
4  echo "<html><head><style type='text/css'>";
5  echo "table.center{ margin-left:auto; margin-right:auto; }";
6  echo "<div style='text-align:center;'>";
7  echo "</style></head><table class='center'>";
8  foreach($xml->CD as $cd)
9  {
10 if($cd->COUNTRY == "EU")
11 {
12 $country = $cd->COUNTRY;
13 echo "<tr><td>";
14 echo $cd->TITLE . ' ' . $cd->ARTIST . ' ' . $cd->COUNTRY;
15 echo ' ' . $cd->COMPANY . ' ' . $cd->PRICE . ' ';
16 $cd->YEAR . "<br />";
17 echo "</tr></td>";
18 }
19 }
20 echo "</table></div></html>";
21 ?>
```

I use the same logic as 'cat_simple.php' but only displays data from 'COUNTRY' 'EU' by using an 'if' statement (line 10).

Load 'xml_simple.php' to invoke the application. Click the drop-down menu arrow and choose 'All Customers'. Figure 7.6 shows the results.

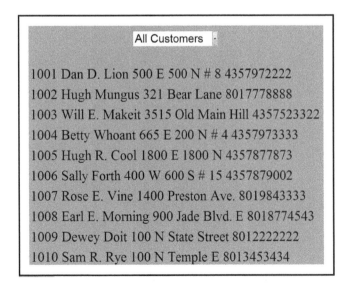

Figure 7.6 Output 'All Customer' Data Using 'SimpleXMLElement' Class

Notice that the display is a bit cleaner than the 'DOMDocument' application. This is because I added a bit of CSS. To view the entire catalog, USA entries, UK entries, or EU entries, click on the appropriate menu item.

XML Tree Application

The previous two applications extracted data from XML documents using the 'DOMDocument' and 'SimpleXMLElement' classes, respectively. The intention of the application I am about to build is to display the schema (tree) of an XML document. An *XML tree* is the structure of an XML document. XML documents form a tree structure that starts at the root and extends through branches to the leaves.

The XML documents I use are 'customer.xml' and 'catalog.xml'. Both documents are available on the companion website.

Application Scripts for XML Tree

I use six scripts in this application – 'tree.php', 'select_tree.js', 'get_tree.php', 'error.php', 'customer.php', and 'catalog.php'.

PHP file 'tree.php' provides a drop-down menu for choosing the XML tree to display and a JavaScript event handler to handle the event.

```php
1  <?php
2  // File tree.php
3  ?>
4  <html><body style="background-color:BURLYWOOD;">
5  <head><script src="select_tree.js"></script></head>
6  <body><div style="text-align:center;">
7  <form>
8  <h3 style="color:crimson;">Select XML Tree:  </h3>
9  <select name="rpt" onchange="showRpt(this.value)">
10 <option value=999 selected="SELECTED">CHOOSE ONE</option>
11 <option value="All">Customer Tree</option>
12 <option value="Catalog">Catalog Tree</option>
13 </select>
14 </form>
15 </div></body></html>
```

The JavaScript event handler (line 9) invokes function 'showRpt()' from 'select_tree.js' (line 5) when a menu choice is selected. The menu (lines 9–13) includes three options – '999', 'All', and 'Catalog'. If the '999' option is chosen, a message is given to choose one of the other two options.

JavaScript file 'select_tree.js' processes the AJAX HTTP request.

```javascript
1 // File select_tree.js
2 var xhr;
3 xhr = new XMLHttpRequest();
4 function showRpt(str)
5 {
6 var url="get_tree.php";
7 xhr.open("POST",url,true);
```

```
 8 xhr.setRequestHeader("Content-Type",
 9 "application/x-www-form-urlencoded");
10 xhr.onreadystatechange=function()
11 {
12 if (xhr.readyState==4 || xhr.readyState=="complete")
13 window.location = xhr.responseText;
14 }
15 xhr.send("response="+str+"&sid="+Math.random());
16 }
```

I begin by creating a new instance of 'XMLHttpRequest' as 'xhr' (lines 2 and 3). I continue with a function that processes the AJAX request (lines 4–16). I open a new request (line 7), set the request header information (line 8), test if the request is complete (lines 10–12), place the response in 'window.location' (line 13), and send the request (line 15). By using 'window.location', I tell the browser to replace what is currently being displayed with the tree structure of the XML document. The 'window.location' object allows you to redirect the browser from the current page address (URL) to a new page.

PHP file 'get_tree.php' processes the AJAX response.

```
 1 <?php
 2 // File get_tree.php
 3 $response = $_POST["response"];
 4 if ($response == 999)
 5 { echo "error.php"; }
 6 else
 7 {
 8 if ($response == "All") { echo "customer.php"; }
 9 else if ($response == "Catalog") { echo "catalog.php"; }
10 }
11 ?>
```

I begin by posting 'response' into '$response' (line 3). If '$response' is '999', I redirect to 'error.php' (lines 4 and 5). If not, I redirect either to 'customer.php' or 'catalog.php' (lines 6–10).

PHP file 'error.php' displays an error (lines 6 and 7) if the user chooses this item from the drop-down menu.

```
 1 <?php
 2 // File error.php
 3 ?>
 4 <html><body style="background-color:BURLYWOOD;">
 5 <div style='text-align:center;'>
 6 <h3 style='color:RED;'>
 7 Choose one of the reports Silly!</h3>
 8 </div>
 9 </body></html>
```

PHP file 'customer.php' displays the tree structure of 'customer.xml'.

```
1  <?php
2  // File customer.php
3  $xml = simplexml_load_file('xml_docs/customer.xml');
4  header('Content-Type: text/xml');
5  echo $xml->asXML();
6  ?>
```

I begin by placing 'customer.xml' in a 'SimpleXML' object as '$xml' (line 3). I then tell the browser to display the contents of the object (lines 4 and 5).

PHP file 'catalog.php' displays the tree structure of 'catalog.xml'.

```
1  <?php
2  // File catalog.php
3  $xml = simplexml_load_file('xml_docs/catalog.xml');
4  header('Content-Type: text/xml');
5  echo $xml->asXML();
6  ?>
```

I begin by placing 'catalog.xml' in a 'SimpleXML' object as '$xml' (line 3). I then tell the browser to display the contents of the object (lines 4 and 5).

Load 'tree.php' to invoke the application. Figure 7.7 shows the initial menu.

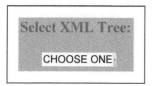

Figure 7.7 Display AJAX-Enabled Form with Drop-Down Menu of XML Tree Options

Click the drop-down menu arrow and choose 'Customer Tree'. Figure 7.8 shows a partial display of the XML tree for 'customer.xml' (there should be ten 'row' nodes displayed).

```
<row>
   <ID>1001</ID>
   <FIRST_NAME>Dan D.
   </FIRST_NAME>
   <LAST_NAME>Lion</LAST_NAME>
   <ADDRESS>500 E 500 N # 8</ADDR
   ESS>
   <PHONE>4357972222</PHONE>
</row>
```

Figure 7.8 Output Showing Partial XML Tree of Customer Data

Click the 'back' arrow on the browser to return to the menu. Click the drop-down menu arrow and choose 'Catalog Tree'. Figure 7.9 shows a partial display of the XML tree for 'catalog.xml' (all catalog contents should be displayed).

```
<CD>
   <TITLE>Empire Burlesque</TITLE
   >
   <ARTIST>Bob Dylan</ARTIST>
   <COUNTRY>USA</COUNTRY>
   <COMPANY>Columbia</COMPANY>
   <PRICE>10.90</PRICE>
   <YEAR>1985</YEAR>
</CD>
```

Figure 7.9 Output Showing Partial XML Tree of Catalog Data

The only drawback is that the displayed XML tree is outside the application. That is, once a choice is made from the drop-down menu, the application no longer controls processing. In the next section, I use 'iframes' to rectify this drawback.

Incorporate 'iframes' into the XML Tree Application

The '<iframe>' tag specifies an inline frame. An ***inline frame*** is used to embed another document within the current HTML document. With 'iframe' technology, the tree display can be kept inside the application. The XML documents used are 'customer.xml' and 'catalog.xml'. Both documents are available on the companion website.

Application Scripts for 'iframes'

I use three scripts in this application – 'iframe.php', 'customer.php', and 'catalog.php'.

PHP file 'iframe.php' provides a drop-down menu for choosing the XML tree to display, a JavaScript event handler, and the 'iframe' logic.

```
1  <?php
2  // File iframe.php
3  @$choice = $_POST['choice'];
4  ?>
5  <html>
6  <head>
7  <style type="text/css">
8  table.center {
9  margin-left:auto;
10 margin-right:auto;
11 }
12 </style>
13 <script type="text/javascript">
```

```
14 function clear_screen()
15 {
16 document.getElementById("area").innerHTML = "";
17 alert("Screen information cleared...");
18 }
19 </script>
20 </head>
21 <body style="background-color:burlywood;">
22 <div style="text-align:center;">
23 <form method="post" action="iframe.php">
24 <h3 style="color:crimson;">Select XML Tree:  </h3>
25 <table class="center"><tr>
26 <td><select name="choice" onchange="this.form.submit()">
27 <option value="999" selected>Make a Choice</option>
28 <option value="1">Customer Tree</option>
29 <option value="2">Catalog Tree</option>
30 </td></select></tr>
31 </table>
32 </form>
33 <p>
34 <input type="button" onclick="clear_screen();"
35 value="Clear Screen" />
36 <div id="area">
37 <p>
38 <?php
39 if($choice == "1")
40 {
41 echo "<iframe src='customer.php' width='50%' height='85%' ";
42 echo "name='t1' id='t1'><p>iframes are not supported by your ";
43 echo "browser.</p></iframe>";
44 }
45 if($choice == "2")
46 {
47 echo "<iframe src='catalog.php' width='50%' height='85%' ";
48 echo "name='t1' id='t1'><p>iframes are not supported by your ";
49 echo "browser.</p></iframe>";
50 }
51 ?>
52 </div></div>
53 </body></html>
```

I begin by posting 'choice' as '$choice'. This is necessary because the page must submit to itself to enable creation of an 'iframe' within the current document. I include JavaScript function 'clear_screen()' (lines 14–18), which clears the screen. Within the drop-down menu (lines 26–30), I include a JavaScript event handler (line 34) that submits the form when a change is made.

Below the form, I use an '<input>' tag (lines 34 and 35) to display the button that, when clicked, runs the 'clear_screen()' function. I continue by creating an 'iframe' that holds the 'customer' XML tree if the 'choice' is

'1' (lines 39–44) or an 'iframe' that holds the 'catalog' XML tree if the 'choice' is '2' (lines 45–50). The '<iframe>' tag identifies the PHP file that creates the XML tree through the 'src' attribute (lines 41 and 47).

 PHP file 'customer.php', converts 'customer.xml' to an object and displays its tree structure.

```
1  <?php
2  // File customer.php
3  $xml = simplexml_load_file('xml_docs/customer.xml');
4  header('Content-Type: text/xml');
5  echo $xml->asXML();
6  ?>
```

PHP file 'catalog.php' converts 'catalog.xml' to an object and displays its tree structure.

```
1  <?php
2  // File catalog.php
3  $xml = simplexml_load_file('xml_docs/catalog.xml');
4  header('Content-Type: text/xml');
5  echo $xml->asXML();
6  ?>
```

Load 'iframe.php' to invoke the application. Figure 7.10 shows the initial menu. Click the drop-down menu arrow and choose 'Customer Tree'. The tree structure is displayed inside the application. Click the drop-down menu arrow and choose 'Catalog Tree'. The tree structure is displayed inside the application. Click the 'Clear Screen' button and click 'OK' to continue. By using 'iframes', I can maintain control of processing.

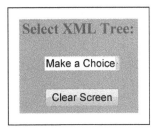

Figure 7.10 Display Showing Iframe-Enabled Form

Summary

The goal of this chapter was to gain skills in creating XML from a database and vice versa, and in creating AJAX-driven applications to generate reports from XML documents. By following the modular approach I present, you should be able to build other applications much more easily.

8 Really Simple Syndication and PHP Data Objects

Overview

Two topics are covered in this chapter – Really Simple Syndication (RSS) and PHP Data Objects (PDO). The topics are grouped together because, although very different, they offer advanced capabilities for working with the Oracle database.

RSS provides an easy way to share and view content on the Internet and is written in XML. It was designed to show selected data. RSS is often called a news feed or RSS feed. People can check a website at any time to see updates because an RSS feed is linked to a database.

The PDO extension defines a lightweight, consistent interface for accessing databases in PHP. PDO provides a data-access abstraction layer, which means that the same functions are used to issue queries and fetch data regardless of the database software.

Learning Objectives

After completing the chapter, you will gain skills in two areas. First, you will create an RSS feed. Second, you will use the PDO extension to communicate with the Oracle database. Skills are enhanced through explanation and code examples. The following objectives summarize the skills the chapter will help you develop:

1 Learn the definition and characteristics of RSS.
2 Learn how to create an RSS feed application.
3 Learn the definition and characteristics of PDO.
4 Learn how to display data using PDO.
5 Learn two ways to prepare a SELECT statement using PDO.
6 Learn two ways to prepare an INSERT statement using PDO.
7 Learn two ways to prepare an UPDATE statement using PDO.
8 Learn two ways to prepare a DELETE statement using PDO.
9 Learn how to use PDO methods with transactions.

Definition of Really Simple Syndication

Really Simple Syndication (RSS) is a dialect of XML and provides a format for web content syndication. I use RSS 2.0 format because it is newer and eliminates the need for namespaces.

Characteristics of Really Simple Syndication

An RSS feed must be a valid XML document. The root element must be '<rss>' and contain the attribute 'version="2.0"'. The root element must have a single child element called '<channel>'.

The '<channel>' element has three required elements that contain information about the feed – '<title>', '<link>', and '<description>'. Element '<title>' is the name of the channel (feed). Element '<link>' is the URL of the website corresponding to the channel. Element '<description>' describes the channel. Sixteen optional elements are available if desired.

A channel may contain any number of '<item>' elements. These elements represent the data pulled from an Oracle database. The '<item>' element must contain either a '<title>' or '<description>' element, but can also contain seven optional elements.

For Google Chrome users, install the extension to auto-detect RSS feeds available (at the time of writing) at the following URL:

https://chrome.google.com/webstore/detail/nlbjncdgjeocebhnmkbbbdekmmmcbfjd

Really Simple Syndication Feed Application

I begin by building an RSS application with three classes – 'dbAggregation', 'dbIterator', and 'rss_feed'. The 'dbAggregation' and 'dbIterator' classes were introduced and explained in Chapter 6. The application creates an RSS feed using information from an Oracle database table to populate the '<item>' elements.

The 'dbAggregation' class sets the username, password, and host server. It also connects to Oracle, gets SQL from the calling environment, instantiates a 'dbIterator' instance, and returns the result set based on the SQL.

The 'dbIterator' class implements an Iterator interface, accepts the connection to Oracle from 'dbAggregation', parses, and executes the SQL. The class also contains the Iterator interface logic.

The 'rss_feed' class builds an RSS feed. The class sets the result set, choice to either display or save the feed, and file name if the feed is to be saved. In addition, the class contains six methods. Four methods are simple getters for channel information. The 'write()' method contains logic for building an RSS feed. It relies on the 'XMLWriter' extension to generate XML for the RSS feed. The 'flush()' method contains logic for displaying or saving the feed.

Before introducing the PHP scripts for building the feed, I create a table in Oracle to hold feed information. I use 'Oracle SQL Developer' software to create the table. Be sure to remove the line numbers before running any SQL!

```
1  CREATE TABLE blog
2  (
3  article_id CHAR(3),
4  title VARCHAR2(25),
5  article VARCHAR2(30),
6  created DATE,
7  url VARCHAR2(40)
8  );
```

The 'blog' table includes five fields (lines 3–7). Fields 'title', 'article', and 'url' are variable-length strings. Field 'article_id' is a fixed-length string. Field 'created' is a date type.

Populate the 'blog' table. Each record spans two lines. For instance the first record (lines 1 and 2) place values into each of the fields. Line 9 saves the data to Oracle. Again, be sure to remove the line numbers before running the SQL.

```
1  INSERT INTO blog VALUES
2  ('001','Get er Done','Just Do It!', '12-JAN-10','http://www.usu.edu');
3  INSERT INTO blog VALUES
```

```
4 ('002','Where Yall At?','We Be Here!', '03-FEB-10','http://www.amazon.com');
5 INSERT INTO blog VALUES
6 ('003','Yoo Hoo','Owwie, Owwie!', '28-FEB-10','http://www.audiogon.com');
7 INSERT INTO blog VALUES
8 ('004','Home Run', 'Fly Out', '11-SEP-11','http://www.w3schools.com');
9 COMMIT;
```

PHP file 'dbAggregation.php' contains the 'dbAggregation' class. Add your username, password, and host server to the 'setParms()' method. These fields are left blank because users should each have their own connection information.

```php
1  <?php
2  // File dbAggregation.php
3  class dbAggregation
4  {
5  private $_schema;
6  private $_password;
7  private $_host;
8  protected $_connection;
9  public function __construct()
10 {
11 $this->setParms();
12 $this->connDB();
13 }
14 public function setParms()
15 {
16 $this->_schema = '';
17 $this->_password = '';
18 $this->_host = '';
19 }
20 public function connDB()
21 {
22 $this->_connection = oci_connect($this->_schema,
23 $this->_password, $this->_host);
24 }
25 public function getResultSet($sql)
26 {
27 $results = new dbIterator($sql, $this->_connection);
28 return $results;
29 }
30 }
31 ?>
```

The constructor (lines 9–13) automatically runs the 'setParms()' and 'connDB()' methods. Method 'setParms()' (lines 14–19) sets the appropriate connection information. Method 'connDB()' (lines 20–24) connect to Oracle. Method 'getResultSet()' (lines 25–29) invokes 'dbIterator' and returns the results generated from this class. For a more detailed explanation, review Chapter 6.

PHP file 'dbIterator.php' contains the 'dbIterator' class.

```php
1  <?php
2  // File dbIterator.php
3  require_once 'dbAggregation.php';
4  class dbIterator implements Iterator
5  {
6  public $sql;
7  public $connection;
8  protected $_result = array();
9  protected $_valid;
10 private $_stmt;
11 public function __construct($sql, $connection)
12 {
13 $this->sql = $sql;
14 $this->connection = $connection;
15 if(!$this->_stmt = oci_parse($connection, $sql))
16 { echo "failed to parse"; };
17 if(!oci_execute($this->_stmt))
18 {echo "failed to execute"; }
19 }
20 public function next()
21 {
22 $this->_result = oci_fetch_assoc($this->_stmt);
23 if(!$this->_result)
24 { $this->_valid = false; }
25 else
26 { $this->_valid = true; }
27 }
28 public function current()
29 {
30 return $this->_result;
31 }
32 public function key()
33 {}
34 public function valid()
35 {
36 return $this->_valid;
37 }
38 public function rewind()
39 {
40 if(!($this->_result))
41 {
42 oci_free_statement($this->_stmt);
43 if(!$this->_stmt = oci_parse($this->connection,
44 $this->sql))
45 { echo "failed to parse"; };
46 if(!oci_execute($this->_stmt))
```

```
47  {echo "failed to execute"; }
48  }
49  $this->_result = oci_fetch_assoc($this->_stmt);
50  if(!$this->_result)
51  { $this->_valid = false; }
52  else
53  { $this->_valid = true; }
54  }
55  }
56  ?>
```

The constructor (lines 11–19) parses the query. The remaining code implements the Iterator interface. The 'next()' method (lines 20–27) sets each row of data with API 'oci_fetch_assoc' as long as there are data left to be fetched. The 'current()' method (lines 28–31) returns the current row of data. The 'key()' method does nothing in Oracle. The 'valid()' method (lines 34–37) checks if there are any data left in the result set. Finally, the 'rewind()' method (lines 38–54) sets the pointer to the first record of the result set. Review Chapter 6 for a detailed explanation.

PHP file 'rss_feed.php' contains the 'rss_feed' class. This class contains quite a bit of code, but is relatively straightforward except for the 'write()' method.

```
1   <?php
2   // File rss_feed.php
3   class rss_feed
4   {
5   private $_result;
6   private $_rss;
7   private $_choice;
8   private $_rssfile;
9   protected $_feedTitle;
10  protected $_feedLink;
11  protected $_feedDescription;
12  protected $_lastBuildDate;
13  public function __construct($result, $choice, $rssfile)
14  {
15  $this->_result = $result;
16  $this->_choice = $choice;
17  $this->_rssfile = $rssfile;
18  }
19  public function setFeedTitle($title)
20  {
21  $this->_feedTitle = $title;
22  }
23  public function setFeedLink($link)
24  {
25  $this->_feedLink = $link;
26  }
27  public function setFeedDescription($description)
```

```
28 {
29 $this->_feedDescription = $description;
30 }
31 public function setLastBuildDate($lastBuildDate)
32 {
33 $this->_lastBuildDate = $lastBuildDate;
34 }
35 public function write()
36 {
37 $this->_rss = new XMLWriter();
38 if($this->_choice == "see")
39 { $this->_rss->openMemory(); }
40 else
41 {
42 $this->_rss->openUri($this->_rssfile);
43 $this->_rss->setIndent(true);
44 }
45 $this->_rss->startDocument();
46 $this->_rss->startElement('rss');
47 $this->_rss->writeAttribute('version', '2.0');
48 $this->_rss->writeAttribute('xmlns:atom',
49 'http://www.w3.org/2005/Atom');
50 $this->_rss->startElement('channel');
51 $this->_rss->writeElement('title', $this->_feedTitle);
52 $this->_rss->writeElement('link', $this->_feedLink);
53 $this->_rss->writeElement('description',
54 $this->_feedDescription);
55 $this->_rss->writeElement('lastBuildDate',
56 $this->_lastBuildDate);
57 $this->_rss->writeElement('docs',
58 'http://www.rssboard.org/rss-specification');
59 foreach($this->_result as $row)
60 {
61 $this->_rss->startElement('item');
62 foreach($row as $field => $value)
63 {
64 $field = strtolower($field);
65 $this->_rss->writeElement($field, $value);
66 }
67 $this->_rss->endElement();
68 }
69 $this->_rss->endElement();
70 $this->_rss->endElement();
71 $this->_rss->endDocument();
72 }
73 public function flush()
74 {
```

```
75  return $this->_rss->flush();
76  }
77  }
78  ?>
```

The 'write()' method (lines 35–72) begins by creating an instance of 'XMLWriter' (line 37). If the RSS feed is to be displayed (line 38), the 'openMemory()' method (line 39) is invoked, otherwise the 'openURI()' and 'setIndent()' methods (lines 42 and 43) are invoked to appropriately set up the XML for saving. The 'startDocument()' method (line 45) is next, followed by the 'startElement()' and 'writeAttribute()' methods (lines 46–49), which build the front end of the RSS feed. The 'channel' is started in line 50. Next, the 'title', 'link', 'description', 'lastBuildDate', and 'docs' are written (lines 51–58).

In the next part of the method, items are created from the result set built from the database table. Specifically, an outer 'foreach' loop (lines 59–68) creates each 'item' (line 61) and uses an inner 'foreach' loop (lines 62–66) to add values to each 'item' element. The outer loop closes each item element in (line 67).

The method ends by closing the feed (lines 69–71). The 'flush()' method (lines 73–76) returns the RSS feed.

To test the application, save 'dbAggregation.php', 'dbIterator.php', and 'rss_feed.php'. Next, decide if you want to display the RSS feed in a browser or save to a file.

PHP file 'rss_flush.php' displays the RSS feed.

```php
1   <?php
2   // File rss_flush.php
3   require_once 'dbAggregation.php';
4   require_once 'dbIterator.php';
5   require_once 'rss_feed.php';
6   $tbl = "blog";
7   $query = "SELECT title, article description, ";
8   $query .= "url link FROM $tbl";
9   $conn = new dbAggregation();
10  $result = $conn->getResultSet($query);
11  $rss = new rss_feed($result,"see",'');
12  $rss->setFeedTitle('PHP Object-Oriented Programming with Oracle');
13  $rss->setFeedLink('http://dnet.brigham.usu.edu/');
14  $rss->setFeedDescription('Get the lowdown on OOP and PHP');
15  $rss->setLastBuildDate('Sun, 14 Sep 2012 13:24:38-0700');
16  $rss->write();
17  $see = $rss->flush();
18  echo $see;
19  ?>
```

The SQL query selects 'title', 'article', and 'url' from the 'blog' table, and renames the columns to be consistent with RSS tag names (lines 6–8). A new instance of 'dbAggregation' is created (line 9) and the 'getResultSet()' method is invoked to return the result set to '$result' (line 10). Next, a new instance of 'rss_feed()' is created (line 11) with arguments '$result', 'see', and ''. String 'see' tells the program to display the feed. Since no file is saved, nothing is sent as the third parameter. The next four lines (lines 12–15) are just simple setters. The 'write()' method is called to build the feed (line 16) and the 'flush()' method is called (line 17) to send the result.

Load 'rss_flush.php' in a browser. Figure 8.1 shows the results.

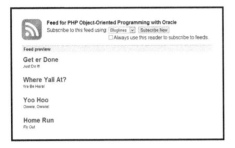

Figure 8.1 Display Showing RSS Feed

Before attempting to save the file, check permissions. If needed, use the following Linux commands. In this case, 'xml_docs' is the folder where I have the files for the application saved and where I want to save the RSS feed. Of course, your directory may be named what you wish.

chmod 777 xml_docs

PHP file 'rss_save.php' saves the RSS feed to a file.

```
1  <?php
2  // File rss_save.php
3  require_once 'dbAggregation.php';
4  require_once 'dbIterator.php';
5  require_once 'rss_feed.php';
6  $tbl = "blog";
7  $query = "SELECT title, article description, ";
8  $query .= "url link FROM $tbl";
9  $conn = new dbAggregation();
10 $result = $conn->getResultSet($query);
11 $rss = new rss_feed($result,"save",'xml_docs/rss.xml');
12 $rss->setFeedTitle('OOP News');
13 $rss->setFeedLink('http://php.net/manual/en/language.oop5.php');
14 $rss->setFeedDescription('Get the lowdown on OOP and PHP');
15 $rss->setLastBuildDate('Sun, 14 Nov 2010 13:24:38-0700');
16 $rss->write();
17 $dir = 'xml_docs/rss.xml';
18 if(is_writable(dirname($dir)))
19 { $save = $rss->flush();
20 echo 'RSS file created'; }
21 else
22 { echo 'Problem with directory permissions'; }
23 ?>
```

There are two differences between displaying and saving. First, the final two arguments passed to object 'rss_feed' are 'save' and 'xml_docs/rss.xml' (line 11). The 'save' argument tells PHP to save the file and the 'xml_docs/rss.xml' argument tells PHP the file name to use. Second, the name of the directory is checked to see if it is writable (line 18).

Load 'rss_save.php' in a browser. Figure 8.2 shows the results. Verify the contents of 'rss.xml' in the 'xml_docs' directory.

```
RSS file created
```

Figure 8.2 Display Showing that RSS Feed Was Created and Saved

Definition and Characteristics of PHP Data Objects

The **PHP Data Objects** (PDO) extension defines a lightweight consistent interface for accessing databases in PHP. PDO provides a data-access abstraction layer, which means that, regardless of database, the same functions are used to issue queries and fetch data. So, PDO provides an object-oriented alternative to APIs. PDO is very fast because it is written in the 'C' language. PDO supports most databases, including Oracle, MySQL, PostGres, DB2, and MS SQL Server.

Display Data with PHP Data Objects

A major advantage of using PDO is that it is object-oriented. As such, it contains a set of methods that work with all supported databases. For instance, the 'query()' method executes an SQL statement and returns a result set as a 'PDO' object. The 'exec()' method executes an SQL statement and returns the number of affected rows. The 'fetch()' method fetches the next row from a result set.

PHP file 'select_pdo.php' displays data from the 'web_site' table (created in Chapter 3). Fill in your specific username, password, and host server information before running the code.

```php
1  <?php
2  // File select_pdo.php
3  $user = '';
4  $pass = '';
5  $host = '';
6  $sql = "SELECT * FROM web_site";
7  try
8  { $db = @ new PDO("oci:dbname=$host",$user,$pass); }
9  catch(PDOException $e)
10 { die('Connection error => ' . $e->getMessage()); }
11 $result = $db->query($sql);
12 if(!$result)
13 {
14 $error = $db->errorInfo();
15 die('Execute query error => ' . $error[2]);
16 }
17 $db = null;
18 while($row = $result->fetch(PDO::FETCH_ASSOC))
19 {
20 $id = $row['VID'];
21 $user = $row['VUSER'];
```

```
22 $pswd = $row['PSWD'];
23 $lvl = $row['LVL'];
24 echo $id . '  ' . $user . '  ';
25 echo $pswd . '  ' . $lvl . '<br />';
26 }
27 ?>
```

I begin by setting the Oracle host server, username, and password information (lines 3–5), and the SQL query (line 6). I use a 'try–catch' block to trap connection errors (lines 7–10). In line 8, I assign '$db' the new instance with '@ new PDO("oci:dbname=$host",$user,$pass);'. The '@' symbol suppresses error messages. PDO knows that the connection is to Oracle because "oci:dbname=$host" is included as the first parameter in the PDO object.

I continue by using the 'PDOException' class in the 'catch' (line 9) to handle errors. If there is an error message, I get it with the 'getMessage()' method (line 10) and stop processing with 'die()' (line 10).

In line 11, I use the 'query()' method to place the result set into '$result'. If the result set is empty, I prepare the '$error' array to hold the error message with the 'errorInfo()' method (line 14), create the message and place it in '$error' as the third element (line 15), and stop processing with 'die()' (line 15).

I assign 'null' to the '$db' object (line 17) to close the connection. If the result set is not empty, I use the 'fetch()' method (line 18) to grab each row. I use the 'PDO::FETCH_ASSOC' directive so I can use the field names from the database to identify field values.

Be sure to capitalize field names from the Oracle database table! For instance, in line 20, '$id = $row['VID'];' returns the value of the 'VID' field from the table. If you don't capitalize the field name, an error is *not* generated, but no output is displayed because Oracle only recognizes capitalized field names. Using a 'while' loop (lines 18–26), I fetch each row from the database, set variables from the 'fetched' database row (lines 20–23), and display results (lines 24 and 25). Load 'select_pdo.php' into a browser. Figure 8.3 shows the results.

```
001  ben    1649869de3d29daab675ad252b9bd02248fd9ea7  1
002  dandy  85aa14a772c00238f44f5a2b4edee7b9602aee2d  2
003  sally  ae79c3ab02ccd046df6f0ba809c753fef7b1d44f  2
004  oliver 82008b43682796ae6255c402eec2e49bea6904ad  2
005  betty  f11d88e5c0ca93d109c9c4af63a3155bd749f0e5  2
```

Figure 8.3 Output Showing 'web_site' Data Using 'PDO' Class

With PDO, a database connection class is not needed. In addition, PDO is built into the PHP core.

Prepare a SELECT Statement with PHP Data Objects

PDO offers an object-oriented solution to mitigating SQL injection. There are two ways to prepare SQL statements against injection – 'named' and 'unnamed'.

PHP file 'select_named.php' uses a 'named' bind variable to prepare a SELECT statement. Fill in your specific username, password, and host server information before running the code.

```
1  <?php
2  // File select_named.php
3  $user = '';
```

```
 4  $pass = '';
 5  $host = '';
 6  $sql = "SELECT * FROM web_site WHERE VID = :id";
 7  $id = '001';
 8  try
 9  { $db = new PDO("oci:dbname=$host",$user,$pass); }
10  catch(PDOException $e)
11  { die('Connection error => ' . $e->getMessage()); }
12  $stmt = $db->prepare($sql);
13  $stmt->bindParam(':id',$id,PDO::PARAM_STR,3);
14  $stmt->execute();
15  if(!$stmt)
16  {
17  $error = $db->errorInfo();
18  die('Execute query error => ' . $error[2]);
19  }
20  $db = null;
21  $row = $stmt->fetch(PDO::FETCH_ASSOC);
22  echo $row["VID"] . ' ' . $row["VUSER"] . ' ' .
23  $row["PSWD"];
24  echo ' ' . $row["LVL"];
25  ?>
```

The logic is the same as the previous example except for the binding logic, and since only one record is returned, there is no need for a 'while' loop. I use the 'named' bind variable ':id' for the 'VID' field (line 6). SQL injection is mitigated because the value of the named bind variable is not determined until after the Oracle execution plan is finished. If a hacker attempts to inject SQL, Oracle does not interpret it.

I use the 'bindParam()' method (line 13) to bind the value in '$id' into the 'named' variable ':id'. The directive 'PDO::PARAM_STR' tells the method that the bind variable is a string. The parameter '3' tells the method that the field has three characters. PDO method 'execute()' (line 14) runs the SQL and returns the number of affected rows. Load 'select_named.php' into a browser. Figure 8.4 shows the results.

```
001 ben 1649869de3d29daab675ad252b9bd02248fd9ea7 1
```

Figure 8.4 Output of Record Using 'PDO' Class and 'string' Named Binding

In the previous example, I used a string for the bind value. In this example, I need to use a number (integer) for the bind value, so I have to change the 'bindParam()' directive. I also need a 'while' loop because more than one record is returned.

```
1  <?php
2  // File select_named_int.php
3  $user = '';
4  $pass = '';
5  $host = '';
```

```
 6  $sql = "SELECT * FROM web_site WHERE LVL = :lvl";
 7  $lvl= 2;
 8  try
 9  { $db = new PDO("oci:dbname=$host",$user,$pass); }
10  catch(PDOException $e)
11  { die('Connection error => ' . $e->getMessage()); }
12  $stmt = $db->prepare($sql);
13  $stmt->bindParam(':lvl',$lvl,PDO::PARAM_INT);
14  $stmt->execute();
15  if(!$stmt)
16  {
17  $error = $db->errorInfo();
18  die('Execute query error => ' . $error[2]);
19  }
20  $db = null;
21  while($row = $stmt->fetch(PDO::FETCH_ASSOC))
22  {
23  $id = $row['VID'];
24  $user = $row['VUSER'];
25  $pass = $row['PSWD'];
26  $lvl = $row['LVL'];
27  echo $id .' ' . $user .' ' . $pass .' ' . $lvl .
28  '<br />';
29  }
30  ?>
```

Instead of using a bind variable for the 'VID' character string field, I use a 'named' bind variable for the 'LVL' number field (line 6). Also, I change the directive in the 'bindParam()' method to 'PARAM_INT' (line 13). Finally, I add a 'while' loop (lines 21–29) to process the results. The rest of the logic is the same as the previous example in 'select_named.php'. Load 'select_named_int.php' into a browser. Figure 8.5 shows the results.

```
002 dandy 85aa14a772c00238f44f5a2b4edee7b9602aee2d 2
003 sally ae79c3ab02ccd046df6f0ba809c753fef7b1d44f 2
004 oliver 82008b43682796ae6255c402eec2e49bea6904ad 2
005 betty f11d88e5c0ca93d109c9c4af63a3155bd749f0e5 2
```

Figure 8.5 Output of Record Using 'PDO' Class with 'integer' Named Binding

In the next example, I use the '?' symbol to indicate that a bind variable is 'unnamed'. Fill in username, password, and host server information before running the code.

```
1  <?php
2  // File select_unnamed.php
3  $user = '';
```

```
 4 $pass = '';
 5 $host = '';
 6 $sql = "SELECT * FROM web_site WHERE VID = ?";
 7 $id = '001';
 8 try
 9 { $db = new PDO("oci:dbname=$host",$user,$pass); }
10 catch(PDOException $e)
11 { die('Connection error => ' . $e->getMessage()); }
12 $stmt = $db->prepare($sql);
13 $stmt->bindParam(1,$id);
14 $stmt->execute();
15 if(!$stmt)
16 {
17 $error = $db->errorInfo();
18 die('Execute query error => ' . $error[2]);
19 }
20 $db = null;
21 $row = $stmt->fetch(PDO::FETCH_ASSOC);
22 echo $row["VID"] . ' ' . $row["VUSER"] . ' ' .
23 $row["PSWD"];
24 echo ' ' . $row["LVL"];
25 ?>
```

In line 6, I use '?' for an 'unnamed' bind variable. The 'bindParam()' method is even simpler (line 13). The first parameter is '1' because only one bind variable is used. The second parameter is '$id' to indicate the value to use. With unnamed bind variables, the type of data doesn't matter. So, you do not need to change the parameters for method 'bindParam()' to bind to a number field. Load 'select_unnamed.php' into a browser. Figure 8.6 shows the results.

```
001 ben 1649869de3d29daab675ad252b9bd02248fd9ea7 1
```

Figure 8.6 Output of Record Using 'PDO' Class with Unnamed Binding

Prepare an INSERT Statement with PHP Data Objects

PHP file 'insert_named.php' uses 'named' bind variables to prepare an INSERT statement. Fill in your specific host server, username, and password information before running the code.

```
1 <?php
2 // File insert_named.php
3 $user = '';
4 $pass = '';
5 $host = '';
6 $sql = "INSERT INTO web_site VALUES
7 (:vid, :vuser, :pswd, :lvl)";
8 $data = array('006','Mark D.','Spot',2);
9 try
```

```
10  { $db = @ new PDO("oci:dbname=$host",$user,$pass); }
11  catch(PDOException $e)
12  { die('Connection error => ' . $e->getMessage()); }
13  $stmt = $db->prepare($sql);
14  $result = $stmt->execute($data);
15  if(!$result)
16  {
17  $error = $db->errorInfo();
18  die('Query error => ' . $error[2]);
19  }
20  $db = null;
21  ?>
```

The named bind variables are ':vid', ':vuser', ':pswd', and ':lvl' (line 7). Keep in mind that bind variables can be given any name, but I use the same names for the bind variables as the database fields for convenience. I use array '$data' (line 8) to hold the values for the bind variables. I use the 'prepare()' method (line 13) to ready the 'INSERT' statement for binding. I use the 'execute()' method (line 14) to complete the binding process.

Load 'insert_named.php' into a browser. An 'INSERT' statement adds data to a table, but doesn't create a result set so nothing is displayed on the browser. So, use 'Oracle SQL Developer' to check the table for a new record.

PHP file 'insert_unnamed.php' uses an 'unnamed' bind variable to prepare an INSERT statement. Fill in your specific host server, username, and password information before running the code.

```
1  <?php
2  // File insert_unnamed.php
3  $user = '';
4  $pass = '';
5  $host = '';
6  $sql = "INSERT INTO web_site VALUES (?,?,?,?)";
7  $data = array('007','Rosy','Palms',2);
8  try
9  { $db = @ new PDO("oci:dbname=$host",$user,$pass); }
10  catch(PDOException $e)
11  { die('Connection error => ' . $e->getMessage()); }
12  $stmt = $db->prepare($sql);
13  $result = $stmt->execute($data);
14  if(!$result)
15  {
16  $error = $db->errorInfo();
17  die('Query error => ' . $error[2]);
18  }
19  $db = null;
20  ?>
```

The only difference between this code example and the 'named' one is that the bind variables are question marks '?' (line 6).

Load 'insert_unnamed.php' into a browser. Use 'Oracle SQL Developer' to check the table.

Prepare an UPDATE Statement with PHP Data Objects

PHP file 'update_named.php' uses a 'named' bind variable to prepare an UPDATE statement. Fill in your specific host server, username, and password information before running the code.

```
1  <?php
2  // File update_named.php
3  $user = '';
4  $pass = '';
5  $host = '';
6  $sql = "UPDATE web_site SET pswd = 'Spots'
7  WHERE vid = :vid";
8  $vid = '006';
9  try
10 { $db = @ new PDO("oci:dbname=$host",$user,$pass); }
11 catch(PDOException $e)
12 { die('Connection error => ' . $e->getMessage()); }
13 $stmt = $db->prepare($sql);
14 $stmt->bindParam(1,$vid);
15 $result = $stmt->execute();
16 if(!$result)
17 {
18 $error = $db->errorInfo();
19 die('Query error => ' . $error[2]);
20 }
21 $db = null;
22 ?>
```

The logic is the same as the 'insert_named.php' example except that the SQL statement is an 'UPDATE' (lines 6 and 7). Load 'update_named.php' into a browser. Use 'Oracle SQL Developer' to verify the results.

PHP file 'update_unnamed.php' uses an 'unnamed' bind variable to prepare an UPDATE statement. Fill in your specific host server, username, and password information before running the code.

```
1  <?php
2  // File update_unnamed.php
3  $user = '';
4  $pass = '';
5  $host = '';
6  $sql = "UPDATE web_site SET pswd = 'Palm' WHERE vid = ?";
7  $vid = '007';
8  try
9  { $db = @ new PDO("oci:dbname=$host",$user,$pass); }
10 catch(PDOException $e)
11 { die('Connection error => ' . $e->getMessage()); }
12 $stmt = $db->prepare($sql);
13 $stmt->bindParam(1,$vid);
14 $result = $stmt->execute();
15 if(!$result)
```

```
16 {
17 $error = $db->errorInfo();
18 die('Query error => ' . $error[2]);
19 }
20 $db = null;
21 ?>
```

The logic is the same as the 'insert_unnamed.php' example except that the SQL statement is an 'UPDATE' (lines 6 and 7). Load 'update_unnamed.php' into a browser. Use 'Oracle SQL Developer' to verify the results.

Prepare a DELETE Statement with PHP Data Objects

PHP file 'delete_named.php' uses a 'named' bind variable to prepare a DELETE statement. Fill in your specific host server, username, and password information before running the code.

```
1  <?php
2  // File delete_named.php
3  $user = '';
4  $pass = '';
5  $host = '';
6  $sql = "DELETE FROM web_site WHERE vid = :vid";
7  $vid = '006';
8  try
9  { $db = @ new PDO("oci:dbname=$host",$user,$pass); }
10 catch(PDOException $e)
11 { die('Connection error => ' . $e->getMessage()); }
12 $stmt = $db->prepare($sql);
13 $stmt->bindParam(1,$vid);
14 $result = $stmt->execute();
15 if(!$result)
16 {
17 $error = $db->errorInfo();
18 die('Query error => ' . $error[2]);
19 }
20 $db = null;
21 ?>
```

The logic is the same as the 'update_named.php' example except that the SQL statement is a 'DELETE' (line 6). Load 'delete_named.php' into a browser. Use 'Oracle SQL Developer' to verify the results.

The next example deletes a record using an 'unnamed' bind variable. Fill in your specific host server, username, and password information before running the code.

```
1  <?php
2  // File delete_unnamed.php
3  $user = '';
4  $pass = '';
```

```
 5  $host = '';
 6  $sql = "DELETE FROM web_site WHERE vid = ?";
 7  $vid = '007';
 8  try
 9  { $db = @ new PDO("oci:dbname=$host",$user,$pass); }
10  catch(PDOException $e)
11  { die('Connection error => ' . $e->getMessage()); }
12  $stmt = $db->prepare($sql);
13  $stmt->bindParam(1,$vid);
14  $result = $stmt->execute();
15  if(!$result)
16  {
17  $error = $db->errorInfo();
18  die('Query error => ' . $error[2]);
19  }
20  $db = null;
21  ?>
```

The logic is the same as the 'update_unnamed.php' example except that the SQL statement is a 'DELETE' (line 6). Load 'delete_unnamed.php' into a browser. Use 'Oracle SQL Developer' to verify the results.

Transactions with PHP Data Objects

A *transaction* comprises a unit of work performed within a database management system (DBMS) against a database. Transactions have two main purposes. First, they provide reliable units of work that allow correct recovery from failures and keep a database consistent even in cases of system failure. Second, they provide isolation between programs accessing a database concurrently.

A database transaction must be atomic, consistent, isolated, and durable (ACID). An *atomic transaction* is one that either completes all of its database operations or none of them. A *consistent transaction* is one where results are predictable. An *isolated transaction* is one where any changes made are independent and visible from other concurrent operations. A *durable transaction* is one that, once committed (saved to the database), will survive permanently.

ACID Test

Databases use two mechanisms to ensure that transactions pass the ACID test – rollback and commit. *Rollback* is an operation that returns the database to a previous state and ends the transaction. *Commit* is an operation that ends the transaction and makes all changes visible to other users.

By using rollback and commit with transactions, the integrity of a database can be ensured. If a transaction fails to complete, rollback can be used to restore the database to a previous, clean state. If a transaction completes successfully, commit can be used to save changes to the database.

PHP file 'transaction1.php' shows how transactions work in PDO. Fill in your specific database information before running the code.

```
1  <?php
2  // File transaction1.php
3  $user = '';
```

```
 4  $pass = '';
 5  $host = '';
 6  $db = new PDO("oci:dbname=$host",$user,$pass);
 7  $sql1 = "INSERT INTO web_site VALUES ('006','Mark D.','Spot',2)";
 8  $sql2 = "INSERT INTO web_site VALUES ('006','Eileen','Down',2)";
 9  $sql3 = "UPDATE web_site SET pswd = 'Downe' WHERE vid = '006'";
10  $db->beginTransaction();
11  $result = $db->exec($sql1);
12  $db->rollback();
13  $db->beginTransaction();
14  $result = $db->exec($sql2);
15  $result = $db->exec($sql3);
16  $db->commit();
17  $db = null;
18  ?>
```

I begin by creating a new PDO object and assigning it to '$db' (line 6). I use three SQL statements as transactions and assign them to '$sql1', '$sql2', and '$sql3', respectively (lines 7–9). The first two are INSERT statements, and the last one is an UPDATE statement. I begin a new transaction by invoking the 'beginTransaction()' method (line10). I execute the first SQL statement of the transaction in line 11. I then 'rollback' the transaction in line 12. I begin a new transaction in line 13 and execute the second and third SQL statements in the transaction. I end by saving the transaction (line 16).

So, the data associated with the 'INSERT' statement assigned to '$sql1' is not reflected in the database because the first transaction was rolled back. When a transaction is rolled back, it is like nothing happened! The second transaction was saved so the SQL in lines 8 and 9 were saved. When a transaction is committed, the results are saved to the database.

Load 'transaction1.php' into a browser. Use 'Oracle SQL Developer' to verify the results.

What Happened with Transaction 1?

Since the first 'INSERT' statement is rolled back (in the first transaction), the database does not reflect the change. The second and third SQL statements are saved to the database (in the second transaction). As a result, the 'Eileen' record is added to the database and its password is modified to 'Downe'.

Like the previous example, PHP file 'transaction2.php' starts two transactions. However, the first transaction executes two 'INSERT' statements. This transaction is reversed because of the 'rollback'. The second transaction deletes the record with 'VID' of '6', executes the second 'INSERT', updates the password, and commits.

```
1  <?php
2  // File transaction2.php
3  $user = '';
4  $pass = '';
5  $host = '';
6  $db = new PDO("oci:dbname=$host",$user,$pass);
7  $sql1 = "INSERT INTO web_site VALUES ('006','Eileen','Down',2)";
8  $sql2 = "DELETE FROM web_site WHERE vid = '006'";
9  $sql3 = "INSERT INTO web_site VALUES ('006','Mark D.','Spot',2)";
```

```
10  $sql4 = "UPDATE web_site SET pswd = 'Spots' WHERE vid = '006'";
11  $db->beginTransaction();
12  $result = $db->exec($sql1);
13  $result = $db->exec($sql3);
14  $db->rollback();
15  $db->beginTransaction();
16  $result = $db->exec($sql2);
17  $result = $db->exec($sql3);
18  $result = $db->exec($sql4);
19  $db->commit();
20  $db = null;
21  ?>
```

Load 'transaction2.php' into a browser. Use 'Oracle SQL Developer' to verify the table contents.

What Happened with Transaction 2?

Since both 'INSERT' statements are rolled back (in the first transaction), the database does not reflect these changes (line 14). The second, third, and fourth SQL statements (lines 8–10) are saved to the database (in the second transaction). As a result, the 'Eileen' record is deleted from the database, the 'Mark D.' record is added to the database, and its password is modified to 'Spots'.

Like the previous example, PHP file 'transaction2.php' starts two transactions. However, the first transaction executes two 'INSERT' statements. This transaction is reversed because of the 'rollback'. The second transaction deletes the record with 'VID' of '6', executes the second 'INSERT', updates the password, and commits.

The final example, PHP file 'transaction3.php' restores the database to its original state by deleting the record with 'VID' of '6' and saving changes with commit (lines 8–10).

```
 1  <?php
 2  // File transaction3.php
 3  $user = '';
 4  $pass = '';
 5  $host = '';
 6  $db = new PDO("oci:dbname=$host",$user,$pass);
 7  $sql1 = "DELETE FROM web_site WHERE vid = '006'";
 8  $db->beginTransaction();
 9  $result = $db->exec($sql1);
10  $db->commit();
11  $db = null;
12  ?>
```

Load 'transaction3.php' into a browser. Use 'Oracle SQL Developer' to verify the table contents.

Summary

The goal of this chapter was to gain skills in two areas. First, I provided instruction on how to create an RSS feed. Second, I provided instruction on how to use the PDO extension to communicate with the Oracle database.

Index